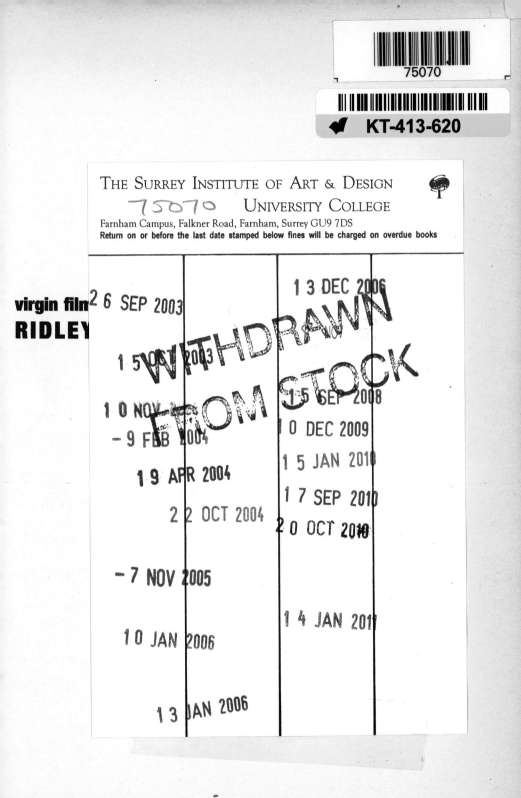

virgin film

RIDLEY

virgin film

RIDLEY SCOTT

James Clarke

First published in Great Britain in 2002
by Virgin Books Ltd
Thames Wharf Studios
Rainville Road
London
W6 9HA

ISBN 0 7535 0731 5

Typeset by TW Typesetting, Plymouth, Devon
Printed and bound in Great Britain by Mackays of Chatham PLC

Dedicated to

Tim, Sarah, Catie and Ben and my good pal Oliver
– keep on trucking

Contents

Introduction: Welcome to Ridleyville

'Light is beautiful' – Ridley Scott

On his commentary to the film *Thelma & Louise*, Ridley Scott makes a definitive comment about his work. It is also the kind of thing you would expect, or rather would hope, any true director in command of all the resources at their disposal to say: 'My performance is everything you see on the screen.'

As with so many of the best Hollywood directors, there is a totality to the way Scott works. He is unafraid of integrating effects, of maximising the voice of the music, of amplifying the impact of lighting and camera moves. Throughout the process of drawing these diverse pieces together, he roots the illusion in the believability of the actors he has cast. Scott is as impassioned about filmmaking as his movie heroes are about fulfilling the demands of their missions, journeys and destinies.

In late April 2002 the film fan community was abuzz with news about a possible new Ridley Scott movie. It came at a time when his career was benefiting from its second wind after the one-two-three punch of *Gladiator*, *Hannibal* and *Black Hawk Down*. So many directors seem to have this experience, where their work is somehow revived and reinvigorated. It happened with Spielberg on *Schindler's List* (1993), with Scorsese on *GoodFellas* (1990), with Lynch on *The Straight Story* (1999).

After 25 years, Ridley Scott, the director of smart and snazzy popular movies, continues to elicit excitement. Like his hotshot contemporaries Scorsese, Spielberg, Lucas, Cameron and Tarantino, just the mere thought of what a new Scott film will *look* like is enough to whip film fans into a frenzy of debate and anticipation, as evidenced by so many messageboards on the Internet and column inches in magazines.

On 15 July 2002, somewhere in LA, the cameras rolled on Ridley Scott's new movie *Matchstick Men*. It tells the story of a con-artist named Roy (Nicolas Cage) who has a host of phobias. He and his protégé Frank (Sam Rockwell) are about to pull off a lucrative con when Roy's teenage daughter Angela (Alison

1

Lohman) turns up and throws everything into disarray. The screenplay has been written by Ted and Nick Griffin from the novel by Eric Garcia, and the film's producers are Robert Zemeckis and Jack Rapke. Scott reteams with John Mathieson, cinematographer on *Gladiator* and *Hannibal*, and, in a break from Scott's recent and brilliant collaboration with Pietro Scalia, *Matchstick Men* is to be edited by Dody Dorn, whose highest profile credit so far has been his editing work on *Memento* (Christopher Nolan, 2000). Already, the film has been described as being in the same vein as Peter Bogdanovich's terrific comedy drama *Paper Moon* (1973). *Matchstick Men* began shooting in July 2002 with Nicolas Cage in the main role. The premise of a control freak clearly losing control continues a fine Scott tradition of characters.

Scott's immediate follow-up will then reunite him with Russell Crowe for the film *Tripoli*.

In late May 2002 it was also announced that Scott had finally expressed interest in a Western from a pitch by writer Bruce C McKenna. The other project Scott was connected to in spring 2002 was an adaptation of Patrick Suskind's novel *Perfume*, originally published in 1976. Stanley Kubrick, one of Scott's big influences, had once shown interest in adapting the material. Other directors had considered the project, including Martin Scorsese, Shekhar Kapur, director of *Bandit Queen* (1994) and *Elizabeth* (1998), Jean-Pierre Jeunet, director of *Delicatessen* (1991), *City of Lost Children* (1995) and *Alien: Resurrection* (1997), and Tim Burton, director of *Beetlejuice* (1988) and *Sleepy Hollow* (1999). *Perfume: The Story of a Murderer* is set in eighteenth-century France where a baby is born with no scent. However, he grows up with a perfect sense of smell and can identify his origin immediately. The boy is an outsider. One night, he follows the scent of a beautiful girl through Paris and her odour is so sublime it overwhelms him and he kills her. He becomes obsessed with copying her smell and will do anything in his quest to do so. One scene has the protagonist about to be hanged. He unleashes a perfume which is so powerful it throws the assembled crowd into an orgy. This premise seems ripe for Scott's eyes, ears and cinema savvy. *Perfume* is also the latest in a long line of possible projects for the director that have emerged over the past year and a half (for more on this see **Ridley's Unrealised Visions**).

At the Top of His Game

'I find it hard to be disapproving. The movies would be duller without Scott's chronic eye for flash, sheen and instant spectacle,' writes David Thomson in *A Biographical Dictionary of Film*. It is common knowledge that everyone loves a comeback kid and currently Ridley Scott is experiencing something of a return to form and popularity. Call it Ridley's Renaissance if you want.

Scott has reasserted his place as a major popular moviemaker, with all that entails in terms of the kinds of projects available to him and a way of translating them to the screen with a big budget and the brightest acting talent.

With *Gladiator*, *Hannibal* and *Black Hawk Down*, Scott's career has reclaimed the prominence it had in the late 1970s and early 1980s. In February 2001 at New York City's Screening Room there was a *Ridley Scott Retrospective* which showcased a selection of his best films.

As with many directors, it is a small number of films that have shaped Scott's reputation. With this book all of his films are treated with equal interest regardless of their cinematic and pop culture standing. The idea here is to take a look at what binds the films together. What is Scott's approach to storytelling? What seem to be his favourite kinds of characters? What kind of situations and – deep breath, here – themes preoccupy his films? What kind of settings does Scott seem to favour as part of his work? What cinema techniques and smoke and mirrors does he draw on to create a vivid illusion as he repeatedly thrills, scares, astounds and moves you?

Before getting to grips with Ridley's cinema stylings there's an influence that needs a name check and a quick look at what that influence was about. The person in question may be unexpected, given the emphasis on Scott's visual focus. Nonetheless, a love of one art form does not exclude an appreciation of the others and one of the key influences on his work is not even a cinematic one. Instead, it comes in the form of one of the great early twentieth-century novelists. One of his works, a novella entitled *Heart of Darkness*, ultimately led to Francis Coppola's *Apocalypse Now* (1979). The writer in question is Joseph Conrad, a Polish author who advanced the art of English literature in the late nineteenth and early twentieth century and who believed firmly in the possibility of unity amongst men.

Conrad wrote numerous novels and short stories. One of his biggest novels was *Nostromo*, a film adaptation that had once been due for David Lean to direct, with Steven Spielberg producing. It now looks as though Martin Scorsese may work on it, using Lean's notes as a starting point. Of course, Scott's debut feature, *The Duellists* (1977), was an adaptation of a Conrad short story. The director's affinity for Conrad seems to go to the heart of many of the films he has chosen to direct.

Frequently, the stories that Scott tells focus on the inherent corruptibility of man. This is a theme played out in *G.I. Jane*, *Gladiator*, *The Duellists* and *Hannibal* at the most obvious. Indeed, Scott's heroes often possess that Conradian sense of men (and women) who must redeem themselves, or their larger society, and find the means to act honourably against other, less honourable forces.

Like Hitchcock, Kubrick, Ford, Cronenberg and Spielberg, to name just a few, Scott is a total filmmaker, utilising all the toys and tools of filmmaking at his disposal. Refreshingly, Scott is a director who acknowledges that film is about more than just the actor's performance. He comes from a tradition of filmmakers that emphasises the craft element of building a film, of creating a world beyond the written and spoken word – though Scott, like any filmmaker, has his critics, who regard his work as frequently lacking coherence and for being predictable and lacking in subtlety.

Ridley Scott is able to make visual effects expressive and has worked with some of the great visual effects designers, notably Doug Trumbull, HR Giger and Rob Bottin. In his book *The Biographical Dictionary of Film*, writer David Thomson describes Scott as being very much in the mould of an old time Hollywood director like Michael Curtiz who directed, amongst others, *Casablanca* (1942), *The Adventures of Robin Hood* (1939), *Mildred Pierce* (1945) and *Yankee Doodle Dandy* (1942). In the June 2002 issue of *Premiere* movie magazine, Scott gets a listing in their fun, but ultimately facile, Power List for Hollywood, a slight guestimation about influence in the industry. Speaking about Scott with *Premiere* movie magazine on the release of *Black Hawk Down* (2001), Joe Roth said, 'He's a guy who, at 64, is right at the top of his game.'

British film producer David Puttnam has been famously quoted as referring to Scott's 'erratic greatness'. For some, Scott is just too commercial a director who is only ever able to make places, people and situations look very appealing and attractive, rather like a commercial is always in the business of making you want to get what you are being shown. There is a similar kind of reservation towards his contemporary Steven Spielberg. Scott, too, has found ways to reinvigorate genre material to such an extent that it redefines a given genre for a whole generation of filmgoers.

Like Spielberg, Scott, at a certain point, began to diverge from the path that had made his name. Scott began his career by making what he calls 'fairly exotic movies'. In 1987, after four very fanciful features, Scott released *Someone to Watch Over Me*, followed by *Black Rain* and then *Thelma & Louise*. With *Someone to Watch Over Me* and certainly *Thelma & Louise*, Scott began to shift the audience's perception of him with a story that was really just about two characters. Scott has always tried to promote some form of female equality and this is no clearer than in his landmark film, *Blade Runner*.

As with many film directors, at least in American cinema, Scott celebrates the individual effort. His romantically informed heroes overcome the challenges of the threatening and disorientating world through a combination of resolve and intelligence. Scott's movies follow genre formulae but do the right thing by using these frameworks to tell stories about compelling characters. With *Gladiator*, for example, Scott revived the Roman epic genre (partly due to the economic benefit of computer-generated environments) through a combination of spectacle and stirring personal drama. For some critics, though, Scott's eye for the memorable image is not enough. Where is the coherent drama? they ask. Where is the complexity? Maybe a film does not have to be complex, though; perhaps it is enough that the situations and images resonate with the audience. That is why Maximus in his moment of death strikes a chord – he wants to go home to his family. That is why, in *Blade Runner*, Roy Batty, for all his futuristic theatrics, stays with us – he wants to find out who he is. That is why Chuck Gieg's upbeat voice-over to close *White Squall* rings true – he now has a better sense of what his place in the world is, having survived the adventure.

Scott may be synonymous with science fiction and fantasy themes but his work is also bound up in a Romantic sensibility. This Romantic tradition places an emphasis on humans returning to nature in some way, on the relationship between man and nature, though not necessarily literally. The other key interest of Romanticism is its images of the unconscious. Many of Scott's films draw on both these outlooks, notably his earliest films most fully, but the strains remain in his later work too. *Legend*, *Alien*, *Blade Runner* and *Hannibal* all put different spins on these issues within the demands of their genres. The Romantic tradition also explores a certain sense of doom; Pauline Kael called Ridley Scott a 'visual hypnotist'.

Ridley Scott makes fairy tales, make no mistake about that. Every film he has directed has this element. Scott's heroes are frequently strong individuals, and sometimes innocents abroad in a world of darkness. In all his films there is a clash between the civilised and the wild. The director also brings to his work a connection and fondness for literature and, most significantly, visual art. Alongside Joseph Conrad, the other literary influence on Ridley Scott, directly or otherwise, is Friedrich Nietzsche, a German philosopher who developed the concept of the Superman, driven by force of will. Whilst working in a cinema financed by American studios and, for the most part, drawing on American ways of storytelling, Scott's British origins and broader European sense shines through in all his work. Yes, it is mainstream Hollywood moviemaking, but never completely. His films have a certain kind of restraint and willingness to explore the shadows. In an interview during the release of *Black Hawk Down*, Scott said he was keen to tell more stories based on events that have actually occurred, contrasting with the impulse of his earlier, more fanciful movies.

One of the key influences on Ridley Scott's cinema must be German Expressionism with its emphasis on décor, lighting, props and costumes rather than just traditional, stage-inspired dramatics. German Expressionist cinema is characterised by movies like *The Cabinet of Dr Caligari* (Robert Wiene, 1919) and the films of Fritz Lang, who directed *Metropolis* (1926), and who many years afterwards emigrated from Germany to America.

Scott is an inherently cinematic director because he absorbs influences and precisely because of the factor he is often criticised for: an appreciation for the dramatic potential of décor and artifice to enhance the human drama. Hollywood directors of European origin, like Josef von Sternberg, Alfred Hitchcock and Vincente Minnelli, worked in the same way during Hollywood's Golden Age. Stanley Kubrick, Jean Cocteau, Andrei Tarkovsky

(*Solaris*, 1972) and Ingmar Bergman, whose *Summer with Monika* (1952) was the first Bergman film Scott saw, can all be pointed to as key moviemakers for Scott.

There is a feeling of the baroque in so much of Scott's work. Over the years, interviews with Scott have also made clear his deep-rooted interest in architecture. All of his films show an affinity to and interest in shapes and structures as important elements in telling the story and suggesting the mood of an environment. In his talk about scripts, Scott has frequently referred to them as blueprints from which you build a film. One of his acknowledged favourite parts of the process is the script read-through stage, just prior to filming.

Like any director, the films Scott has not been able to make are as telling as those he has. The undeveloped projects remain like B-sides, offering further clues to the preoccupations of this storyteller. For more on these see **Ridley's Unrealised Visions**. Scott has openly stated that he thinks audiences should walk away with something after watching a film.

Since he is famous for his background in directing commercials, you could say a snobbery to this form has meant that critics have had their eyes covered by prejudice and have not been able to fully acknowledge Scott's achievements. For Scott, commercials were the perfect training ground and he felt unfazed by the experience of making his first feature.

When people call Scott a stylist it is not a specific enough description. You could say anyone is a stylist. But the style of Ridley Scott's movies is based around artifice and the fantastic in its broadest sense and neither of these things are crimes of cinema. Far from it. Scott draws on the tools of filmmaking, amplifying them and combining them to support the drama of the characters. Artifice is what art is, the act of interpretation.

Throughout his feature career, Scott has continued directing commercials, including those Guinness ads starring Rutger Hauer and more famously, in America at least, an ad for Chanel back in the 1970s entitled 'Share the Fantasy'. In 1986, Scott directed an ad for Pepsi, 'The Choice of a New Generation', that featured Don Johnson and Glenn Frey. Frey's song 'You Belong to the City' was the soundtrack for the ad. Ridley Scott excels at combining and referencing a vast range of art. In the best tradition of postmodernism, for Scott there is no distinction or problem in mixing some piece of classical music with the story of a rampaging space monster. Scott's heroes are frequently mavericks challenging the accepted order. Sometimes they are something of the wild child, other times they are absolutely of the civilised world. For Scott the wilderness is environment, character and situation.

Whether it is a creative sensibility or more a turn of character, Scott's films, for their frequently larger than life stories, are not as 'bubblegummy' as the adventure and fantasy movies of Spielberg and Lucas who were making their mark on popular cinema at the same time as Scott directed his debut feature. Ridley Scott had begun to wonder if he ever would direct a feature film. He is more interested in the elemental and psychological than the social. In this way, he differs considerably from many British film directors, particularly the generation that came to prominence ten years before he did, filmmakers such as Lindsay Anderson, Karel Reisz, Tony Richardson and Ken Loach.

Scott's films have a more sombre quality and as such are more akin to the films of James Cameron, who of course in 1986 made the terrific sequel to Scott's *Alien*. Maybe it is just that American popular stories have an inherently fun and carefree aspect; there is melancholy in all of Scott's films.

Working within the classic genres of cinema (horror, epic, war movie, adventure, science fiction, road movie) Ridley Scott has injected these tried and trusted formats with vigour and his trademark panache. In doing so he has shown himself to be as vivid and powerful a film director as Cameron, Lucas, Scorsese and Spielberg. Like those directors his work has influenced not just other films, in terms of the kinds being made but also their look, television programmes, music videos and commercials. Over the course of his 25-year feature career, Scott has told stories set in the past, present and future, crossing a range of exciting and intriguing settings. Movies such as *Black Rain* and *Black Hawk Down* are in stark contrast to those such as *Legend* and *The Duellists*. Or are they more similar than a first glance would allow us to see?

Like all of the celebrated cinema directors, Scott synthesises genres, styles, narrative tricks and conventions. The world shown in Scott's cinema is unmistakeably his. As his track record indicates, Scott has repeatedly fused commercial imperatives with an approach that is singular and unpatronising. His work exemplifies intelligent mainstream cinema and in some ways his

RIDLEY SCOTT Introduction: Welcome to Ridleyville

films have frequently been attuned to the kinds of concerns and hopes that seem to be looming large in the public consciousness at a given point in time.

Scott has never failed to make intelligent popular films and lend them an adult sensibility, even in his most fanciful work. 'You're the central artery,' is how Scott has described the director's role. Scott's *Black Rain* star Michael Douglas has said of the director, 'Ridley can see things that I can't see. When the celluloid comes back, there are things there that you don't see with the naked eye – it's a really incredible talent.'

Scott's movies centre on protagonists who are driven by deeds not words. Thankfully action, décor and composition all inform the narrative. From Maximus's quest to win his freedom and return home, to the urgency of Ripley going up against the alien, the heroes of Ridley Scott's films are heroic, stoic, determined and always able to rise to the challenge. Regardless of their settings, each film is a true adventure piece. Known for his whizz bang visuals and his background in commercials, Scott has proved his skill at fusing powerful images with rich drama and even some neat symbolism. He is equally at home on the desert highways of *Thelma & Louise* as he is on the high seas of *White Squall*. In each film, the environment is very much a character.

One of Scott's great skills that frequently gets overlooked is in his casting and directing of actors. He has worked with many of contemporary cinema's most accomplished stars and in several instances provided them with opportunities to revise their image. Just consider Harrison Ford's work in *Blade Runner*. Repeatedly, Scott has also cast actors who have gone on to big-time careers that continue today.

In all of his movies, Scott acknowledges the rules of the genre game whilst also pushing its limits. Regarding science fiction, the genre he has so boldly contributed to, Scott once said, 'I'm beginning to wonder if, frankly, some of the best material isn't emerging from the SF field . . . Some of the most original thinking and ideas are in fact emerging from the SF genre.' One day, we can only hope Scott will return to the genre whose potential for human drama and intriguing speculation he has done so much to promote.

Ridley Scott's cinema emerges as a cinema of archetypes rather than more obviously apparent social milieux. Refreshingly, Scott's cinema circumvented naturalism for something more symbolic and heightened, as such making him a stylist and fabulist rather more in the grain of Michael Powell. In his stellar career Michael Powell advanced British cinema with films such as *The Life and Death of Colonel Blimp* (1943), *A Matter of Life and Death* (1947) and *The Red Shoes* (1948), all of them combining real world settings with a more Romantic sensibility and an affinity for the fantastic. Powell's films, in collaboration with his co-screenwriter and producer Emeric Pressburger, held a huge influence over directors such as Martin Scorsese and Francis Ford Coppola.

Over the past 25 years of Scott's feature-directing career he has moved confidently and always intriguingly between distinct genres, ranging from historical drama (*The Duellists, 1492, Gladiator*) to contemporary drama (*Black Rain, Thelma & Louise*) and perhaps most famously science fiction (*Alien, Blade Runner*). As with all directors, it is frequently the less remembered films that engage most. Consider *Legend*, starring a very young Tom Cruise, or *Someone to Watch Over Me*.

Scott's work, perhaps a symptom of nationality and all the tensions and freedoms that can bring, does not do what a lot of other mainstream genre movies do which is to take a triumphalist approach to the action, to make it all dazzlingly comic book and thrilling. Scott's emotional palette tends towards the muted and sombre. Given that everyone is the sum of their experiences, Scott's art school background perhaps lends his work a wider range of informing sources, a finer sense of combing forms and fusing functions giving maturity and intensity to genres previously treated pejoratively. *Alien* is both a science fiction film and a horror movie, dripping with allusion and suggestion.

In his book, *Film as Film*, the writer VF Perkins says of mainstream movies, 'The belief that popularity and excellence are incompatible dies hard. It survives in the pejorative undertones of the word "commercial" and in the equation of significance with solemnity and obscurity.'

Scott's films run a little against the grain of most genre cinema, going for a strongly muted tone right across the board. In 1982, *ET: The Extra-Terrestrial* was the big movie. *Blade Runner*, released the same summer, just didn't have enough smiles for many people; it went for something less surefire.

Scott has hit the highway and the stars, taken us to enchanted forests and bloody war zones and every time he has made us root for the underdog as they find a way to make their mark. This might be a little surprising but, for Scott, part of the mission for him is to tell stories that are life affirming. As he himself said of his make-the-most-of-life outlook, 'That is a point in all my films. It's my philosophy . . .'

Born on 20 November 1937, Ridley Scott grew up in South Shields in northeast England. Scott's father Frank Percy Scott was a partner in a successful shipping business and was then in the military and involved in preparations for the Normandy landings. From all accounts, Scott grew up in an environment of order and discipline. About his mother, Scott has said that it was her strong character which gave him his admiration of powerful women. A child of the Second World War who, with his military father, lived in several places both in the UK and abroad, Scott grew up in an age of apocalypse and mighty machinery. Surely these things must have tattooed themselves on his young imagination.

After what seems to have been a fairly mundane school life, Scott attended art school at West Hartlepool College of Art. In 1958, he was all geared up for the military but his father dissuaded him. In a neat moment of destiny calling, Scott received a scholarship to the Royal College of Art, going in as a graphic designer. As part of his study he was able to study film and in doing so the potential of cinema opened up to him.

At the RCA, Scott made his first film. He wrote, directed and shot a film, called *Boy on a Bicycle*, which told the story of a boy, played by Tony Scott (Ridley's brother), bunking off school and exploring his seaside town. The short was in a sense an environmental film, a melancholy mood piece that indicated things to come, and which Scott has said focuses on being isolated. Like *Blade Runner*, the film features a sequence where old photographs play a major part in the main character's memories of his mother. Scott's father appeared as the tramp in the film and his mother appeared as the boy's mother. In a display of perseverance typical of many of his movie characters, Scott persuaded John Barry to provide music for the short: Barry specially recorded a condensed version of his tune *Onward, Christian Spacemen* after Scott hassled him for about seven months.

At art school Scott was able to pursue his love of art and in conversations and interviews he has described it as a passion.

Many of the heroes of Scott's films exhibit a passion for something – sometimes for better, sometimes for worse.

Like his on-screen heroes, as a director Scott works with efficiency. He has acknowledged many times that he does not like to hang around and just prior to *Gladiator* made the decision to ramp up the number of movies he would look to make in the future. Thus, the sudden torrent of Scott films since 2000.

After completing his studies at the RCA, Scott went on to a travelling scholarship with TIME Life publications to New York and worked in magazines for a short time and then in the production company run by documentary filmmaker hotshots Richard Leacock and DA Pennebaker, who most recently directed *Down from the Mountain* (2001), the concert film showcasing music from the Coen Brothers film *O Brother Where Art Thou?* (2000). Scott worked as an editor at the company, developing a familiarity with documentary aesthetics that has stayed with him and benefited all of his drama films. At the same time, he was being asked by the BBC when he would return to take up a position in the art department.

Before heading back to London, Scott took off on a road trip around America and then returned to the UK and worked as an art director at the BBC. Soon after he had the chance to enrol on the broadcaster's trainee director scheme and began working in episodic television, rather like Spielberg and John Frankenheimer had done in America in the 1960s. As the summation of the training programme, each aspiring director had to make a test episode. Scott chose to adapt a piece of literature, as he has done several times since in his feature career. In what might have been a little homage to one of his movie heroes, Stanley Kubrick, Scott chose to adapt Humphrey Cobb's *Paths of Glory* which Kubrick had made in 1957 with Kirk Douglas. Scott's version starred Keith Barron. The material was rehearsed for one day and then shot the night of that same day. Scott directed, designed, scripted and secured the props for the piece and the show was recorded, making a positive impact on the BBC producers. Scott swiftly found himself working on shows including *Adam Adamant Lives*, *Z Cars* and *The Informers*.

Alongside his episodic television work, Scott began art-directing commercials. He soon found himself frustrated by the limits of television drama and he made the jump into full-time work in advertising. The first commercial he directed was for Gerber's baby food and he was off and running. In 1967 he established Ridley Scott Associates (RSA). The company continues today with great success. At this time, other British directors were also breaking through, notably Alan Parker with whom Scott felt a healthy sense of competition. Parker made the break into features first. Like many directors, Ridley Scott has opted to work with a core team over the years on a series of films. He has also worked with many of the biggest names in the Hollywood film industry, and in each chapter there is an overview of the people whose work you will have seen or heard before and since working with Scott. Notably, Scott has frequently supported the careers of colleagues who began working with him on commercials.

Scott became a big name in commercials directing and would frequently shoot an ad in a day for clients including Levi's, Chanel and Hovis. By the mid-1980s, an established and successful feature film director, Scott would continue to direct commercials as a way of maintaining his skills and updating in the longeurs between feature projects. Scott's '1984' ad for the debut of the Apple Mac is considered a commercials classic, paving the way for the kind of event advertising we are now so familiar with.

Feature Future

In 1971 Scott was getting hungry to make the break into directing feature films. He self-penned *Running in Place*, a low-budget heist film in which Michael York was interested in starring, though in time it was *The Duellists* that would prove to be Scott's debut.

As of 1977, Scott's feature directing career was up and running. By the mid-1990s he was in a position to extend his activity to embrace more work as an executive producer or a producer with both feature films and television series. As such he is a mini movie mogul in a very American tradition. In the late 1990s, Ridley teamed up with his brother Tony Scott on the TV series *The Hunger* – Tony Scott had directed the feature back in 1983. Together the brothers head up a consortium which owns Shepperton Studios (see **Ridley Scott's Business Ventures**) and Scott has interests in London and LA-based visual effects house The Mill. Ridley Scott now stands where he once did before as a major box office draw, his name alone promising a cinematic treat which will never be boring.

So, how does this book work? This book follows a similar pattern to previous titles in the series. Each of Scott's films gets placed within a sense of his consistency and repetition of themes and forms. The different aspects of interest about each of Ridley Scott's films are broken down. Each chapter deals with an individual film and the chapters are arranged in chronological order. Like the other titles in this series the fun of the format is that you can go from one film to another regardless of chronological order. Read where you are most interested. Think of it is a free association guide to Ridley Scott's movies. You're the boss and soon you'll find yourself making connections between the movies.

These film-by-film chapters follow a general structure. Where appropriate certain chapters contain further subdivisions. All chapters include the name of the studio that originally released the film, the running time for each film and also their original American (MPAA) and British (BBFC) certification. Basically, the format goes like this:

CREW AND CAST: this lists the folks behind and in front of the camera.

SUMMARY: this provides an outline of each film's storyline.

THE CONCEPT: this takes you through the development of the idea for each film prior to the director's involvement and then how things progressed once Ridley Scott became attached. In certain cases, Scott developed a film from scratch, notably *The Duellists* and *Legend*.

CASTING: this takes a look at certain actors involved in a given film, including references to other notable films you may have seen them in.

MAKING IT: this concerns itself with the key stages that the film developed through. In some cases this process was especially labyrinthine and on others appears to have been a walk in the park. Basically, though, getting a film made is just plain difficult. Or challenging, depending on your point of view.

THE SHOOT: this section charts the course of the filming of each film. As with the **MAKING IT** section, some projects had their share of drama while others ran more quietly. In certain chapters, this section is further subdivided to make the amount of information more reader friendly.

COLLABORATORS: a look at the talent who teamed up with Scott to realise each film. As with many top directors, a core team emerges through the years.

MUSIC: Ridley Scott describes music as the final adjustment to his film and its performances and his movies brim with strong music scores. Later in the book (see **Soundtrack Listing**), each film's soundtrack is noted including their track listings.

THE OPENING: being such a visually driven director, Scott always makes the most of his opening credits or opening sequences to reel in his audience. In some cases they are like mini movies all by themselves – not surprising given the director's commercials background.

ON THE SCREEN: this explores the visual design of the film, considering the way that the visual elements come together to create drama and meaning.

HEROES AND VILLAINS: this explores the key characters of each film. In certain cases, this segment is broken down further.

PICTURE PERFECT: this explores Scott's visual motifs and tricks.

TECH TALK: this explores the frequent and dazzling use of special effects in Ridley Scott's movies. The section also notes any other quirky details in the nuts and bolts department of getting a film made.

MOVIE TALK: a listing of memorable dialogue from each Scott film.

THE BIG IDEA: this section explores the bigger themes of each film and sure enough you'll see that auteur spirit come shining through across the span of Scott's movies.

CRITICAL CONDITION: excerpts from reviews of each film and, in certain cases, other comments.

GROSSES: a note about the film's budget and then what it pulled in at the box office.

POSTER: a note about the image comprising the film's promotional posters.

HOME ENTERTAINMENT: details about the availability of each film for viewing at home and a mention about what extras you can find on the DVD releases. Let it be said here that Ridley Scott is a big fan of the DVD format.

AWARDS: a listing of those nominations and awards given for each film.

GREAT SCOTT: an overview and opinion of the individual film within the bigger Scott picture.

SCOTT FREE: a Scott quote about each of his films rounds out each film analysis.

The Duellists (1977)

(Colour, 95 minutes)

CIC Release of an Enigma Production
Producer: David Puttnam
Screenplay: Gerald Vaughan-Hughes from the story *The Duel*
by Joseph Conrad
Cinematographer: Frank Tidy
Editor: Pamela Power
Production Designer: Peter J Hampton
Art Director: Bryan Graves
Music: Howard Blake
Fight Arranger: William Hobbs

CAST: Keith Carradine (*D'Hubert*), Harvey Keitel (*Feraud*), Cristina Raines (*Adele*), Edward Fox (*Colonel*), Robert Stephens (*Treillard*), John McEnery (*Commander*), Albert Finney (*Fouche*), Diana Quick (*Laura*), Tom Conti (*Dr Jacquin*), Alun Armstrong (*Lacourbe*), Meg Wynn Owen (*Leonie*), Jenny Runacre (*Mme de Lionne*)

BUDGET: $1.2 million

MPAA: R

BBFC: A

SUMMARY: 1800, Strasbourg: on a quiet country lane a gooseherd girl comes across a duel between French soldier, Feraud, and the local mayor's nephew. Feraud severely injures the man and causes a ruffle in the local military garrison. D'Hubert, a higher ranking soldier in the same regiment as Feraud, is charged with bringing Feraud in for a hearing. Feraud is something of a firebrand and ladies' man and has gone to spend time with Madame de Lionne but D'Hubert tracks Feraud down and arrests him. Feraud is furious and, against D'Hubert's wishes, they duel. D'Hubert defeats Feraud, but D'Hubert's friend, Jacquin, a doctor, later advises him that he has heard that Feraud intends to kill D'Hubert.

1801, Augsburg: a soldier's tent in the battlefield of a Napoleonic campaign. There is a break in hostilities, and under these circumstances duels are permitted. Feraud sends an officer to trail D'Hubert and soon D'Hubert is duelling with Feraud again. This time Feraud wounds D'Hubert.

A colleague, Lacourbe, tells D'Hubert that one more duel would make his reputation. D'Hubert's lover, Laura, then tries to convince him not to fight again but he resists her plea. Laura goes to the soldiers' camp to find Feraud, who she tells, 'I believe you feed your spite on him.' Laura has her fortune read by a card lady and the foretelling is not good so she leaves D'Hubert. Another duel occurs between D'Hubert and Feraud and the meeting has a real savagery to it. Laura watches from the shadows, unseen. D'Hubert is seen by the General who orders him to duel no more. D'Hubert also learns he has been promoted to command a troop.

1806, Lübeck: in a boarding house/inn, D'Hubert, now a major, learns that Feraud is in the same room having not initially seen him. Attempting to make a getaway, D'Hubert is sighted by Feraud. D'Hubert walks away. He later bumps into Laura who has left France. D'Hubert and Lacourbe talk about Feraud and duelling. Clearly, D'Hubert has misgivings. Another duel is arranged, this time on horseback. D'Hubert and Feraud charge at one another and D'Hubert wins this challenge and rides to victory.

1812, Russia: amidst the snow and cold of a camp at night, D'Hubert sights Feraud watching him. They are both bearded and exhausted and go to duel again, this time using pistols. Their duel is cut short by Cossacks before it even begins and D'Hubert and Feraud fight side by side for a moment, firing at the Russians.

1814, Tours: D'Hubert is limping now and is spending time with his sister and family at her chateau. She tells her brother he should think about marriage. There is a neighbouring family who have a daughter – D'Hubert meets the young woman and sure enough they fall in love and marry. Napoleon's reign ends and Louis is once more the King of France. D'Hubert is visited by the Colonel who informs him he is not a Napoleonic supporter, despite fighting in his army. Feraud describes D'Hubert as a traitor to Treillard.

1816, Paris: D'Hubert comes across the Colonel again who informs D'Hubert that Feraud has been arrested as a Napoleon sympathiser. D'Hubert goes and sees Fouche, the commander of the army, and has him strike Feraud's name from the list of suspected dead men, though he says Feraud should never know he has done this. Feraud walks the streets and is informed of where D'Hubert is based.

At home, D'Hubert takes a walk and is met by two of Feraud's associates who say a final duel is necessary. D'Hubert is reluctant but accepts and he and Feraud duel once more in the woods and the grounds of a castle. When the moment comes, D'Hubert has the advantage but chooses not to kill Feraud.

D'Hubert returns to his family and Feraud wanders alone through the countryside.

THE CONCEPT: Scott teamed up with writer Gerald Vaughan-Hughes and they developed two screenplays: one based on the the Gunpowder Plot of 1605, one of the first terrorist efforts in British history in which a group of Catholics led by Guy Fawkes tried to blow up the Houses of Parliament. The other project, which Hollywood studios felt was too intellectual, was a drama based on a real nineteenth-century palaeontologist in America: 'Indian' Capwell. A keen reader, Scott had also recently been going through the works of Joseph Conrad and was excited by the possibilities of his short story, *The Duel*.

The film was originally to have retained the original title, but Scott and Vaughan-Hughes began working up a script entitled *The Duellists*. It was initially intended as a sixty-minute TV drama piece and they pitched it to French television company Technicinol. The company put up a budget of around £150,000 but soon the script mushroomed and Technicinol were unable to remain committed to the project at its new scale. Scott then took the project to America to Hallmark Hall of Fame who had moved into producing TV drama. Again, the proposed budget proved too high for TV. However, Scott was advised by the Americans to pitch it as a theatrical feature and so he returned to London and went to David Puttnam and his company Enigma. Puttnam agreed to produce the film.

Puttnam had been in Cannes with *Bugsy Malone* (Alan Parker, 1976) when David Picker of Paramount Pictures asked if he knew any other hot directors and Puttnam put Ridley Scott's name forward. He then called Scott urging him to come and meet with Picker. Scott jumped on a plane and flew to Cannes the next day. Puttnam and Scott offered Picker *The Gunpowder Plot* and *The Duellists*. *The Gunpowder Plot* film was budgeted at about $2 million and *The Duellists* at $1.2 million. Picker went with the cheaper production.

The film got good reviews but not such good distribution. There were only seven prints ever made.

CASTING: Scott cast upcoming star Harvey Keitel, who felt he was wrong for a film with such an explicitly European setting. Keitel had just appeared in Martin Scorsese's *Mean Streets* (1974) and *Taxi Driver* (1976). He would also go on to appear as Judas Iscariot in *The Last Temptation of Christ* (1988) for Scorsese and also work with Scott again in *Thelma & Louise*.

Keith Carradine had just starred in Robert Altman's *Thieves Like Us* (1974) when Scott cast him.

Supporting characters were played by established and new British actors who included Edward Fox, Albert Finney, Pete Postlethwaite (as a barber) and Tom Conti. By this time Finney had starred in *Saturday Night and Sunday Morning* (Karel Reisz, 1960), *Tom Jones* (Tony Richardson, 1963) and *Charlie Bubbles* (directed by Finney, 1967). He went on to appear in *Murder on the Orient Express* (Sidney Lumet, 1974), *Miller's Crossing* (Joel Coen, 1990) and *The Browning Version* (Mike Figgis, 1994) amongst others. *The Duellists* marked Pete Postlethwaite and Tom Conti's feature film debuts. Postlethwaite went on to star in *In the Name of the Father* (Jim Sheridan, 1993), *The Lost World: Jurassic Park* (Steven Spielberg, 1993), *The Usual Suspects* (Bryan Singer, 1995) and *Brassed Off* (Mark Herman, 1996). Tom Conti starred in *Merry Christmas, Mr Lawrence* (Nagisa Oshima, 1983) and *Reuben, Reuben* (Robert Ellis Miller, 1983). He also appeared as the father of the bride when Ross and Emily got married in the wedding episodes of American sit-com *Friends*. Diana Quick continues to act, and appeared in the feature *Affair of the Necklace* (2002) and featured in *Brideshead Revisited* and the *Inspector Morse* TV series.

MAKING IT: By the early 1970s, Scott was hungry to develop his first feature film project. His work in commercials had been massively successful. Scott began considering scripts but none of them satisfied him and so he chose to develop his own material. He began by writing his own screenplay, a heist film, entitled *Running in Place*, which he anticipated Michael York starring in.

After a year of development, however, the budget fell through and the project went no further. What also became apparent was that because of his hectic schedule, Scott had no time to really devote to writing himself and so he began casting about for a writer to draft a screenplay from his ideas. Scott's first collaborator was John Edwards who co-wrote a screenplay with Scott entitled *Castle X*, a horror film with a medieval setting. The project generated some interest, notably from Robert Stigwood, the musical producer, who bought the screenplay by Scott and Edwards. The intention was to make a film from the script which would star the Bee Gees. Scott spent some time working with the Bee Gees on the project but finally Stigwood pulled out and the funding was no longer available. Scott was beginning to wonder if his chance might ever come (see **THE CONCEPT**) while his contemporary and friend, Alan Parker, was beginning to get feature projects up and running.

THE SHOOT: Against Puttnam's wishes, Scott worked as camera operator on the film. Initially David Puttnam was concerned that this would slow down the film's production and so he and Scott agreed to a test case which was that if, after five days, the shoot was behind schedule then Scott would no longer direct and camera operate. However, Scott's experience and confidence doing both jobs never wavered and the shoot stayed on course.

The film was shot on location between September and December 1976 in northern Scotland, which doubled for the Russian Steppes. The other key location was Sarlat in the Dordogne region of France. For the sequence set in the Russian Steppes, crew and producer David Puttnam had to don hotel blankets to portray soldiers; the budget could not cover more costumes. *The Duellists* was poorly marketed in 1978 and failed to hit the mass audience it was intended for. Interestingly, during the making of the film Scott regarded the project as something of a Western; instead it was promoted as an art house film.

COLLABORATORS: Producer David Puttnam went on to produce *Midnight Express* (Alan Parker, 1980), *Chariots of Fire* (Hugh Hudson, 1981), *Local Hero* (Bill Forsyth, 1983), *Memphis Belle* (Michael Caton-Jones, 1990) and *Being Human* (Bill Forsyth, 1993). Composer Howard Blake had worked on the TV series *The Avengers* and went on to score *The Riddle of the Sands* (Tony Maylam, 1979), *Flash Gordon* (Mike Hodges, 1980) and *A Midsummer Night's Dream* (Adrian Noble, 1996).

MUSIC: With *The Duellists*, Scott applied Howard Blake's period-flavoured score judiciously but powerfully. Blake's score – anachronistic with its twentieth-century tone – was performed by the National Philharmonic Orchestra, and the film concludes with a suitably brooding and grand Wagnerian-style theme.

INFLUENCES: As with all his films, one of Scott's starting points where appropriate is to look at paintings produced in the era in which the story is set – for this that meant referring to Napoleonic-era painters. One of Scott's informing film sources was Kubrick's gorgeous *Barry Lyndon* (1975); the work of eighteenth-century painter Georges de la Tour was an influence, notably for de la Tour's skill at creating a sense of subjects illuminated by candlelight.

THE OPENING: The film begins with a voice-over by Stacy Keach explaining that 'The duellist demands satisfaction. Honour for him is an appetite'. Honour is not an appetite just for the duellist, though. In Scott's subsequent feature films it will emerge as central to virtually all of the characters.

ON THE SCREEN: The first image is a wide shot of a country glade and pathway into which enters a goosegirl. It is a beautiful, gorgeous shot, almost too much so, as is the rest of the film with its brooding skies, filter shots and wide vistas. The film's penultimate scene is similarly beautiful. It is an incredible wide shot of Feraud looking out over a river. It looks like a painting. The last shot though is an intense close-up of Feraud looking bleak, angry and sad – an era has ended. The image is intensified by the melancholy of the film's score.

Contrasting with the static and stately shots of landscapes are the handheld, down-and-dirty shots of the duels, investing each one of them with energy and a sense of uncertainty. Scott also shoots parts of the duels using a long lens that gives the footage a documentary feel. It is as though we are observing the duellists from a safe distance. *The Duellists* introduces us to Scott's taste for kinetic action and willingness to portray violent behaviour as believably painful, both physically and emotionally. It is not comic book action.

HEROES AND VILLAINS: In keeping with the whole idea of the civil and the wild (the forces of order and society versus the laws of nature and chaos) that Scott will go on to develop in this film and in many of his later films, the character name of Feraud suggests the word *ferocious* and the character is very animal-like and wild. One of D'Hubert's soldier friends says of Feraud, 'He'll hunt you out in the end.' This observation only adds to Feraud's animal persona.

Even the way Feraud holds his free hand during the first duel resembles a claw ready to maul a victim. Feraud is a man of few words and his broad face and stocky frame contrast with D'Hubert's lanky body and long and more delicate face. Feraud is a fierce, strong person whilst D'Hubert is more fragile. One funny moment in the film focuses on D'Hubert's masculinity and sense of honour being compromised because he is suffering from a cold. D'Hubert's uneasiness with the duelling comes out further when he is shown wearing a glove for his first planned duel with Feraud.

As their conflict escalates over the years the story does have a comic streak like a Road Runner/Wile E Coyote cartoon albeit with pig-tails. Feraud and D'Hubert are not so much realistic and naturalistic figures as they are archetypal. They are like superhumans in their focus on duelling and the codes of professionalism. D'Hubert's mission to bring in the loose cannon Feraud at the beginning of the film is similar to Deckard being charged with bringing in the rogue replicants at the beginning of *Blade Runner*. Feraud is a maverick figure, a classic Ridley Scott hero; D'Hubert is the weaker duellist but stronger person because he questions the duels, at one point saying that he is 'far from certain' about why he does it.

Feraud is angry when D'Hubert's weakness wins out and abruptly brings an end to their second duel. Feraud shouts at D'Hubert, 'Don't expect decency from his kind,' and taunts D'Hubert in the same way that Batty taunts Deckard in *Blade Runner*.

These are men of action but D'Hubert is a man of thought too. He has to reconcile the personal and professional. There is a lot at stake when D'Hubert fights one last time. There is a family to live for, just as Maximus has a family to live for at the start of *Gladiator*.

The final duel in the forest and around the castle ruins emphasises the cat and mouse conflict between the main characters and Feraud is shown to be more at home in the wilderness whereas D'Hubert is more clumsy amongst the trees and bushes. At the critical moment D'Hubert does not kill Feraud. Scott's storytelling panache comes through as D'Hubert's decision is shown in a brief flashback so that initially it is not clear if Feraud is still alive. Then we see Feraud walking through the forest and Scott cuts back to the moment where D'Hubert points the gun at him.

You can draw a direct line from the soldier ethic of *The Duellists* through to Ripley in *Alien,* Deckard in *Blade Runner,* Keegan in *Someone to Watch Over Me,* Conklin in *Black Rain,* Columbus in *1492,* Sheldon in *White Squall,* Urgayle in *G.I. Jane,* Maximus in *Gladiator,* Starling in *Hannibal* and the soldiers of *Black Hawk Down.*

WOMEN: The film features several strong women characters, such as Laura, who can stand their ground with confidence in the male-orientated society that is the heart of the story. This is very much a Scott issue; see, for example, **G.I. Jane.**

PICTURE PERFECT: A lot of the film's lighting feels as though it has been sourced naturally with sunlight frequently pouring in through windows. Shot during the autumn of 1976, the film has a cold feeling to it that culminates in the Russian Steppes sequence in all its apocalyptic grandeur.

Scott's undeniable ability to compose a frame and image that looks great is on show throughout the film. A shining example of this is the shot that establishes the location of Feraud and D'Hubert's second duel with its background and foreground action and the men small against the landscape. Feraud starts in the foreground, up close to the camera before turning and walking into the background.

For all the historical setting there is the quality of a fairy tale in the story, especially in one key scene when Laura gets her fate read by visiting a tarot card reader – an old woman in a shadowy, but ornate, room. Of course, both D'Hubert and Feraud also fit this fairy-tale mould, particularly Feraud. Like Roy Batty in *Blade Runner,* Feraud is something like a Dark Angel for D'Hubert, a necessary evil who compels the 'weaker' man to act strongly.

The *Barry Lyndon* influence is also evident in the scenes that begin almost as still lifes of fruit and food before zooming out slowly to the master shot. Another shot in the *Barry Lyndon* mode is of D'Hubert and his sister Adele sitting, tableau like.

There is a humorous payoff when Adele, pregnant, feels the baby kick and she says 'perfect discipline'. The tradition that has caused so much grief for D'Hubert is going to continue in the next generation.

In contrast to the Russian sequence is the subsequent Tours 1814 phase of the film in which the action plays out in sunshine and against the delicate surroundings of a country chateau. During this part of the film, Scott uses trees and carriages to frame shots. The rooms are like the room in *Blade Runner* with all of the dolls and the Napoleonic teddy bear. The interiors are light and the story focuses on D'Hubert as his sister Adele encourages him to marry. It is a brighter part of the character's life. Adele says to D'Hubert that marriage is sensible and that 'Nothing sensible goes out of fashion'. She likens moss to marriage as a process of settling down. It is not the first time a Scott character will refer to nature to explain their behaviour. Tellingly, when D'Hubert fights the final duel, he pauses and looks at moss on a tree.

TECH TALK: Famously, the swords were hooked up to batteries in order to create the sparks. More than once the charge sent the duelling actors to the ground.

MOVIE TALK:
Feraud (to D'Hubert): 'You have insulted me.'
D'Hubert: 'I have strained my patience in order not to do so.'

D'Hubert: 'The only way out is to go through with it.'

The General (to D'Hubert): 'You persistently behave like a wild beast.'

D'Hubert: 'I'm not fanatical enough to persevere in this absurdity.'

D'Hubert: 'I'm a temperate man.'

D'Hubert: 'The king's army will have more realists than royalists.'

Chevalier: 'Honour before everything.'

THE BIG IDEA: Honour, dignity and fidelity to the unit propel the drama in which the men meet only ever with beautiful women, all of them proactive and strong, notably Laura and D'Hubert's sister Adele. The women are frustrated by the men's codes. Laura does not want D'Hubert to duel any more. He isn't as masculine as Feraud and explains to Laura that 'Honour is indescribable, unchallengeable'. Laura confronts Feraud about the duels saying that, 'I believe you feed your spite on him.'

Scott even finds a chance for a painfully romantic moment when Laura writes the word 'goodbye' in lipstick on D'Hubert's sword leaving him to find it after she has gone. D'Hubert is emotionally restrained when he sees Laura again, shot in very tight close-ups, and the physical restraint imposed by the military fashion adds to the moment. 'There's only grief to be got from following soldiers,' D'Hubert says to Laura. There is a frailty to their relationship as its lost love plays out.

All of Scott's films have a standout action set piece though in a film whose entire plot revolves around fights, this might be hard to define. However, the sequence that stands out is the duel on horseback (see **Top Shots**). Scott makes it work so well because of the detail, such as the shot of D'Hubert's hands shaking before the duel commences. The quick intercut with a few frames from past encounters emphasises D'Hubert's anxiety without resorting to dialogue. Scott creates a sense of chaos and the horse duel is over in a flash, as if we almost have not really seen it. It suggests the frenzy of the moment and it feels more like a nightmare than something that really happened.

The voice-over introducing us to 1806, Lübeck says that 'the map of Europe changed and so did military fashion'. The fashion seems more interesting to the director than any sense of history.

The most telling voice-over of the many in the film is the one that is the most Ridley Scott in its style. It's the introduction to the 1812 Russian Steppes sequence when the narrator says, 'The Emperor's grand army regrouped for Armageddon.' The Armageddon image and idea carries on into *Alien*, *Blade Runner*, *Legend* and *1492*. The whole Russian sequence feels intensely desolate and even has a fantasy quality about it too, especially in the shot of the frozen soldier. The images of the freezing faces of the soldiers lit by campfire light make them seem more like cavemen, in contrast to their elegant and decorative appearance earlier in the film. Feraud and D'Hubert are both like bears as they eye one another up across the fire.

All first films are essential viewing because they tend to contain all of the basic character types and ways of telling a story that get developed down the line in often more remembered films. First

films are like forgotten treasures. Just as George Lucas's
THX-1138 (1971) sows the seeds for the *Star Wars* double trilogy
(1977–2005), just as *Boxcar Bertha* (Martin Scorsese, 1972)
anticipates *Taxi Driver* (1975) and just as *The Sugarland Express*
(Steven Spielberg, 1974) sets the trail followed by his most recent
film *Catch Me If You Can* (2002), so too does Ridley Scott's *The
Duellists* set out his cinematic pitch. *The Duellists* is a mood piece
film, like *Blade Runner* and *Legend*, and the setting is very much a
character itself.

Howard Blake's score really plays up the film's melancholy and
the entire piece has the same control exerted by the characters in
the film. There is precision and technological skill, and enough
warmth and human frailty on display to match and make the
story ring true beyond its storyworld.

CRITICAL CONDITION: 'Exciting enough in adventure story
fashion thanks to its series of vividly staged duels, Ridley Scott's
film is shot in a style that all too clearly betrays the dampening
influence of television . . . Moreover it confirms once again that
Conrad at his best does not translate to the cinema too easily,'
was the *Monthly Film Bulletin*'s comment on this debut.
According to *Time Out*, 'The filmmakers dubiously opt for a kind
of Napoleonic Western . . .' while the *Chicago Reader*'s Dave
Kehr concluded that 'The pleasures are mainly pictorial: damp
green landscapes and heavy gray skies.'

POSTER: The faces of Feraud and D'Hubert dominate the upper
part of the image while the bottom part of the photo montage
shows horses riding through the grounds of a country house.

HOME ENTERTAINMENT: *The Duellists* has turned up on
television occasionally, usually in a late-night slot, typically billed
as a cult classic, but otherwise it has been hard to track down. In
spring 2002 it was released on VHS, making this wonderful film
available again. From all accounts, a DVD release of *The Duellists*
is due for 2003.

AWARDS: The film was a big shot in the arm for Ridley Scott's
feature career as it was screened at the Cannes Film Festival in
1977 and won the award for Best First Work. It was also
nominated for the Palme d'Or at Cannes.

GREAT SCOTT: A highly assured debut movie which sets in place many of the themes and motifs that will recur in Scott's subsequent films. It is an essential Ridley Scott film, of economical and powerful storytelling. The performances testify to Scott's skill with actors and while the pretty pictures sometimes get the better of him they are, at the least, atmospheric. With its military setting the film is the perfect companion piece to *Gladiator*. Like that film too, the story is set against men pitched one on one when certain codes prevail. *The Duellists* is gorgeous to look at and frequently feels like a painting. Like so many great films, *The Duellists* is so simple in its structure, each segment of the film another riff on the themes and characters at work in the story. One of Ridley Scott's finest hours. A quiet classic.

SCOTT FREE: '. . . the Sarlat locations were so beautiful, it was like stepping back in time'.

Alien (1979)

(Colour, 124 minutes)

20th Century Fox
A Brandywine-Ronald Shusett Production
Producers: Gordon Carroll, David Giler and Walter Hill
Executive Producer: Ronald Shusett
Associate Producer: Ivor Powell
Screenplay: Dan O'Bannon
Cinematographer (Eastman Color): Derek Vanlint
Editor: Terry Rawlings
Sound: Derrick Leather
Production Design: Michael Seymour
Art Direction: Les Dilley and Roger Christian
Special Effects: Brian Johnson and Nick Allder
Costumes: John Mollo
1st Assistant Director: Paul Ibbetson
Music: Jerry Goldsmith

CAST: Tom Skerritt (*Dallas*), Sigourney Weaver (*Ripley*), Veronica Cartwright (*Lambert*), Harry Dean Stanton (*Brett*), John Hurt (*Kane*), Ian Holm (*Ash*), Yaphet Kotto (*Parker*), Bolaji Badejo (*Alien*)

RIDLEY SCOTT Alien

BUDGET: $8.5 million

MPAA: R

BBFC: X

TAG LINE: In space, no one can hear you scream.

SUMMARY: It is the future: a hulk of a spaceship called the *Nostromo*, a commercial towing vehicle, drifts through space. Inside the ship the crew of seven – five men and two women, and one cat – awake from deep sleep and start their working day. The crew gripe about work for the Company and are then informed by Captain Dallas that they have a mission to check out a distress call from a nearby planet. Some of the crew are willing and others more reluctant.

Three of the crew, Kane, Lambert and Dallas, go on to the planet's surface and explore. Kane discovers a bizarre egg nest but on closer inspection is attacked by one of the creatures as it hatches. Kane is brought back on board, against the wishes of Warrant Officer Ripley, who says he should be quarantined first. Dallas and Ash remove the creature from Kane's helmet and examine it, in an effort to assess its origin and function. Soon after, the creature breaks free and is loose in the quarantine bay.

Tension builds between the crew as they try to find the creature. The *Nostromo* takes off from the surface of the planet. Some crew want to eject the creature into space but Ash insists they take it home for study. Kane eventually awakes but soon after dies, bloodily. He is buried in space and the crew then set about tracking down the alien which is somewhere on the ship. The oldest crew-member, Brett, is the alien's next victim. The crew then design a tracking device to find the alien and hatch a plan to trap the beast in the ship's airlocks. Ripley offers to go into the airlocks but is denied. Captain Dallas does this and pays the price when confronted by the alien. Throughout the trauma, Ash seems spookily unruffled. With Dallas dead, Ripley assumes responsibility. She co-ordinates the effort to defeat the alien. Ash's cold behaviour is then explained when he short circuits after an argument with Ripley, revealing himself to be a robot. The robot Ash is apparently on board to ensure the Company's protocol is maintained. Ash therefore quotes the crew contract and expresses a disquieting and unquestioning fidelity to the Company throughout the film.

Lambert and Parker team up to explore and are killed by the alien. Ripley is the sole survivor. With her incinerator gun, she determinedly tracks the alien. Ripley then sets the *Nostromo*'s self-destruct system and she goes to board the escape shuttle (see **Top Shots**). Once aboard the shuttle Ripley is sure her trauma is over; she has even found the energy to save the *Nostromo*'s cat Jones. The *Nostromo* finally explodes. Ripley prepares to sleep, but realises she is not alone. The alien is on board the shuttle. Ripley finally kills the beast and sleeps peacefully.

THE CONCEPT: Back in America, after the shutdown on *Dune* (see **MAKING IT**), Dan O'Bannon teamed up with his screenwriter friend, Ron Shusett, and they began developing ideas for new material. One of the pieces they began changing was the script that O'Bannon had half completed under the title of *Memory*. This became the first part of what would become *Alien*. O'Bannon was not sure of how to finish this script until Shusett reminded his friend of his other idea of gremlins on board a B17 bomber during World War II. Interestingly, Roald Dahl had also written a story for Walt Disney back in the 1940s, as part of the war effort, entitled *The Gremlins* in which woodland creatures wreak havoc on the airmen who have built an air hangar in the woods. Shusett suggested this 'gremlins' premise would fit well with the first half of *Memory*. The initial full draft was titled *Star Beast*. One of the great things of writing is that you sometimes bump into a really smart idea that you never saw coming. It was only when O'Bannon was working on dialogue for the script that he came up with titling it *Alien*. There is a starkness to the film's title, reflected in the simple font used for the lettering and the far from thrills and spills tone of the poster.

At this stage, a key factor in O'Bannon's work on the script (and prior to Ridley Scott coming on board) was the work of HR (Hans Rudi) Giger that he had seen back in 1975. In *The Book of Alien* by Paul Scanlon and Michael Gross, O'Bannon says, 'I had never seen anything that was quite as horrible and at the same time as beautiful as his work.'

In O'Bannon's mind *Alien* would be a low-budget movie. To fuel interest in the screenplay, O'Bannon called on his illustrator friend Ron Cobb to render several production illustrations. Script and pictures were sent out and there was swift and serious interest. Brandywine Productions bought the material and made a deal with 20th Century Fox. Walter Hill and David Giler reworked O'Bannon's script: a major subplot around the alien was dropped and the android/Ash subplot was added.

At about this time, in Britain, Ridley Scott had seen his *Tristan and Isolde* (see **Ridley's Unrealised Visions**) fold up after initial interest from Paramount, which had reached the point where Scott had even begun developing the project. Simultaneously, the head of 20th Century Fox in London, Sandy Leiberson, had been impressed by *The Duellists* and the studio had a film they wanted to make but no director attached. Lieberson felt Scott might be the man for the job.

The script for *Alien* was sent to Scott who read it with real excitement and soon after joined the project. He storyboarded the entire film and the executives at 20th Century Fox were apparently so impressed they happily pumped the budget up from $4.2 million to $8.5 million.

With the original Dan O'Bannon draft rewritten by Walter Hill and David Giler, who changed not so much structure but dialogue and detail and made Ripley a woman, Scott had released himself from the fading *Tristan and Isolde* project, *Knight* (see **Ridley's Unrealised Visions**), and, in transferring to the *Alien* production, he brought with him many collaborators and associates from his years in advertising. A notable talent in this respect was Scott's RSA colleague Michael Seymour who served as production designer on the film.

CONCEPTUAL ART: As with *Star Wars* and so many other big-budget fantasy movies, the developmental artwork for *Alien* is an eye candy explosion and a saga in itself. Looking through the images it is astonishing to see the density and expanse of thought that went into designing the look of the film. Chris Foss was charged with designing the exteriors of what was eventually called the *Nostromo,* and its shuttle craft the *Narcissus*. The *Nostromo* had previously been called the *Leviathan*. One of Foss's most striking images was of refinery platforms built on asteroids. The artist also designed a fixer robot for a sequence where the badly damaged ship needs attending to. An early design for the ship had a snakelike form. It always seems to be the case that so much pre-production art that never got taken further feels more intriguing than what was finally approved.

Foss's designs were then synthesised with Cobb and Ridley Scott's concepts. Close to production, there was still no approved alien design. One attempt resulted in a kind of space octopus while another resembled a small dinosaur. It was at this point that Dan O'Bannon showed Scott the collection of Giger's art in the book *Necronomicon*. Scott responded particularly to the feel of two images in that book: *Necronom IV* and *V*. Like everyone who saw the film, Scott was affected by Giger's primal quality and the undeniably disturbing connotations of the design. Over the years, Giger's work has been likened to that of Hieronymus Bosch and Francis Bacon. There is a grotesquerie to the film which, in a way, Scott returned to with *Hannibal* in 2001.

The original face-hugger design was much bigger than the form it takes in the film. An initial concept was for it to use a large muscular tail to spring out of its egg. It was Scott who pushed for it just being face sized. The look of not only the fully grown alien but also its early versions was to become an iconic and genre-defining image, paving the way for a run of movie monsters. Giger's alien was not just frightening; it was far removed from the bug-eyed aliens of old. There was something truly primal about it, like a shark. The concept of the beast was powerfully elevated by the sexual subtext of the design. This sensibility carried over into the wider design of the film and continued to shape the look and feel of the three films that followed in the series.

In a creepy way, the set for *Alien* included real bones. Scott, Giger and the design team created a primitive, viscous world that has since provoked an ongoing interest in the power of the film's images. Giger self-dubbed his design style as biomechanics.

In an interview with *Starlog* magazine in 1986, at the time of the release of the sequel, *Aliens* (James Cameron), Sigourney Weaver recalled working on *Alien* and described the fully evolved alien as 'this huge, erotic creature, a wonderful exploitation of everybody's darkest fears'. One of the concepts that Giger was interested in was the degree to which humans and their efforts are perishable.

Giger designed the alien in its three phases and also envisioned the planet the crew land on, the calcified 'space jockey' and cannon. Once the film went into production, Giger took responsibility for sculpting and constructing the face-hugger and big alien – O'Bannon felt the big alien was 'not only savage, it's also ignorant'.

Giger's nickname for the big alien was Alien Dessert. In his 1986 sequel, James Cameron elaborated further on the suggestions of motherhood through the interface between Ripley as woman and the concept of the alien eggs and birth. He also took the last twenty minutes of *Alien* with Ripley running wildly around the ship and made it the guiding principle for the entire film.

At one point Giger had designed an egg chamber that resembled a breast. Just as Giger was a major influence on *Alien*, Giger's big influences included the fiction of Edgar Allan Poe and HP Lovecraft. At one point in his life, Giger had kept a dream book to record images that carried a real intensity for him.

Ridley Scott was unable to find the right space in the story to show the alien culture, as much as he wanted to. For him, though, the coating of slime on the alien towards the end of the film indicates the commencement of its life cycle again by going into a cocoon.

At the time of *Alien*'s release, Timothy Leary delighted in the creature's power to evoke thoughts about what was beautiful and what was beastly. Acclaimed American writer Harlan Ellison put it most acutely in his foreword to the book HR Giger's *Biomechanics* (1990): 'The man is trying to unnerve us.'

The film showed cinema audiences that, among many other strengths, one of Ridley Scott's great skills would be in pumping fresh blood into familiar genres. *Alien*, like the subsequent *Blade Runner*, impacted massively on the look of many science fiction films to come. Along with *Star Wars* (George Lucas, 1977) and then *Close Encounters of the Third Kind* (Steven Spielberg, 1977) it was the high-profile film that let science fiction, in its broadest sense, become a staple of mainstream movie going. For many people *Alien* was the Rolling Stones to *Star Wars*'s The Beatles.

Alien was Scott's second feature and was the film that blasted him into the movie major league. 20th Century Fox distributed the film, adding to their contribution to great science fiction and fantasy movies of our time. Produced by Walter Hill, Gordon Carroll and David Giler the film was shot in England. *Alien* went on to do what several other Scott movies would: it broke out of its cinema origins and became an icon in pop culture (Weaver would get letters from fans). The film has been endlessly referenced, discussed and alluded to in other films, stories and even computer games.

In keeping with Hollywood tradition, and fuelled by the success of *Star Wars*, there were numerous tie-in products, including a novel by film-novelisation king Alan Dean Foster (who also adapted *Aliens* to novel form in 1986). There were also behind-the-scenes guides, typical press packs produced by the studio. *Heavy Metal* magazine published *Alien: The Illustrated Story* by comic book kings Archie Goodwin and Walter Simonson. There was even a chestburster T-shirt. Perhaps the Holy Grail of collectibles which never made it to consumers was an action figure line by Kenner Toys who had struck gold with *Star Wars*.

With *Alien*, Scott initiated his conscious programme of 'layering' whereby every frame contained a density of detail.

From the first image, the film is engaging and innovative, reflecting Scott's commitment to a total kind of filmmaking. He gave Steve Frankfurt and Richard Greenberg the task of creating the film's opening titles where the word ALIEN appears by degrees across the screen. Originally, Frankfurt and Greenberg were working just on the poster campaign (see **POSTER**) but Scott wanted there to be a consistency with the print material and the on-screen credits: the poster-egg suspended in darkness, cracking, light emitting and smoke/mist. The film's trailers hint at menace and monsters with cracking egg, light, smoke and eerie animal-like wail.

CASTING: *Alien* introduced movie audiences to Sigourney Weaver and it remains perhaps the role with which she is most identifiable. She returned as Ripley in James Cameron's *Aliens*, David Fincher's *Alien³* (1992) and Jean-Pierre Jeunet's *Alien: Resurrection* (1997).

From all accounts, Ridley Scott and Sigourney Weaver collaborated well, and pursued the image of space pirates. Weaver had initially wanted to play Lambert because in the draft she first read Lambert was always cracking jokes. This initial version of the character is clearly very different from the Lambert we see in the film, who is not really what you would call a joker.

John Hurt was already an established screen actor by the time of *Alien* but since then he has gone on to ever-greater success in films and television. He has starred in *The Elephant Man* (David Lynch, 1980), *Captain Corelli's Mandolin* (John Madden, 2001) and cameoed in *Harry Potter and the Philosopher's Stone* (Chris Columbus, 2001).

Yaphet Kotto had made his mark in *Blue Collar* (Paul Schrader, 1978) and can also be seen in, among many others, *Stolen Hearts* (Ralph Portillo, 1996), *Homicide: Life on the Street* (TV, 1993–99), *Freddy's Dead: The Final Nightmare* (Rachel Talalay, 1991), *The Running Man* (Paul Michael Glaser, 1987), *Roots* (TV, 1977) and *Brubaker* (Stuart Rosenberg, 1980).

Prior to the *Nostromo* being invaded, Veronica Cartwright had appeared in *Invasion of the Body Snatchers* (Philip Kaufman, 1978) and has since gone on to appear in *The X-Files* (TV, 1993–2002), *LA Law* (TV, 1986), *The Witches of Eastwick* (George Miller, 1987) and *The Right Stuff* (Philip Kaufman, 1983).

Tom Skerritt remains a high-profile actor having appeared in *Contact* (Robert Zemeckis, 1997), *A River Runs Through It* (Robert Redford, 1992), *Steel Magnolias* (Herbert Ross, 1988), *Top Gun* (Tony Scott, 1986) and even two seasons of classic 80s sitcom series *Cheers*.

Ian Holm can also be seen in *Oh! What a Lovely War* (Richard Attenborough, 1969), *Mary, Queen of Scots* (Charles Jarrott, 1971), *Robin and Marian* (Richard Lester, 1976) and post-*Alien* went on to appear in *Chariots of Fire* (Hugh Hudson, 1981), *Time Bandits* (Terry Gilliam, 1982), *Greystoke* (Hugh Hudson, 1984), *Brazil* (Terry Gilliam, 1985), *Kafka* (Steven Soderbergh, 1991), *Naked Lunch* (David Cronenberg, 1991) and *The Lord of the Rings: The Fellowship of the Ring* (Peter Jackson, 2001).

Harry Dean Stanton has appeared in *Cool Hand Luke* (Stuart Rosenberg, 1967), *Dillinger* (John Milius, 1973), *The Missouri Breaks* (Arthur Penn, 1976), *Escape From New York* (John Carpenter, 1981), *Paris, Texas* (Wim Wenders, 1984), *The Last Temptation of Christ* (Martin Scorsese, 1988), *Wild at Heart* (David Lynch, 1990) and *The Straight Story* (David Lynch, 1999).

MAKING IT: *Alien* is a seminal science fiction movie, the genesis of which goes back to 1975. In France, screenwriter Dan O'Bannon and a legendary posse of designers were huddled to develop Frank Herbert's novel *Dune* for the screen with Jodorowsky on board to direct. The artists in question were all leaders in their field. There was British artist Chris Foss, French artist Jean 'Moebius' Giraud (see also **Blade Runner**) and Swiss artist HR Giger. Sadly, all of this talent could not wrangle Herbert's immense novel into a viable film form at the time and the *Dune* adaptation fell through. Dan O'Bannon returned to America and the team of artists disbanded. It would not be until the early 1980s that producer Dino De Laurentiis would bring David Lynch on board for a lavish and quixotic take on the novel (1984).

In 1974, O'Bannon had collaborated with John Carpenter on the film *Dark Star* from a story by O'Bannon who also appeared in the film as an astronaut who smuggles an alien on board the ship.

As he had done with *Star Wars*, it was Alan Ladd Jr who gave the go ahead to *Alien* from 20th Century Fox's Hollywood studio base. Ladd Jr has an astounding track record, having been the guy behind *Star Wars*, then this film, then *Blade Runner* and many years later *Thelma & Louise*.

THE SHOOT: Gordon Carroll and Ivor Powell, Ridley Scott's associate, served as the film's line producers, handling the day to day running of the production that began on 3 July 1978 and concluded on 21 October 1978. When Scott saw the miniature photography that had been initially completed he was so unsatisfied he scrapped it entirely and personally supervised the effects reshoots.

As with all his films, Scott spent much energy shaping the environments in which the drama played out. To support him in the development of the film's look Scott brought on board designer Ron Cobb, who had worked on *Star Wars*, notably designing some of the cantina boozers. Cobb was responsible for designing the film's interior environments and Moebius designed the space suits. Scott had long been a fan of Moebius's work and Moebius went on to work on other American movies, including Steven Lisberger's *Tron* (1982) and the George Lucas–Ron Howard movie *Willow* (1988).

Alien is as fully a designed world as that of *Blade Runner*, *2001: A Space Odyssey* (Stanley Kubrick, 1968) and *Star Wars*, immersing the audience in an utterly believable world. Roger Christian (who went on to direct movies such as *Battlefield Earth*, 2000) oversaw the ship interior work with Leslie Dilley responsible for the realisation of the alien. The shuttle set was constructed by rearranging elements of the bridge set and simply redressing them. The detail of the production design extended to logos and even down to the word *Nostromo* being stamped on fictional pieces of equipment and the creation of a Middle Heavens starchart. One logo for the film was comprised of Giger forms for each letter.

It was Ridley Scott who suggested the *Nostromo* be a tug, thereby steering the look of the vessel in a new direction.

Scott screened *Dr Strangelove* (Stanley Kubrick, 1963) because he wanted the sense of the military in space.

Actual medical equipment and real aeroplane panels were gathered and used for monitors and control decks on the ship set. From floor to ceiling the set stood six foot six inches high.

Ron Cobb designed the autodoc, air lock and Ash's blister capsule. Scott pushed for a cathedral effect in lighting the storage area. Roger Christian was responsible for props and guns. On one day, the flamethrower almost barbecued Scott.

As the script developed the hypersleep scene was alternately deleted and included in the film, more than anything else because it proved difficult to design an appropriate look for the space.

MAKE BELIEVE: Three *Nostromo* models were built: a twelve-inch model for medium and long shots; a 48-inch for rear shots and for realistic jet burn shots and there was a model attached to a seven-ton rig for an undocking sequence.

John Mollo designed the costumes for the film, having served in this capacity on films including *Star Wars*. Moebius worked for just a few days on the film, designing the space suits, many of them in bright pinks and yellows on the page. It was the intricacy of his design, the number of components, that stayed with the film. For a director so easily pigeonholed for his apparent artifice Ridley Scott has always elicited very naturalistic performances from his actors, notably rooting his more fanciful films in something real.

At one point there may have been more nudity in the film, showing the crew being so comfortable with one another. The *Alien* cast complained about the slim characterisation in the script. On film, however, their characters are rich and testify to the difference between the film and the script. It is not all on the page. Scott's skill at casting the right kind of face contributes hugely to the drama (see **CASTING**).

To make the planet on which the *Nostromo* lands look spherical the special effects crew spray-painted the planet model white and then projected transparencies of coloured dyes and chemicals on to it and mounted a camera over a tank to film it.

Wind, ice and fog machines were used for the creation of the planet surface and true to the film's detailed design philosophy the space suits even vented carbon dioxide through the helmets.

For the now legendary and intense scene of Kane's death, John Hurt's fake chest cavity was stuffed with offal flesh. Famously, Scott had not told the cast quite what was about occur when Hurt began writhing on the table top so the reactions of the actors are true to the moment it was filmed. Genuine shock horror is what we are seeing. The other greasy, gruesome scene was when Ash short circuits in a grand guignol of spaghetti and onions. The physical element of pre-digital effects has a lot to do with adding visceral energy to a scene.

To portray the fully formed alien, the film hired a 7ft 2in tall African performer named Bolaji Badejo. The costume was a full body cast. For close-ups, a specially designed animatronic head was designed and built by Carlo Rambaldi who had worked his magic on Steven Spielberg's *Close Encounters of the Third Kind* (1977) and would go on to further alien adventures with *ET: The Extra-Terrestrial* (1982).

Scott had been inspired by *The Day The Earth Stood Still* (Robert Wise, 1951) and the work of his contemporary George Lucas on *Star Wars*. The other films Scott was informed by were *The Texas Chainsaw Massacre* (Tobe Hooper, 1974) and *The Exorcist* (William Friedkin, 1973). Other influences included the Howard Hawks-produced *The Thing From Another World* (Christian Nyby, 1951), *20 Million Miles to Earth* (Nathan Juran, 1957), and *It! The Terror From Outer Space* (Edward L Cahn, 1958). In his book, *The Alien Quartet*, David Thomson also comments on *The Quatermass Experiment* influence on *Alien* in terms of the connection between a space traveller turning into something slimy and organic.

Rightly or wrongly, the impact of *Alien* hung around the director's neck. Critics would continually say that style won out over substance. It is the argument of a verbally driven culture who think meaning only comes through words. George Lucas has had to put up with the same reservation for most of his career. The content of a film is more than just what the characters say; if it could just be reduced to words then maybe it should really have been a radio play. A film's meaning comes through the way characters are placed in the shot, how they move, what they don't say and how they look.

Scott's interest and affinity for the work of Joseph Conrad got a further nod in *Alien* when Scott named the main ship *Nostromo* after the Conrad character and novel about a mine in South America. The conflict between big business and workers that features in *Nostromo* finds its way into the blue-collar world of the film. This is not a film about *Flash Gordon*-styled heroes. This is a film about regular people working in space. Scott also used the name Weyland Yutani Corporation for the company who own the *Nostromo* – the name is borrowed from Conrad's *Heart of Darkness*, famously the inspiration for *Apocalypse Now* (Francis Ford Coppola, 1979) and Orson Welles's abandoned adaptation. The *Narcissus* shuttle alludes to Conrad's novel *The Nigger of the Narcissus*, the plot of which revolved around a ship's crewman who becomes infected with a deadly disease; a neat tie-in with the *Alien* premise.

Over the years the resonances of the chestburster have seeped into popular culture with its associations of birth and fluids. The subsequent *Alien* films would continue to explore this image and its connection to Ripley as an emerging mother figure across the films. There is also a sexual element to the alien creature with its phallic-like tongue and its penetrative allusions.

When Scott presented his cut of the film, the studio were uneasy about its first 45 minutes, claiming that nothing happened. In this opening phase of the film, Scott establishes the character tensions, gives us a powerful and uneasy sense of the ship's environment and one killer jump scene. What more can a movie do in its first 45 minutes? *Alien* is a haunted house movie and Scott shows us around the house.

Another reservation that Scott negotiated with typical skill was around the ending. The producers wanted the film to end in the shuttle with Ripley escaping to safety. Scott pushed for the alien to be on board for a final confrontation.

The film was released on 25 May 1979 and was a massive hit, 20th Century Fox proving themselves as a studio who knew how to make science fiction movies, following on from *Planet of the Apes* (Franklin J Schaffner, 1967) and *Star Wars* (George Lucas, 1977).

COLLABORATORS: Early in his career, Scott worked with several big names in special visual effects. There was British effects ace Brian Johnson who began on films such as *When Dinosaurs Ruled the Earth* (Val Guest, 1970) and *Taste the Blood of Dracula* (Peter Sasdy, 1970) before working on *Space 1999* (TV series, 1975–77) and then going on to work on *Star Wars: Episode V – The Empire Strikes Back* (Irvin Kershner, 1980), *Dragonslayer* (Matthew Robbins, 1981), *The Neverending Story* (Wolfgang Petersen, 1984), *Aliens* (James Cameron, 1986), *Spies Like Us* (John Landis, 1985), *Slipstream* (Steven Lisberger, 1989), *Space Truckers* (Stuart Gordon, 1997) and *Dragonheart* (Rob Cohen, 1996).

This was Scott's first collaboration with Adrian Biddle, who went on to work as cinematographer on *Thelma & Louise* and *1492: Conquest of Paradise*, as well as *101 Dalmatians* (Stephen Herek, 1996), *The Mummy* (Stephen Sommers, 1999) and *The World Is Not Enough* (Michael Apted, 1999).

Derek Vanlint was cinematographer on Matthew Robbins and Hal Barwood's fantasy film *Dragonslayer* (1981) and in 2000 shot and directed *The Spreading Ground*.

Art director Les Dilley had worked on *Star Wars* (George Lucas, 1977) and went on to be involved with *Indiana Jones and the Raiders of the Lost Ark* (Steven Spielberg, 1981) and *Deep Impact* (Mimi Leder, 1998). He also worked with Scott on *Legend*.

Both Ivor Powell and Jerry Goldsmith worked with Scott again: Powell was the associate producer on *Blade Runner* while Goldsmith scored the European version of *Legend*. Terry Rawlings, editor also of *Blade Runner* and *Legend*, continues to cut big films, especially those shot in Britain. His credits include *The Core* (2002), *The Musketeer* (Peter Hyams, 2001), *Entrapment* (John Amiel, 1999), *US Marshals* (Stuart Baird, 1998), *The Saint* (Philip Noyce, 1997), *GoldenEye* (Martin Campbell, 1995), *Alien³* (David Fincher, 1992), *Slipstream* (Steven Lisberger, 1989), *The Lonely Passion of Judith Hearne* (Jack Clayton, 1987), *FX* (Richard Franklin, 1986), *Yentl* (Barbra Streisand, 1983) and *Chariots of Fire* (Hugh Hudson, 1981).

MUSIC: Scott's collaboration with Hollywood movie music legend Jerry Goldsmith was their first. Goldsmith had been scoring films and TV shows since the early 1960s. His credits include the theme for *The Waltons* TV series and movie such as *The Blue Max* (John Guillermin, 1966), *Patton* (Franklin J Schaffner, 1970), *Papillon* (Franklin J Schaffner, 1973), *Chinatown* (Roman Polanski, 1974), *Logan's Run* (Michael Anderson, 1976), *The Omen* (Richard Donner, 1976), *Poltergeist* (Tobe Hooper, 1982), *First Blood* (Ted Kotcheff, 1982), *Gremlins* (Joe Dante, 1984), *Basic Instinct* (Paul Verhoeven, 1992) and *The Sum of All Fears* (Phil Alden Robinson, 2002). Goldsmith's score for *Alien* captures the emptiness and loneliness of space with a surprising lyricism.

Though Jerry Goldsmith provided a vintage score, the film closed off with American composer Howard Hanson's Symphony Number 2: Romantic and also included Mozart's *Eine kliene Nachtmusik*. Scott had even considered a synthesiser version of Holst's *The Planets* being used for the film. During the part of the film where Ripley races around trying to kill the alien, Scott played *The Planets* live on set.

With the release of *Alien* on DVD, a bootleg soundtrack is available based on the material available as an isolated score on the DVD. More interesting, though, is that not all of Goldsmith's score is fresh to *Alien*. Goldsmith had previously scored a film called *Freud* and several pieces from that score are used in *Alien*. These excerpts feature during the shaft sequence, the moment where the face-hugger spills blood and the scene where Ripley is searching for Jones the cat just prior to the death of Parker and Lambert.

THE OPENING: The first 45 minutes of the film are dedicated to immersing us in the environment and rules of the ship so that the following action is utterly believable. Scott, like any strong filmmaker, will show you the world of their story rather than have it described in dialogue. He contrasts between the pristine white of the medical areas with the greys of the bridge and the light and shadow of the places below deck.

The film starts with a very slow pan right across the stars to reveal a ringed planet. This is not the gee whiz outer space of 1977's *Star Wars*. The title ALIEN appears incrementally. Scott wanted the design here to suggest hieroglyphics, so that the monster is suggested as from a culture and is therefore intelligent and not just an eating machine.

Scott's trademark use of well-placed sound is at work here. An eerie, unsettling sound runs over the credits and woven into this is an occasional heartbeat sound. The final piece of sonic layering in this opening sequence is Jerry Goldsmith's score as it begins to emerge.

Scott uses layers of sound to create atmosphere so that there is a powerful contrast between the hum and silence inside the ship and the hellish storm sound of the planet which makes it seem like it is screaming and alive. This silence on the ship is in striking comparison to the end of the film when all hell breaks loose as Ripley races around the ship – claxons wailing, footsteps on metal.

ON THE SCREEN: Scott's use of a dissolve to the establishing shot of the ship drifting through space continues the film's sense of menace and slumber. Once inside the ship, he takes us on a tour of the empty corridors and chambers and lets us take in the great detail of the ship's design. It is like being on board an intergalactic *Marie Celeste*. It's a full spaceship set, floor to ceiling and completely believable through the skilful lighting and camera placement.

A slow tracking camera moves through the ship to establish the environment and the deathly silence is finally explained: the crew are in hypersleep in their white and pristine bay. Ridley Scott has described the first shot of the crew in the film as showing 'seven babies all slumbering'. Scott uses a dissolve as Kane awakes, enhancing the sense of just waking; a dreamlike feel. There is the menacing chattering of the computer as it wakes up. All of the gliding shots during this part of the film make the viewer wonder if it is not the point of view of some visitor on board. Scott gives the film a wide range of textures from the video and monitor readouts to planet landscape in all its apocalyptic fury. There is something cosy about the working and domestic quarters of the ship though its engine areas and ducts are very threatening and certainly industrial.

The breakfast scene with the camera at head height, circling the table, has a real documentary feel to it as this very homely, domestic scene unfolds. These are real, earthy people not glossy space adventurers.

In keeping with images of birth and wombs, the Mother computer room is a chamber. The film has a running motif of woman with its Mother, eggs, genital-like openings of the discovered ship and of course Ripley notably in the last part of the film. The pod that extends from the ship is attached by an umbilical cord. Ripley is a mother figure and she is shown as protective of Jones the cat but she also emerges as the one able to be concerned for the crew as the trauma develops. 'You bitch!' Ripley wails at Mother during an especially fraught moment. Ripley is Scott's first big-time classically strong woman in a world of men.

Alien builds on the military sensibilities shown in *The Duellists* but in *Alien* the drama centres around the crew as a unit under threat.

HEROES AND VILLAINS: Scott elicits powerful performances from all his cast, with looks and visual work taking precedence over dialogue. In Sigourney Weaver and Veronica Cartwright he cast women with strong faces.

Parker, the engineer, is like the moaning child who objects to having to be involved in checking out the 'transmission of unknown origin' saying, 'It is not in my contract to do this kind of duty.' Parker complains about his work conditions to which Captain Dallas replies, with a sense of typical Scott duty and leadership, 'You get what you're contracted for like everyone else.'

Ash says there is a clause to go and do such work with no sense of real emotion.

When the alien is brought back on board, attached to Kane, Dallas agrees with Ash that the creature has to go back. Dallas does what the rules set down by the company employing them say. This implies the tyranny of capitalism over the workers. Adding interest to the science fiction and horror element is the way Scott brings out the mundane sense of boredom that will soon be shattered by something far more exciting, a rampaging monster. In his cool unflappability Captain Dallas is very much like Captain Sheldon in *White Squall* and Columbus in *1492: Conquest of Paradise*.

Little details enhance the characters such as Lambert being given a nervous tic as she totes on a cigarette. In contrast Ash is a figure of control just like a robot would be. He is more than human – in a way a precursor to Roy Batty in Scott's follow-up film, *Blade Runner*.

Dallas stays very calm about the face-hugger attack and remains so throughout the film. He abides by a sense of professionalism that ultimately he takes too far. Parker and Brett are in stark contrast to Dallas and Ripley particularly. Parker and Brett behave like kids and are apparently the least professional. All Parker does for much of the film is say that he wants to go home.

As the crew member who is in charge when Dallas and Kane are offboard Ripley stringently abides by the codes in place. She stresses that 'If we break quarantine we could all die.' She is the one with the clearest sense of responsibility to the unit. In Scott's movie world this sense of honour and professionalism is what makes her the hero. Ripley also emerges as a woman who can hold her own in male company just like G.I. Jane can (*G.I. Jane*). She is also something of a maverick who is frustrated by Dallas and Parker. As the crew fret about how to deal with the alien Ripley says to Parker, 'We'll blow it the fuck out into space. Is that acceptable to you?' Like Maximus in the arena with his gladiator team (*Gladiator*), Ripley pulls her unit together in the face of great adversity and they go up against the enemy with logic, courage and ferocity. Ripley insists, 'We have to stick together.'

Ripley's hard face in combat and her hair tied up for her end battle amplifies her strength. She becomes quite feral as she carries her incinerator gun. Scott uses a fire and ice colour scheme in this last part of the film, suggested by the flame and blue light. We see Ripley just sitting and crying with Jones, thinking she has killed the alien. When she strips down to her underwear and vest to prepare for hypersleep Ripley's vulnerability is enhanced just as the alien attacks one more time with its phallic-like inner jaw.

For all her strength and resolve, Ripley is fragile too and this is what endears us to her. She is almost in tears when alone in the Mother chamber, like a little girl lost in the woods. Ripley's drama takes her from clean-cut innocence to a very roughed-up and wild experience which James Cameron would ratchet up in his sequel film.

Interestingly, and as a great example of a how film novelisation can work best, Alan Dean Foster opens his adaptation of the *Alien* screenplay with backstory and character definition which explores what the film suggests.

PICTURE PERFECT: Scott's flair for powerful visuals even gets a workout in the points of light on the explorers' helmets. In one shot he uses these to emphasise the scale of the ship they discover. We see tiny points of light bottom left of screen. In this exploration sequence, Scott goes to handheld camera to follow the three of them. It is an organic environment, notably the ship they find. The ship is phallic and calcified, with its dead gunner and huge cannon. To intensify the moment of Kane's discovery of this, Scott has the camera pull back to reveal the immensity of the chamber.

The airlocks of the *Nostromo* are threatening to look at and also have an organic feel as the entrance holes to the Derelict do. The ship is visualised as a beast in the bowels of which the crew move, get lost and get devoured. Scott has created a future gothic world. The use of Mozart's *Eine kleine Nachtmusik* is a neat counterpoint to the grungy, wild and primal action and environment being unleashed. The ship becomes like a cave and the crew become survivors fighting with incinerators. In Scott's films, terror is often beautiful – just check out the shot of the hatchery as Kane descends. Kane describes the egg chamber as 'a cave of some sort'. All horror stories express a fear of the return of repressed events or emotions; *Alien* plays on such fears.

When Brett looks for Jones the cat and is finally attacked by the alien, the tension is created mostly through the near silence. Really, all we hear are Brett's footsteps and there is the occasional slow camera move. Lit from above, Brett's gaunt face is spooky in itself. Scott holds long takes, particularly when Brett freshens his face in the falling water above him.

As in all his films, Scott uses intercutting to increase the drama in the scene between the crew on board and those exploring. James Cameron would use this even more so in his war movie sequel *Aliens*. In the sequence of Dallas in the air vents later in the film, intercutting once again heightens suspense and emphasises characters being cut off from one another. Scott subtly gets the camera to zoom in so as to emphasise tension, notably as Ripley listens and talks to Dallas during his passage through the vents. The camera tightens on her face as she listens with terror. Ripley wants to go and tell the explorers to come back aboard. Scott excels at atmosphere that in itself is dramatic and this film allows him to not shy away from visceral action.

For the scene of Kane in the sick bay asleep the camera is at low height and glides around to find Ash monitoring Kane's condition.

Ripley comes in and they have a very edgy conversation. Ash is something of a neat story red herring. He is almost like the bad guy but he is not.

Scott goes for simple scare effects amidst the more involved tricks so that he uses the it's behind you tactic, as when the alien's tail hangs down behind Ripley. Or the it's above you approach and of course the less well-known it's inside you technique. *Alien* is Scott's first horror movie; *Hannibal* is his second.

As the tension mounts, the characters are lit from below, emphasising the spookiness of the situation as they move through the more shadowy areas of the ship. Lambert looks especially haunted.

The camera's frequent low height suggests something is going to pounce. Scott knows this is a haunted house film, rather like *Jaws* (Steven Spielberg, 1975) was a haunted sea movie. The scene of Lambert being killed really puts us in Lambert's position as the camera is placed behind her right shoulder and the alien rises horrifyingly into view.

Scott emphasises the chilling aspect of the action in the final phase of the film with his use of blue light. The sequence where Lambert and Parker are killed is made more intense and Ripley's feeling of uselessness is amplified because she hears it play out over the ship's communication system.

As Ripley finds herself the sole survivor, and all alone in the corridors of the *Nostromo*, Scott goes for a handheld camera. The endless corridors are like a dark forest that Ripley must get out of. The flashing lights, grilles, steam, light and shadow all add to the sense of claustrophobia, terror, chaos and the apocalyptic.

Scott does not use conventionally creepy music at points where you might expect it. Instead, we have just sound effects, for example when Parker and Lambert go hunting through shafts.

When Ripley is cornered she sings 'You Are My Lucky Star' which in part has a comic effect. Once the trauma is over, Ripley is lit by sunlight on her face as she files her report in voice-over and the camera pushes in gently towards her face.

TECH TALK: One of the *Nostromo* models was twelve feet long. *Alien* is a classic example of pre-digital effects, based instead around model work and low-budget, in-camera practical effects. Where *Star Wars* had a style based largely around speed, befitting its celebration of youthful energy, the ship in *Alien* lumbered through space. Scott builds tension and only in the last twenty minutes does the film unleash itself.

The planet set was constructed on stage H at Shepperton Studios under the personal supervision of HR Giger.

To make the seats of the ship vibrate as the ship takes off, Scott installed paint mixers beneath them and then, when they did not vibrate strongly enough, had to resort to asking the actors to shake around.

The closed circuit TV footage of the crew exploring the planet which Ash watches on his monitor was fed directly from the studio floor to the monitor in real time. In part, the decision to go with this was to disguise a model of the Derelict, an example of necessity and limitation being used to a creative advantage.

Small lead soldiers on a little track were used for the vast wideshot of the three crew members approaching the Derelict at the bottom of the frame.

The Derelict's walls were made of wood that was then covered with lathe and webbing which were then expanded by adding pre-cast plaster shapes. Finally, Giger would add the final layers and detail and the surface was then painted.

As the shoot progressed, Scott would respray parts of the set corridors to create a variety of looks.

It might surprise those familiar with the genteel landmark BBC Television children's programme *Blue Peter* that frequent guest and bird impersonator Percy Edwards provided the sounds of the alien.

Giger and Peter Vosey built a 1/25 scale model of the space jockey as a reference for the creation of the final, full-scale model which was 26 feet high. Giger would work on the detail of the space jockey through much of the film's production until the crew were ready to film it towards the end of the schedule.

For the egg hatchery, the live action plate of Kane descending and tiny against the vast chamber was expanded by a knockout matte painting by Ray Caple.

To make the *Nostromo* landing legs look bigger in one particular shot, Scott dressed three kids in scaled-down space suits for the shot of Kane, Dallas and Lambert going on to the planet surface at the beginning of the film.

For the inside of the face-hugger creature that Ash and Dallas pick over on board the ship, a queasy mix of oysters and clams was used.

To enhance the tension of Kane's exploration of the egg chamber, Scott devised the idea that there should be a kind of trip wire that would alert the eggs to intruders. Using a laser beam, the crew then pumped smoke under it, creating an eerie, otherworldly layer that Kane breaks through. For this scene 130 eggs were constructed and one was made with a hydraulic system in order to open up prior to the deadliest kiss in history.

When studio executives visited the set and watched an assembly of footage they jumped at all the right places. The film worked.

The face-hugger model was a metal skeleton covered with moulded latex. For the acidic blood that eats through the ship's floor a cocktail of chloroform, acetone, cyclohexylamine and acetic acid was made up. The floor for the shots was only made of Styrofoam.

For the egg that Kane discovers, skin from a cow's stomach was used and a sheep's intestine. The egg that Kane sees is rather like a heart beating and Scott intensifies its gooey form with a violent sound as it attacks Kane.

Roger Dicken originally wanted to design the chestburster to pull itself up out of the Kane's chest cavity using its own tiny hands. That's even more disgusting than what indeed happens.

At one point efforts were made to make the alien transluscent.

This sounds apocryphal but apparently one of Scott's early *Alien* notions was to have the alien devour Ripley, her head especially, and then speak with her voice in a message back to earth.

MOVIE TALK:
Ripley (to the alien): 'I got you, sonofabitch.'

Ripley (reprimanding Ash): 'By breaking quarantine you risked everybody's life.'

Ash (to Ripley): 'You do your job, you let me do mine.'

THE BIG IDEA: Where *The Duellists* had the wild spirit of Feraud, in *Alien* there is a monster to test the civilised world. Ash describes the planet that the crew explore as being '. . . almost primordial'. The alien, as an organism that grows dangerously inside a human body, suggests something cancerous and carried even more currency in an age of AIDS. *Alien's* horror film credentials are assured.

As in *The Duellists,* the clash between personal sense and professionalism is part of the drama. In keeping with the overriding sense of duty, for better or worse, Kane says, 'We got this far, we have to go on,' as he, Dallas and Lambert explore the uninviting planet. Duty over personal fear is central to the drama of *Alien.* Dallas says he'll take responsibility for Kane when they return on board the ship.

The film's drama also involves moments that characterise the relationship between humans and machines and the frustrations that ensue. There is Ripley's anger at Mother late in the film. There is Dallas's sense of comfort in being able to go to Mother. There is Ash, the android, who short circuits, casting his behaviour into a whole new light for the crew.

RELEASE: For the film's premiere at the Egyptian Theatre in Hollywood, a mock-up of the egg chamber, the Mother set and most astonishingly a three-quarter scale model of the space jockey were all arranged at the cinema.

CRITICAL CONDITION: 'As a science fiction film, it's seriously flawed, but as a horror film it works perfectly,' said *Starburst*. The *Monthly Film Bulletin* agreed, 'What keeps it going are the shock disclosures of the ever enlarging alien . . . there is precious little else to engage the attention,' as did *Time Out*: 'The limited strengths of its staple sci fi horrors . . . always derived from either the offhand organic/Freudian resonances of its design or the purely manipulative editing and pacing of its above average shock quota.'

GROSSES: *Alien* was the fourth biggest hit of 1979, behind *Rocky II* (Sylvester Stallone), *Every Which Way But Loose* (James Fargo) and *Superman: The Movie* (Richard Donner). It opened in 91 cinemas and then extended wider – by the late 1970s audiences were once more enthusiastic for the promise and uncertainty of space. The film grossed $60 million on its initial release and established itself as a bona fide science fiction classic, endlessly referenced by other movies. It was the first of several times that Ridley Scott would redefine a genre and make it stick. By 2000, *Alien* had grossed $165 million.

Upon the film's release, science fiction author AE Van Vogt issued a lawsuit claiming plagiarism of his 1939 story *Discord in Scarlet*. The lawsuit was settled out of court.

POSTER: *Alien* was a massive hit. Its poster was very different to the high-spirited images becoming associated with the revived science fiction genre of the late 1970s. This poster was stark, dark and menacing with the alien egg suspended in darkness with a crack emitting an unfriendly-looking glow. The development of *Alien*'s advertising always centred on the menace of the alien. An early poster design featured a silhouette of Kane with a hole ripped in his chest. The tag line reads: 'Once again, something has come from space and this time it's not a friend.' It was a smart riposte to the benevolence of 1977's *Close Encounters of the Third Kind* which would still be very fresh in audiences' collective memory in 1979. Further designs included statements such as Prepare Yourself. Another poster concept featured just a close-up of Ripley taken from late in the film as she confronts the alien.

HOME ENTERTAINMENT: *Alien* remains available on VHS, either individually or as part of the *Alien* quartet box set. The *Alien* DVD features a commentary by Ridley Scott, production photographs, conceptual art, trailers, promotional art, deleted scenes and a huge number of Ridley Scott storyboards visualising the entire span of the film. The disc also features an isolated score track.

DELETED SCENES: Inevitably a fair few scenes were cut from the final edit of the film. This material includes:

A dropped scene would have had a love scene in the blister with Kane's body floating by.

Before going to the planet, Lambert plots the course. Instead, the action cuts straight to the planet.

One of the scenes Scott cut was of Lambert discovering the fully grown alien watching her and then skittering towards her, its tail rising suggestively. Scott cut the scene because the creature looked too human.

When Dallas and Ash first examine the face-hugger, Lambert challenges Ripley for not allowing the search party back on board. In the final edit, we get hints of tension between Lambert and Ripley that are left over from this.

At one point, a scene was to have hinted at a relationship between Dallas and Ripley.

After the chestburster scene there was a scene filmed of the crew talking about their next strategy. Instead it goes straight to Kane's funeral.

After Dallas's death, Ripley and Lambert have a reconciliation. Ripley also alludes to Ash's robot status. Lambert is the more frail of the two women. Ripley says to her, 'Will you hang in there?' Ripley is strong and sensitive at this point. She asks if Lambert ever slept with Ash.

Inevitably, all films develop ideas and sequences that are then jettisoned prior to shooting even beginning. For *Alien* there was a fascinating subplot that never made it which focused on the explorers sighting a pyramid. The plucky explorers then investigate. Inside, they find a huge chamber full of statues and hieroglyphics representing the alien life cycle. In this dark place are the alien spores. As much as he wanted to explore this territory, Scott had to cut the scene because of its potential expense.

An action scene that was never filmed has Parker watching the alien as it enters the airlock. It gets wounded and spills acid. The ship's pressure level is threatened and the Alien escapes into the air vent.

The most famous deleted scene is where Ripley finds Dallas in an alien cocoon. This is an intense scene because Dallas is so utterly helpless and near death. The scene is shot as though only illuminated by flame so that the chamber feels like a Hell-hole. In part, the scene describes an alien's lifecycle and a heartbeat sound on the soundtrack plays up the intensity of the moment. In voice-over Dallas groans as Ripley enters the chamber down a ladder. Dallas says pathetically, 'Kill me.' The alien's cocoon chamber is like a rainforest with its primordial condensation. It is very much the alien's womb environment and Ripley is overwhelmed by the might of this natural force in such a hi-tech environment. 'What can I do?' Ripley asks plaintively before resorting to simply torching the chamber. The image has a powerful apocalyptic feel that James Cameron expanded on in his sequel, *Aliens*.

AWARDS: *Alien* won a slew of awards in 1980. It won the Oscar for Best Effects, for Nick Allder, Denys Ayling, HR Giger, Brian Johnson and Carlo Rambaldi. The film was also nominated for an Oscar in Best Art Direction where the nominees were Roger Christian, Leslie Dilley, Michael Seymour and Ian Whittaker. The British Society of Cinematographers awarded Derek Vanlint the Best Cinematography Award.

Jerry Goldsmith was nominated for a Golden Globe in the Best Original Score category. At the 1980 BAFTAs he won the Anthony Asquith Award for Film Music. John Mollo won the BAFTA for Best Costume Design and Terry Rawlings won the BAFTA for Best Editing. The BAFTA for Best Supporting Actor in 1980 went to John Hurt for his role as Kane and the BAFTA for Most Promising Newcomer in a Leading Film Role went to Sigourney Weaver.

TRIVIA: More recently, Scott has been associated with a potential fifth *Alien* film, the predecessors being *Aliens*, *Alien³* and *Alien: Resurrection*. He suggested that a return to the series would focus on the creation of the alien culture, perhaps set around a battleship carrying biomechanical organisms that could be used as weapons.

The film suggests the eggs arrived on the planet in an alien ship. The original script reveals the eggs are part of a genetic engineering experiment being carried out by the company that employs *Nostromo*'s crew.

Alien was originally to have been directed by Walter Hill.

GREAT SCOTT: *Alien* is one of Scott's landmark films and it strikes a perfect balance between characterisation, thrills, scares and a thoughtful script which offers up a range of ideas about what scares us. It proved his ability to combine thrills, tension and believable acting into a compelling whole. Its gore and gross-out level is minimal so that when it does hit the screen it has real impact. The film remains a textbook example of the need to spend time getting to know the characters before plunging them into terror, and it holds its own against the action spectacles of early 21st-century Hollywood. The film excels in its fusion of the atmospheric and claustrophobic production design with the down-to-earth drama where workers are frustrated by the rules imposed by the owners. This is a movie where there is more said in an anxious glance or tic than in any amount of dialogue, so the silence, which particularly defines so much of the opening of the movie, allows the anticipation of terror to grow.

Alien, of course, went on to inspire a whole range of monsters-on-the-loose movies. Movie history came full circle in John Carpenter's stunning horror movie *The Thing* (1982), in which a group of men are picked off one by one by a shape-shifting beast. Paul Anderson's *Event Horizon* (1997) was also clearly indebted to Scott's movie.

Alien continues to have the ability to spook and churn the stomach, and its intelligent and economically drawn characterisations remain a benchmark for the genre.

SCOTT FREE: 'The more sophisticated we make them the more frightening they'd be.'

'Every moment is going to be very slow, very graceful and the alien will alter shape so you never really know what he looks like.'

Blade Runner (1982); (The Director's Cut) (1992)

(Colour, 114 minutes)

A Ladd Company Release in association with Sir Run Run Shaw through Warner Brothers. A Michael Deeley-Ridley Scott production
Producer: Michael Deeley
Executive Producers: Brian Kelly, Hampton Fancher
Screenplay: Hampton Fancher and David Peoples, based on the novel by Philip K Dick, *Do Androids Dream of Electric Sheep?*
Cinematographer (Technicolor, Panavision): Jordan Cronenweth
Editor: Terry Rawlings
Music: Vangelis
Production Design: Lawrence G Paull
Art Direction: David Snyder
Set Design: Tom Duffield, Bill Skinner, Greg Pickrell, Charles Breen, Louis Mann, David Klasson
Set Decorator: Linda DeScenna, Tom Roysden, Leslie Frankenheimer
Visual FX Supervisors: Douglas Trumbull, Richard Yuricich, David Dryer
Visual Futurist: Syd Mead
Costume Design: Charles Knode, Michael Kaplan
Sound: Bud Alper
Associate Producer: Ivor Powell
Assistant Directors: Newton Arnold, Peter Cornberg

CAST: Harrison Ford (*Rick Deckard*), Rutger Hauer (*Roy Batty*), Sean Young (*Rachel*), Edward James Olmos (*Gaff*), M Emmet Walsh (*Bryant*), Daryl Hannah (*Pris*), William Sanderson (*JF Sebastian*), Brion James (*Leon*), Joe Turkel (*Tyrell*), Joanna Cassidy (*Zhora*), James Hong (*Chew*), Morgan Paull (*Holden*), Kevin Thompson (*Bear*), John Edward Allen (*Kaiser*), Hy Pyke (*Taffey Lewis*)

BUDGET: $28 million

MPAA: R

BBFC RATING: AA

TAG LINE: Man has made his match . . . now it's his problem.

SUMMARY: LA, November 2019. The Tyrell Corporation has begun genetically engineering replicants. People are moving Off World – a location free of pollution and filled with plenty. Replicants are used as Off World 'slave labour' and, following 'a bloody mutiny' of Nexus 6 replicants, replicants have been 'declared illegal on earth'. A Blade Runner unit has been put in place to shoot to kill any replicants: 'This was not called execution, it was called retirement.' In an office of the Tyrell Corporation, a man named Leon, a Nexus 6 mutineer, is questioned by a detective named Holden. Using an eye-dilation-based device, Holden attempts to assess the identity of Leon. Is he human or replicant? Leon shoots Holden down and escapes.

Across town, a weary Blade Runner named Rick Deckard is brought in to see his boss Bryant who informs Deckard of the job that has come up and shows him files on each of six wanted replicants. Deckard is reluctant but takes the job. He is sent over to the Tyrell Corporation to assess a woman there named Rachel. Also present at the meeting is Tyrell himself. After the test, Deckard and Gaff (who keeps making origami figures) check out Leon's apartment and Deckard discovers a snake scale in the bath and bags it up. Leon is seen talking to the 'lead' Nexus replicant, Roy Batty.

The Nexus 6 replicants begin to search for their maker Tyrell, beginning at an eyeball maker who they kill before following the piece of information he gave them which was to go and find JF Sebastian. Deckard returns home (see **Top Shots**) and Rachel is there, at first unnoticed by Deckard. She questions him about whether or not he thinks she is a replicant. Deckard says that she is. Rachel then leaves, leaving behind a cluster of photographs, including one apparently of her with her mother.

In an alleyway, a woman replicant, named Pris, curls up in the garbage. She is found by genetic engineer JF Sebastian who invites her up to his apartment in the eerily empty Bradbury Building. Sebastian has Methuselah's syndrome, meaning he ages unnaturally fast.

Deckard taps out a tune on his piano and then studies a photo of Leon's apartment. Using a piece of virtual technology, Deckard is able to chart the photo as though it were a three-dimensional space and sees a woman in the bathroom with snake scales on her skin. Deckard tracks down the guy who engineered the artificial snake and, from there, Deckard's investigation takes him to a club where he finds Zhora, the snake dancer. When she realises she is under threat from Deckard she attacks him but Deckard pursues her through the city, finally shooting her dead. Across the street, Rachel watches and Deckard at the last minute goes to find her. He is intercepted by Leon who tries to kill Deckard but is foiled by Rachel's intervention. Back at his apartment, Deckard freshens up. Rachel is there and they kiss.

At JF Sebastian's apartment, Pris spray-paints her eyes and then Roy Batty turns up. Pris and Batty spend time with JF Sebastian and eventually Batty is taken to Tyrell. Sebastian goes with him. Batty taunts Tyrell and questions him and finally kills him as Sebastian looks on helplessly. Deckard investigates JF Sebastian's apartment and is attacked by Pris who he guns down. Batty returns for the showdown and chases and hunts down Deckard. Finally, Batty dies, but not before rescuing Deckard from death.

Deckard returns to his apartment, where Rachel is and he protectively takes her into the lift to exit the building.

THE CONCEPT: After the huge success of *Alien* in 1979, Ridley Scott was ready to commit to a new feature that wasn't science fiction. Fate had other things in mind for him however. *Blade Runner* may well be Scott's 'masterpiece' and certainly one of his greatest films, combining rich emotional suggestion with stunning images of a not so far-off future world. The film is absolutely a cult piece, a status born out of its story and also its production history. Initially a box office failure in 1982, the film benefited from the burgeoning home video market of the time, which built up a newly appreciative audience able to view the film repeatedly and appreciate its minutiae of detail and design and the strength of its drama. Soon after its original release a movement of supporters and fans developed. Eventually a fanzine committed to the film named *Cityspeak* was launched.

CASTING: Originally, Hampton Fancher had envisioned Robert Mitchum in the role of Rick Deckard, then he considered Tommy Lee Jones and later Christopher Walken. Scott suggested Dustin Hoffman, who came on board for a period of time and worked with him to develop the character. Hoffman finally dropped out and the project was left without a leading man. Director Steven Spielberg had been raving about Harrison Ford during 1980 having just worked with him in *Raiders of the Lost Ark* (1981) and the industry was aware of the buzz. Scott decided that Ford would be their Deckard. (Deckard was originally to have worn a fedora but Scott didn't want to duplicate *Raiders of the Lost Ark*.)

Ford had been in two early movies, both directed by Francis Ford Coppola, but in which he had been far from the star. One was *The Conversation* (1974) and the other *Apocalypse Now* (1979) where he plays Colonel G Lucas. What Scott responded to in Ford in both these cases was a certain kind of creepy menace that certainly also came through at key moments in *Blade Runner*. In *Blade Runner*, though, the director and the actor revised Ford's image, going for something more downbeat and mature – it remains one of Ford's finest hours. Ford continued the popularity of his late 1970s and early 1980s movies with films such as *Presumed Innocent* (Alan J Pakula, 1990), *Working Girl* (Mike Nichols, 1988), *The Fugitive* (Andrew Davis, 1993), *What Lies Beneath* (Robert Zemeckis, 2000) and *K19: The Widowmaker* (Kathryn Bigelow, 2002).

Rutger Hauer had made a name for himself in Holland working with Paul Verhoeven, who also went on to a big-time Hollywood career. For Hauer, *Blade Runner* opened the door to many Hollywood movies, notably *Ladyhawke* (Richard Donner, 1985), *Blind Fury* (Philip Noyce, 1989), *The Hitcher* (Robert Harmon, 1986), the movie *Buffy the Vampire Slayer* (Fran Rukel Kuzui, 1994), *Flesh + Blood* (Paul Verhoeven, 1985), *The Osterman*

Weekend (Sam Peckinpah, 1983) and the high-profile TV movies *The 10th Kingdom* (2000), *Merlin* (1998) and *Fatherland* (1994).

Darryl Hannah received her fair share of recognition for her role as Pris in *Blade Runner* and has since sustained a real presence in a wide range of films and TV projects, which include *Memoirs of an Invisible Man* (John Carpenter, 1991), *Steel Magnolias* (Herbert Ross, 1988), *Legal Eagles* (Ivan Reitman, 1987), *Crimes and Misdemeanours* (Woody Allen, 1990), *Clan of the Cave Bear* (Michael Chapman, 1985), *My Favourite Martian* (Donald Petrie, 1999), *The Gingerbread Man* (Robert Altman, 1998), *Casa de Los Babys* (John Sayles, 2002), *Searching for Debra Winger* (a documentary made by Rosanna Arquette about women in Hollywood, 2002) and Quentin Tarantino's movie *Kill Bill* (2003).

Sean Young's career continues in a range of feature film and TV movie projects. Her credits since *Blade Runner* have included *Baby: Secret of the Lost Legend* (BWL Norton, 1985), *No Way Out* (Roger Donaldson, 1987), *Wall Street* (Oliver Stone, 1987), *Even Cowgirls Get the Blues* (Gus Van Sant, 1993) and *Ace Ventura: Pet Detective* (Tom Shadyac, 1994).

MAKING IT: At the time of the film's release, special effects co-supervisor on *Blade Runner*, Richard Yuricich, commented about Ridley Scott saying, '*Blade Runner* was Ridley Scott's movie all the way – even more so, I think, than Stanley Kubrick's *2001*.'

Blade Runner is science fiction, detective story, future film noir, postmodern, cyberpunk, humanist, fantasy. This chapter can only cover the basic elements of the film; for a grand tour of *Blade Runner*'s concept, realisation and legacy check out Paul Sammon's massive volume *Future Noir*, one of the most comprehensive film companions ever published.

The film's first rough cut screening for financier Tandem was bad news as the narrative was confusing. However, when the author of *Do Androids Dream of Electric Sheep?* on which the film was based, Philip K Dick, saw the film he loved it, especially the sense of the environment he put on paper being so vividly realised. This was an amazing achievement as Dick was vehemently unnerved by Hollywood. Unfortunately, on 2 March 1982, Dick died just a few months shy of the film's North American release, which he had been looking forward to immensely. In 1990, Paul Verhoeven's adaptation of Philip K Dick's work *We Can Remember It For You Wholesale* was released as *Total Recall* (1990) and in the summer of 2002 Steven Spielberg's version of Dick's short story *Minority Report* was released.

Many critics said *Blade Runner* lacked heart and sufficient interest (the *LA Times* called the film 'Blade Crawler'; see **CRITICAL CONDITION**) and yet twenty years later it is the film's *human* sense which is such a part of its popularity. So, quality endures. Sure enough a *Blade Runner* cult began to develop over the years and the fire was fanned by the publication of an academic book entitled *Retrofitting Blade Runner: Issues in Ridley Scott's Blade Runner and Philip K Dick's Do Androids Dream of Electric Sheep?*

The film's genesis is a long and winding road. Way back in 1969, soon after the publication of Philip K Dick's new science fiction novel *Do Androids Dream of Electric Sheep?*, the story had caught the attention of a new filmmaker at the time and his writing partner, Martin Scorsese and Jay Cocks respectively. Scorsese and Cocks were interested in adapting the novel but no more came of it. (Interestingly though, in 1995, the Kathryn Bigelow science fiction film *Strange Days* was released with a script co-written by Jay Cocks with James Cameron. The scenario and feel certainly evokes *Blade Runner*.) It was not until 1974 that Dick's novel was initially optioned but Dick, already cautious about Hollywood and film, was unhappy with the draft as it tended to take the story down an action adventure route. The project's development ground to a halt.

Having initially fallen at the first hurdle in an effort to turn Dick's novel into a movie, the ambition to adapt it was renewed in the late 1970s when an actor and writer approached Philip K Dick. The man's name was Hampton Fancher and, in the long term, the existence of *Blade Runner* goes right back to him. It was a circuitous and tortuous journey, as so many adventures in moviemaking are. Fancher responded particularly to the potential for a film adaptation to carry Kafka-like leanings of paranoia, enclosure and despair. Powell describes Hampton Fancher as 'a very romantic writer'.

After a series of scuffles and negotiations, Fancher and his old friend Brian Kelly (an actor turned producer) secured the rights and work began. Fancher's immediate next step was to secure an established producer with a track record. British producer Michael Deeley was the man they chose – he had produced *The Italian Job* (Peter Collinson, 1969), *The Wicker Man* (Robin Hardy, 1973), *The Man Who Fell to Earth* (Nicolas Roeg, 1976), *Nickelodeon* (Peter Bogdanovich, 1976), *Convoy* (Sam Peckinpah, 1978) and *The Deer Hunter* (Michael Cimino, 1978). Deeley had a commitment to genre efforts with a revisionist slant. By 1978, on the basis of Fancher's screenplay, Deeley was on board and began pitching the project to Hollywood studios for financing. In the very nature of an adaptation, Fancher's draft made significant changes to the source material: San Francisco became LA; the role of Deckard's wife, Iran, was minimised; and the character of Rachel became more prominent. Fancher's own personal enthusiasms featured too, notably the exploration of an ecological subtext.

In this phase of development the script was entitled *Mechanismo* and then *Dangerous Days*, a title that would stick for a while. Somewhat surprisingly, at one point Gregory Peck voiced an interest in the project. Perhaps a future world Atticus Finch, from *To Kill a Mockingbird* (Robert Mulligan, 1962), could have been an iteration of the concept.

At this stage Michael Deeley began considering the emerging new directorial talent of Adrian Lyne, Michael Apted, Bruce Beresford and Ridley Scott who, in 1980, was working on the screenplay for *Dune* with writer Rudolph Wurlitzer.

In keeping with the Gregory Peck connection, the American director of *To Kill a Mockingbird*, Robert Mulligan, was also considered. When Mulligan came on board Fancher developed the script a little more, rewriting the ending so that it finished with something of a Western-style shootout between Deckard and the replicants. In 1978, Mulligan pulled out of the project and once again Deeley was left to find a director with whom to package the screenplay. For a short time, CBS Films also became interested until they recognised they could not finance it at the scale needed.

In April 1979, Deeley sent the script to Ridley Scott with whom he was familiar. Scott initially refused, having recently completed a science fiction film (see **Alien**).

In his interview with *Starburst* in October 1982, associate producer Ivor Powell talks of a film called '*Knight*, a medieval film that Ridley desperately wants to do'. This was probably the *Tristan and Isolde* story (see **Ridley's Unrealised Visions**).

However, Ivor Powell encouraged Scott to read the screenplay. By this time Scott was due to commit to directing *Dune* and was also mulling over what would become *Legend*, though at this time it was called *Darkness*.

But the death of Scott's elder brother Frank appeared to change much. He was looking for some serious diversion; he pulled out of the *Dune* commitment and was without a film to move directly on to. Scott reconsidered the *Dangerous Days* script and expressed an interest in directing the film version. Hampton Fancher and Ridley Scott began revising the script in April 1980 and soon Scott's emphasis on the visual fed into the script development.

One of the key early influences on Scott was the French magazine *Heavy Metal*. At this stage Scott wanted a term other than detective for Deckard's occupation. Fancher cast about and came across a little-known William Burroughs novel called *Blade Runner*. Scott was happy with the name and secured permission to use it. It then became clear that another science fiction novel, this one by Alan E Nouse, was also called *Blade Runner*. Scott and Fancher swiftly secured the rights to this title also. For a brief time, Scott wanted to call the film *Gotham City* but *Batman* creator Bob Kane baulked at the notion and *Blade Runner* remained, with Scott insisting it was only ever going to be a working title.

By 24 July 1980, Scott and Fancher had a revised screenplay to work from and prepare the film around. The draft included six replicants yet only four feature in the film. The fifth replicant had been killed prior to the film-story beginning and for twenty years now people have debated whether or not Deckard is the sixth replicant: screenwriter David Peoples has suggested that Ridley Scott misinterpreted the script and did conceive of Rick Deckard as a replicant; Ford is less sure of Deckard's replicant status: 'My argument with Ridley was that he definitely was not a replicant.'

From all accounts, there was a degree of tension between Fancher and Scott during this period, which in part is the natural course for work between two individual and strongly creative and confident minds. Much later in the film's production, Scott was fired from the set for just a few days. Fancher wanted an essentially lyrical science fiction film and Scott wanted to pursue a thriller-inflected narrative. David Peoples was brought in to revise Fancher's screenplay, pumping up some of the detective elements. Peoples went on to write the stark and rich script for the Clint

Eastwood western *Unforgiven*. Peoples's work on *Blade Runner* appears to have been a process of embellishment and refinement rather than any wholesale reordering of the material – he himself was knocked out by Fancher's draft and, perhaps more than anything, Peoples emphasised Scott's wish for a detective element.

Significantly, the word android became replaced with the word replicant, which met with Dick's satisfaction. Peoples also introduced Deckard into the movie as a divorced man walking through the streets of the city. His early work on the ending of the script had Deckard taking Rachel to the beach and shooting her. After a series of frustrations, Fancher officially left the *Blade Runner* project, doing a few rewrites towards the end of the production on certain scenes. Finally, the project was ready to begin hiring crew and creating sets at the Burbank Studios in Hollywood.

Filmways Productions joined the project as financiers and a firm start date of 12 January 1981 was set with a release date of December 1981. And then, suddenly, Filmways pulled out preferring to back another film, De Palma's *Blow Out* (1981). Deeley was left with not much time to secure new funding for the project. He soon configured a new deal with Sir Run Run Shaw (an Eastern movie mogul), Tandem Productions Inc and the Ladd Company, run by Alan Ladd Jr, who had backed George Lucas so confidently on *Star Wars* during his time at 20th Century Fox.

Scott began investing his time in refining the look of the film, offering up the following comment: 'There should be a total integration on a film . . . every incident, every sound, every movement, every colour, every set, prop or actor is all part of the director's overall orchestration of a film. And orchestration, to me, is performance. Just as performance is everything.'

One of Scott's primary influences was Edward Hopper's painting *Nighthawks*. The science fiction artist John Harris was also an influence on *Blade Runner*'s cityscape. When Syd Mead, an industrial and sci-fi designer, came on board, Scott had found his soulmate. Mead had designed the V'Ger ship in *Star Trek: The Motion Picture* (Robert Wise, 1979). He notably created the Spinner police vehicles in *Blade Runner*. His initial brief had only been to work on vehicles but soon he was brainstorming many of the environments. Lawrence G Paull was signed up as Production Designer and David Snyder as Art Director. Scott had wanted to camera operate on *Blade Runner*, as he had done on *The Duellists* and *Alien*, but American union rules would not allow it. Step forward Jordan Cronenweth as the director of photography. Marvin G Westmore handled make-up chores with other make-up work being done by an uncredited Michael Westmore and even the legendary John Chambers who had supplied all make-up for the original *Planet of the Apes* film of 1967.

With *Blade Runner*, Ridley Scott did what George Lucas had done with *Star Wars* and fused the best contemporary visual talent (including Mentor Huebner on storyboards) with a rich tradition of art and design to create a story wrapped up in a staple generic form of the detective film noir. *Blade Runner* might also be a Western, with its morality play leanings. In this story about robots and humans, it is a neat symmetry that the film's Napoleon Teddy robot anticipates and refers back to the teddy bear in Brian Aldiss's short story 'Supertoys Last All Summer Long' which became the Steven Spielberg film *AI: Artificial Intelligence* (2001).

THE SHOOT: The *Blade Runner* set was built over the Old New York set at the Burbank Studios and an elaborate sprinkler rig was set up above the street to supply the rain, at that time a pragmatic decision to minimise it looking like a set, but a decision which, on screen and within the story world of the film, suggests an ecologically altered world. Dubbed Ridleyville by the crew, the set was highly detailed, even down to fake magazine covers with titles like *Krotch*, *Horn* and *Kill*. The neon cowboy girl came directly from the set of *One From the Heart* (Francis Ford Coppola, 1982).

Lawrence G Paull has commented about *Blade Runner* that 'every *Blade Runner* set was designed to generate an emotional aura'.

While most of the movie was shot in Burbank, the shot of the bird flying up at the end as Batty dies was filmed at Shepperton Studios in England.

The first scene to be shot was of Deckard ordering his meal at the start of the film. To suggest a character who had given up on his appearance, Ford suggested the crew cut which, under Scott's direction, took several hours to get right.

In designing the look for Roy Batty, Scott had devised a series of markings that were like tattoos on the replicant's bare chest when it is exposed late in the film. The idea here was the suggestion of engine demarcations.

The last night of principal photography, 30 June 1981, focused on shooting material for the showdown between Batty and Deckard. Harrison Ford's genuine exhaustion serves the on-screen persona of Deckard well, giving it added believability. It has been well documented that Ford and Scott experienced some creative tension. Scott was composing more than just the actors' performances in the film and from all accounts Ford sounds as though he felt stranded by his director. Whatever occurred, the on-screen result is one of Ford's finest hours, sombre, stark, melancholy, quite at variance with his screen persona at the time.

Several years later, like a river running its course to the sea, *Blade Runner*'s stylings could be seen informing a range of films and TV shows. The film also helped fuel the birth of the cyberpunk genre.

Blade Runner's longevity was further ensured in 1989 when a stereo-film preservationist named Michael Arick found a workprint of the film in the Warner Brothers film vault. Contacting Scott, they prepared a workprint release for 6 May 1990 at the Odeon Fairfax in LA. The workprint had no voice-over or happy ending. The workprint, though, is not the Director's Cut known now to so many. The Director's Cut was later duly prepared, incorporating the now legendary unicorn shot that Scott had photographed back in 1982.

For over twenty years, Scott's film has provided a rich source for scholars and fans to mine, and rightly so. It is science fiction, fantasy, parable, thriller, noir. The film has a cult status and with every year that passes it seems to gain in stature. Twenty years later, space adventure storyteller George Lucas was encouraging his art department on *Star Wars: Episode II – Attack of the Clones* to outdo *Blade Runner*'s megalopolis look.

In his book about the film, Scott Bukatman writes of the source material for *Blade Runner* being concerned with what it is to be 'non-human'. This gives the film a lot of territory to explore and for all its gee whiz design and flash it is ultimately about very human concerns and dilemmas. For Bukatman, one of the film's strengths is that it does not explain everything. It is a film of uncertainty released at a time of certainty in the big popular movies, notably that year *ET: The Extra-Terrestrial*.

Blade Runner has found its way into movie magazine retrospectives, top tens, film festivals and countless academic works. It is a great example of how a film can satisfy so many ranges of interest and enthusiasms and is an especially good example of how intelligent mainstream, genre cinema can be, as rich and stimulating and true as films not bound by genre, a term which increasingly appears to be little more than a marketing tool.

COLLABORATORS: Hampton Fancher, who Ridley Scott has said is the real vision behind *Blade Runner*, wrote and directed a feature in 1999 called *The Minus Man* about a drifter who it transpires is a serial killer. The project was based on the novel by Lew McCreary and starred Owen Wilson. Fancher is currently developing a feature project on his beloved passion of flamenco dancing. He also wrote the screenplay for an early Denzel Washington starrer, *The Mighty Quinn* (Carl Shenkel, 1989).

Associate producer Ivor Powell, nephew of celebrated UK film critic Dilys Powell, had worked on *2001: A Space Odyssey* (1968) as one of the art department. He had also worked with David Puttnam on a documentary called *Memory of Justice*. It was through this that he met Ridley Scott – his first work with Scott was *Alien*.

Douglas Trumbull had begun working with Stanley Kubrick on *2001: A Space Odyssey* and moved on to *The Andromeda Strain* (Robert Wise, 1971). In 1971 he directed cult science fiction favourite *Silent Running* in which an astronaut is adrift in space aboard a ship carrying a real Garden of Eden designed to revive Earth in the aftermath of a nuclear war. Trumbull also worked on *Star Trek: The Motion Picture* (Robert Wise, 1979). Over the last ten years, Trumbull has not worked in motion pictures, or rather he has but of a different sort, providing the images for theme park rides and attractions including Back to the Future . . . The Ride, In Search of the Obelisk, To Dream of Roses and Leonardo's Dream.

Richard Yuricich continues to create visual effects for movies. Most recently he has worked on *Resident Evil* (Paul Anderson, 2002), *Event Horizon* (Paul Anderson, 1997), *Mission: Impossible-2* (John Woo, 2000), *Under Siege 2: Dark Territory* (Geoff Murphy, 1995) and served as matte consultant on *Field of Dreams* (Phil Alden Robinson, 1989).

Jordan Cronenweth was the cinematographer on *Blade Runner*, taking the cinematic look that Scott became known for one step further. Cronenweth had previously shot *Brewster McCloud* (Robert Altman, 1970) and also *Citizens Band* (Jonathan Demme, 1977). After *Blade Runner* his work included the romantic fantasy comedy *Peggy Sue Got Married* (Francis Ford Coppola, 1985) and the Talking Heads film *Stop Making Sense* (Jonathan Demme, 1984). Jordan Cronenweth died in 1996.

David Webb Peoples (here credited as David Peoples) wrote the screenplay for *Twelve Monkeys* (Terry Gilliam, 1995). He also wrote the screenplay for *Soldier* (Paul Anderson, 1998) and directed Rutger Hauer in the film *The Blood of Heroes* (1988). In 1992, Clint Eastwood's *Unforgiven* was released, for which Peoples wrote the screenplay.

Scott's *Alien* editor Terry Rawlings also returned.

MUSIC: For *Blade Runner*, Scott teamed up with Greek composer Vangelis, whose score for *Chariots of Fire* in 1981 – which had been produced by David Puttnam (who had produced Scott's debut feature *The Duellists*) – had really put him on the Hollywood movie map. Vangelis's music for this film has become legendary, in part because of the difficulty there was in it finally being made available to fans. When the score was first released it was an orchestral version of Vangelis's synth-based material. When Scott showed Vangelis the film for the first time in order to begin scoring it, the Greek composer was astounded and in time would generate a score quite in contrast to more familiar and triumphal genre offerings. Vangelis's music was romantic, bluesy, atonal. Over the years the movie's soundtrack release has been a convoluted and confounding affair. The first soundtrack released was merely a copy of the work in the film. Only in June 1994 was the authentic material released under the title *Blade Runner: Vangelis*.

Vangelis's score is expansive and intimate as appropriate. For Deckard's scenes in his apartment it is very melancholy. Bluesy and melancholy music also underscores the scene where Rachel is first at Deckard's apartment and he fixes her a drink.

THE OPENING: *Blade Runner* is legendary in pop culture for the detail of its images. The film starts with the Warner Bros Logo and silence and then the Ladd Company logo. A thunderous and ominous beat starts as the credits begin. The film title appears in red while all the other credits are in white. The choice of red suggests violence and passion, both qualities that the replicants will all display. Text setting up the backstory appears and then the film cuts to its first image and Scott plunges us into something resembling hell, only a hell of glittering lights and immense fireballs. Vangelis's searing synth music adds to the atmosphere of menace and majesty. Scott then throws his audience slightly by cutting to an eyeball reflecting all this dark energy. Scott's affinity for elemental images packs out the beginning of this film. This is a pretty bleak future, always in darkness. Scott has a range of colour schemes going in the film. The bright light, blue and smoke as Deckard and Bryant watch the video files recalls *Citizen Kane* (Orson Welles, 1951).

ON THE SCREEN: There is the muted red of JF Sebastian's room of toys and the burnished look of the skyscape. It is a harsh world. Deckard's apartment is a more muted homely tone, though it is also a place of shadows.

Scott uses candlelight, or the suggestion of it, to illuminate Tyrell's very ornate room. This gives everything a redness that fits with the moment when Batty arrives and destroys his maker. The room becomes more a cave than some swish apartment in a mega skyscraper. Music builds in deathly beats at this point, emphasising the primal moment. Twenty years later, Hannibal Lecter (see **Hannibal**) would be lit by firelight as he writes to his lost love Clarice.

To lend believability to the fantastic world he has created, Scott has the camera move in towards one of the pyramid-ziggurats rather as though being shot from a helicopter.

Scott's interest in stories about very strong and resourceful characters finds its niche in *Blade Runner* with the replicants whom the opening text describes as 'superior in strength and agility'.

The opening text implies that the replicants are not considered living things. All through the film there is a dilemma around what is real, what is artificial, and how you control your feelings in a world where both exist.

Having established the futureworld aspect of the film, Scott then introduces his film noir angle in the sequence with Bryant and Leon. The smoke, the shaft of light and the fan turning all contribute to the sense of noir in our collective moviegoing memory. Later in the film Rachel's hairstyle is very reminiscent of 1940s stylings and there are many scenes where light slices through blinds. Deckard's long coat adds to the atmosphere.

HEROES AND VILLAINS: Deckard is a classic Scott hero, a maverick who wants no more to do with being a *Blade Runner*. Scott defines his personality without dialogue. The first image of Deckard comes as the camera drops down and hunts him out in the city crowd as we watch Deckard wearily scan the skies. Deckard is in some ways an innocent who is professionally terse. His professionalism is compromised by his personal involvement with Rachel. At the end of the film, Gaff shouts out to Deckard, 'You've done a good job, sir'; Rick has been tested. Deckard is like the classic detective: he is the one who links the lonely people of the city together.

The character of Gaff is an almost unworldly presence who always seems to appear as if from nowhere. Gaff makes an origami man figure. Can Gaff read Deckard's reveries? If so, this suggests that Deckard is himself a replicant (see **MAKING IT** for the discussion on this point). In his book about *Blade Runner* Scott Bukatman writes that the film displays a fear of ethnicity in cities, again proving the range of interests the film holds and so assuring its longevity.

'The chance to begin again', the cheesy voice-over on the Off World blimp proclaims. *Blade Runner* is a film about being revived and finding energy in life again, a wild spirit. The detective is an absolute symbol of civilisation. Deckard is confronted and challenged by the wild child, Roy Batty. Like Maximus in *Gladiator,* Jordan O'Neill in *G.I. Jane* and Ripley in *Alien*, an extraordinary situation takes a main character out of their ordinary life. Deckard is a lonely man and fragile too – after the death of Leon, Rick says to Rachel, 'Shakes? Me too. I got 'em bad. Part of the business.'

In *Blade Runner*, Scott's interest in the military code of honour and the unit is less present. In a way both *Blade Runner* and the later *Legend* are atypical Scott films and yet remain two of his very best.

There is a romanticism in this film that Scott repeats in *Someone to Watch Over Me*. Both Claire (in the later film) and Rachel have something of the femme fatale about them and an inevitable sense of doom hangs over Rachel's relationship with Deckard just as it does over the relationship of Claire and Mike in *Someone to Watch Over Me*. Rachel: 'What if I go north? Disappear. Would you come after me? Hunt me?' Rick Deckard replies with, 'No. No I wouldn't.' His delivery of the first 'No' has real frailty to it. The use of the words 'hunt me' suggests something more animal-like and wild. There is also a romantic longing to it. Rachel, like Claire, must get out of town. For all of the emotion in this exchange, Scott suggests Rachel's replicant status with her red pupils and also her mascara which makes her look a little like Pris. However, Scott flips us back out of any definitive view and has Rachel sit at Rick's piano and let her hair down, so she looks much more natural, much less cosmetic. There is an especially lovely moment where Rachel is in profile here and she resembles Laura in *The Duellists*. Deckard joins her and Scott suggests the links between them as they are shot at a three-quarter angle. By contrast their subsequent kissing scene has a violence to it that is unsettling. It's here that Deckard seems less than human. At the end of the film, Deckard is far warmer, nuzzling his face against her body when he comes to take her away from the apartment.

ANDROIDS: The arch nemesis, Roy Batty, is introduced first by a visual showing his clenched, claw-like hand and then we hear his voice saying 'Time enough'. He has the quality of a menacing child, with a disorientating stare. When Roy enters Sebastian's apartment he says, 'Gosh, you really got some nice toys here.' The replicants are like children going up against evil in the form of Tyrell and all that he represents.

There is also a dark playfulness to Roy Batty just as there is to Hannibal Lecter almost twenty years later in *Hannibal*. Batty is perfect in his focus: he is an innocent in a corrupt world. Batty is probably the most authentic and alive character in the film. He would certainly get on well with John Urgayle from *G.I. Jane*. Roy and Urgayle are both associated with birds at some point in their respective stories. These are both nature boys with an intense streak. Urgayle's taunts to Jordan O'Neill recall Batty taunting Deckard. Batty is more than human as Sebastian observes when he says to Roy, 'You're so different, you're so perfect.'

Batty's dialogue almost always feels like poetry: 'Fiery the angels fell, deep thunder rolled around their shores, burning with the fires.' Roy is all about superhuman excellence, such as when he asks JF Sebastian if his chess opponent is good. Batty is a cultured, sophisticated monster continuing the tradition of Feraud (**The Duellists**) and the alien (**Alien**), and who precedes Hannibal Lecter (**Hannibal**).

The key scene where Roy and Pris hang out with JF Sebastian is lit in a kind of grey, ghostly way that is very beautiful.

Pris resembles a doll and so she fits perfectly with the world that JF Sebastian lives in. The shot of her spray-painting her eye sockets suggests an application of tribal make-up as she prepares for the kill. Her white face and black eye make-up suggests a kabuki look, continuing the film's references to Japan – the Orient has consumed Western culture. When Pris dies she is like a thrashing automaton; there are also lots of automata in JF Sebastian's apartment.

PICTURE PERFECT: The film is famous for the design of the futureworld, with its combination of the functional, the exotic, the ancient, the imagined, the industrial, the art nouveau. This adds to the film's drama around classical values and sense of what it is to be human clashing with issues of artificiality and no value. In this early part of the 21st century the film's currency strengthens again as cloning and genetics become ever more part of science.

In this film we rarely see people's faces in full light. The close-up of Rick after his test on Rachel has his face cast half in light, half in shadow. Scott and Jordan Cronenweth backlight many parts of the film such as when Deckard and Gaff prepare to enter Leon's apartment early on. The apartment is certainly creepy, largely because of the flickering light in the bathroom and its near darkness. The whole world shown in the film is one of shadows.

As in *Alien*, Scott uses a dissolve to economically suggest the passing of time when Rachel undergoes her Voigt Kampf test.

Scott has a deft hand at integrating optical effects with live action footage in a very simple and physical way, such as when we see an image of the blimp's lights sweeping the city and then cut to live action and lights sweeping the ground from up above. When Deckard enters the Bradbury Building, Scott enhances the creepiness of the moment with a slowly tracking camera up on the mezzanine looking down, and the image is dominated by a cold blue pallor.

The eyeball guy, Chew, resembles an insect with his microscope goggles and tubes connecting to his big fur coat.

Scott fills the film with moments and shots that do not get fully explained and so remain ambiguous. Gaff makes origami creatures, one of which connects with Deckard's dream. It is left up to the audience to make the connections and judgements. The story lays clues of meaning that keep the audience intrigued. Gaff's origami bird prefigures the dove at the end of the film. The shot of the owl emphasises its red pupils, its artificiality. A shot of Rachel later in the film shows her red pupils but makes no more of it. Tyrell looks artificial with his flamboyant dress sense and glasses.

The film's design remains stunningly believable. During the scene where Deckard takes a virtual trip around a photograph as though it were three-dimensional the audience believes the technology at work while also feeling that it stretches reality just too much. It is the mechanical sound of the machine that keeps the illusion believable. Scott has always known how to give a sense of texture to place. In the nightclub, cutaways to the range of patrons gives the scene a documentary quality. People criss-cross frame all through the film.

When Rick Deckard hangs from the skyscraper at the film's climax we can see the echoes of *Vertigo* (Alfred Hitchcock, 1958) and the art of Moebius in full swing with the plunging, converging vertical lines of the towerblocks. Jean 'Moebius' Giraud was a French comic-book artist and illustrator whose work Ridley Scott had become familiar with in the pages of *Heavy Metal* magazine; some of Scott's storyboards and sketches for *Alien* and *Blade Runner* do show a similarity between his style and Moebius's. Other films to have benefited from Moebius's conceptual design include *Tron* (Steven Lisberger, 1982), the George Lucas-produced fantasy adventure *Willow* (Ron Howard, 1988) and *The Abyss* (James Cameron, 1989). Moebius's comic-book work includes the *Blueberry* Western series in collaboration with writer Jean Pierre Dionet, *The Airtight Garage* and *Arzach*.

In this film, light can represent illumination and also invasion and interrogation. Lights constantly invade Rick's apartment.

For the death of Zhora, Scott gives the brutality of the moment a sense of beauty by filming it in slow motion. It extends the moment of drama. Scott does not resort to the use of obvious chase music and he drops sync sound right down in the moment of Zhora's death. A melancholy, blues-inspired piece of music plays too, accompanied by a heartbeat sound. The melancholy of the film is captured in this sequence and Deckard looks far from pleased to have retired Zhora.

Scott uses slow motion again to give weight to the closing moment between Rick and Roy.

TECH TALK: *Blade Runner* is widely considered one of *the* great visual effects films and came along at a time when visual effects, in the optical, pre-digital age, were really finding their feet in the wake of *Star Wars*'s trailblazing efforts. *Blade Runner*'s effects have a beauty and in places slowness to them, certainly a grace that contrasts with the comic book haste of Lucas's magnum opus.

For *Blade Runner*, Apogee Effects and Industrial Light and Magic had been considered for the visual effects work but Douglas Trumbull's Entertainment Effects Group got the job. For Trumbull the simplest close-up is an effect. Trumbull's overall aesthetic for the effects was to pursue realism and he was especially pleased that it was an effects film set on earth. One effects scene that never came to pass was of Deckard arriving into the movie on a future train from the desert, then getting into his Spinner and getting caught in a traffic jam.

In Philip K Dick's source novel, the story occurs in a post-apocalyptic world in which most animal life does not exist and the great population centres have shrunk because so many people have gone Off World.

Scott had an idea that the police were something of a paramilitary presence in the futureworld and would take the lead. After them, corporate and finally civilian vehicles would be present in the skies. To expand on his concepts, Scott hired Syd Mead whose original brief was to design just six types of vehicle. Mead based the Spinner's ability to fly on the engineering of Harrier Jump Jets and their repulsorlift mechanics.

Initially, Mead's designs were considered too sleek. He revised them, making them clunkier and chunkier, defined by a sense of repairs and additions to the basic units. Mead's enthusiasm was apparent to Scott who then encouraged him to begin designing environments too. In *Cinefex* magazine's *Blade Runner* issue and the subsequent reprint almost twenty years later, Mead explained the design sense for the film saying it was based on a 'social theory . . . that the consumer delivery system had become interrupted . . . we just took all the trends in progress . . . and accelerated them'. Scott encouraged Mead to take photos of the Burbank New York City set and retrofit it. In doing so, Mead developed the notion of an unpleasant future where the oldest parts are nearest the ground. It was production designer Lawrence G Paull's task to translate Mead's concepts into working sets, all of them rich with detail.

The effects work in the film is so detailed that for the Tyrell office sequence the sun changes its position as the scene progresses.

The detail of the film's design goes as far as the inclusion on top of the Tyrell tower model of a fleet of inch-long Spinners.

And how is this for real movie trivia? Some of the flames seen in the opening Hades shot were taken from *Zabriskie Point* (Michaelangelo Antonioni, 1969), in which Harrison Ford appeared early in his career.

Spinner models for the film ranged from one-inch long to full size. The 44-inch quarter-scale model had articulating wheel covers, liquid nitrogen exhaust ports and rotating beacons. The Spinner launch sequence on its readout is the same as the launch sequence for the escape pod in *Alien*.

To enhance believability, the Spinners appear and disappear in the atmospheric conditions depending on whether they are approaching or moving away from camera.

Originally, the opening Hades shot was to have featured just one pyramid and a reveal of a hollow central core with clean air and a landscape garden that connects to the forest landscape we see in Deckard's dream, promising the peace and nurturing of nature. Ironically, Batty, an artificial being, is deeply primal.

Because Doug Trumbull and his collaborator Richard Yuricich had already committed to making their own film, *Brainstorm*, using Trumbull's Showscan process, an agreement was made that they would conceptualise the approach to effects on *Blade Runner* but would hand over all day-to-day management and realisation of this work to a trusted colleague named David Dryer who oversaw miniature photography and matte paintings (photorealistic paintings which expand an environment already recorded by the film camera, usually with actors in the shot).

To enhance the believability of shots most of the miniature work incorporated smoke to suggest the effects of an atmosphere on the clarity or otherwise of objects and models. Fifteen matte paintings were produced for *Blade Runner*.

Scott decided that principal photography and effects shooting should run simultaneously rather than successively. The Hades shot which opens the film is one of *Blade Runner*'s defining images. Designed by Tom Cranham, the model was thirteen feet deep and eighteen feet wide. *Blade Runner* is a vintage pre-digital effects movie, demonstrating the believability that physical and optical effects frequently have over CGI which has an unfortunate weightless quality – they are ultimately virtual and made of nothing. A frightening thought in some ways. All of *Blade Runner*'s matte shots were originally designed by Syd Mead who would take photos of the live action sets, lay transparent paper over them and draw in where the matte painting would be integrated. This information would then be passed on to Richard Yuricich. His matte paintings (done on masonite board measuring $7' \times 3'$) shots in the film are amongst the most beautiful mattes ever committed to film. The 1980s yielded a run of genre movie matte master painters: Yuricich, Albert Whitlock, Mike Pangrazio and Chris Evans.

Saturday 19 December 1981 marked the end of visual effects photography on *Blade Runner*. Scott and Terry Rawlings had from 13 July 1981 until mid-September 1981 to edit the film.

David Dryer, who oversaw effects work on *Blade Runner*, worked mostly with black-and-white images of the film and not colour which led him to comment at the time of the film's original release that it would look beautiful as a black-and-white feature, only adding only to its film noir heritage.

For the sequence where Deckard chases Zhora through the city, Scott and cinematographer Jordan Cronenweth used multiple cameras to capture the action. Cronenweth loved using backlighting because of the theatrical element it gave to the action. Often, he chose to light the actors' faces from below and sometimes even used water to reflect light. The key *Blade Runner* lighting look was to set up a warm, soft uplight in the foreground and a hard blacklight, laced with smoke, in the background.

To create the now famous replicant eye effect a two-way mirror was placed in front of the camera lens at an angle of 45 degrees. A light was then projected into the mirror and this was then reflected into the performer's eye along the optical axis of the lens. Occasionally, coloured gels were used to enhance the effect. The make-up department had created special silver contact lenses for each replicant actor when their replicant had been killed. They were designed to give the replicants a certain look in death but the lenses were never used.

In *Blade Runner*, Deckard finds a snake scale in a bath tub. In *Black Rain*, Conklin finds a sequin in a bath tub. Author KW Jeter's follow-up novels to the *Blade Runner* film are: *Blade Runner II: The Edge of Human, Blade Runner III: Replicant*

Night and *Blade Runner IV: Eye and Talon. The Edge of Human* gets the further adventures of Rick Deckard rolling with him living in rural North America with Rachel who exists in cryogenic suspension. Deckard is then called back to LA in pursuit of the notorious sixth replicant. Mary was the sixth replicant in *Blade Runner* (see **DELETED SCENES**). Scott had considered a *Blade Runner* sequel perhaps set Off World and also based around the issue of cryogenics.

MOVIE TALK:

Deckard: 'I was quit when I came in here, Bryant. I'm twice as quit now.'

Deckard: 'Replicants are like any other machine. They're a benefit or a hazard.'

Leon (to Deckard): 'Painful to live in fear, isn't it? . . . Wake up! Time to die!'

Batty: 'I've seen things you people wouldn't believe . . . I watched C-Beams glitter in the dark near the Tannhauser Gate. All those moments will be lost in time. Like tears in the rain.'

Batty: 'It's not an easy thing to meet your maker.'

Tyrell (to Batty): 'The light that burns twice as bright burns half as long . . . You're the prodigal son. Revel in your time.'

THE BIG IDEA: The film brims with eternal, archetypal questions and accompanying visual elements such as blue skies, a rainbow, fire, even a nail in wood. Memory, death (Leon confronts Deckard asking 'How old am I?' and 'How long do I live?') and the need to belong all collide in the film. They are very traditional values set up in a very non-traditional world. The more things change the more they stay the same. There is even an Oedipal, Greek tragedy aspect in Batty killing his father.

In *Blade Runner*, Scott's preoccupation with the civil and the wild gets a rich rendering. The film constitutes certainly one part of what we could legitimately call Scott's fairy-tale trilogy: *Alien*, *Blade Runner* and *Legend*. When you consider just these three films it is more than understandable to grow excited at the prospect Scott might one day return to the science fiction and fantasy genres, despite a remark he made to *Starlog* magazine that it is becoming increasingly hard to offer up a new view on the future.

This is a very postmodern film, dealing with a world where values have shifted so much from notions of accepted human behaviour. Ziggurat-like buildings rise in their high-tech glory, but recall something far more ancient, so that in the world of *Blade Runner*, as everywhere else, what's new is old. Time eras collide. It is set in the 21st century but all the detectives dress as though it is the 1940s with their hats and long coats. The film's concept and allusions to cyberspace form part of a general, early bird sense about these things in the early 1980s with not only *Blade Runner* but also David Cronenberg's *Videodrome* (1983) and Steven Lisberger's *Tron* (1982) experiencing something of a revival twenty years on, through the miracle of DVD. These films are all progenitors of *The Matrix* (Andy and Larry Wachowski, 1999).

In some ways the film is about freedom and slavery to individuals and to the past. Tyrell says of the replicants: 'If we can gift them the past . . . we can control them better.' So, the film is about maintaining and finding your identity and sense of self.

In the scene where Rachel shows Rick a photograph of her with her mother when Rachel was a child, Rick says, 'Those aren't your memories, they're somebody else's.' We also see Rick sleepily at his piano on which stand photographs apparently from the early twentieth and late nineteenth centuries. The sequence then dissolves to a slow-motion image of a unicorn charging through a forest (see **Legend**). *Blade Runner* and *Legend* are Scott's all-out fairy-tale movies. *Legend* was being developed during the preparation for *Blade Runner* and there must inevitably have been a criss-crossing of ideas and images; no story exists in isolation from all the others.

Beneath the darkness and hostile action is a story about remembering, loving and finding a place in the world, a story common to anyone watching the film. One of the key informing films for *Blade Runner* is *Metropolis* (Fritz Lang, 1926) itself an icon of cinema with its exploration of the modern age. *Blade Runner* captures a similar sense, fused with Philip K Dick's paranoia but also his humanism. For some, *Blade Runner* is most anxious about the increasing ethnic diversity of cities. Notably, and interestingly, one of the post-*Blade Runner* projects Scott had in mind was a *Metropolis* film, a project which has yet to see the light of a projector (see **Ridley's Unrealised Visions**).

Scott uses a handheld camera to add urgency to certain scenes such as the violent confrontation between Leon and Rick on the streets.

Strong women, real or otherwise, feature prominently in *Blade Runner*. Pris and Zhora are almost superwomen while Rachel is more the little girl lost, the innocent. Bryant describes Zhora as beauty and the beast saying that 'she's both'. Scott's fairy-tale leanings are all over *Blade Runner*. The cityscape is believable and utterly fanciful and Roy Batty is like a Dark Angel who has fallen from Off World to the hellish streets amidst the towers.

For all of his rapid aging, JF Sebastian is very childlike as he delights in his robot creations. He is an innocent, fairy-tale-like character and the city is like a fairy-tale forest. Youth and age is another preoccupation of the replicants who are very much like children in an adult world of control. JF Sebastian says to Pris with her eye make-up on, 'You look beautiful.' She is the beautiful beast, rather like the alien is in *Alien*.

The showdown which brings the film to a close is a chance for Scott to stage his regular preoccupation with the conflict between the wild and the civil and find a way to link them too, notably when Roy howls and Rick screams. When Roy goes down to his shorts he is a like a gladiator. This part of the film is very much a mini movie of its own in which the enigma of Batty's aggression and sensitivity comes into its own, culminating with him cradling a dove and saving Rick from falling – in all senses of the word.

There is even a moment which could have come from *The Duellists* when Deckard whacks Batty with a chunk of wood and Batty says, 'That was irrational, not to mention unsportsman-like.'

The film's overall poetic quality is always evident in Batty's statements. It is not so much dialogue that he speaks. Rutger Hauer's performance put him on the Hollywood map (see **CASTING**) and from all accounts he improvised a degree of his lines that are always measured. See how he drops a pause into his line 'Time to die'.

In an interview with Paul M Sammon in his vast book *Future Noir*, Ridley Scott comments: 'It is not the unicorn itself which is important. It's the landscape around it – the green landscape – they should be noticing.'

Like all of Scott's strongest films, *Blade Runner* immerses you in its story world through the density and believability of its design. And again, Scott elicits a range of compelling and very real performances from his actors. There is something total about the film.

RELEASE: On 5 March 1982 a sneak screening of the film was held in Denver and on 6 March 1982 one was held in Dallas. Both of them yielded downbeat audience response. This was in the age of *Star Wars*-style fantasy heroics. *Blade Runner* truly was ahead of its time, by about twenty years. It was after these sneak screenings that a voice-over was decided upon, though Harrison Ford was uncomfortable with the decision feeling a voice-over made the emotions of the film over-emphatic.

Even with the voice-over, however, the film failed to satisfy many people. Interestingly, the audiences' negative test-screening reactions speak volumes about the effect of star power – they were watching Harrison Ford in a very un-Harrison Ford-style piece despite his terrific work in the film.

Scott also shot a new ending which was a variation on an originally scripted scene. The original had Rick and Rachel drive out of a tunnel and race into the woods where they sight a unicorn; the new ending had Deckard put a tinfoil unicorn on the dashboard of the car. Famously, the shots of the snowy wilderness are outtakes from *The Shining* (Stanley Kubrick, 1980). In March 1982, a final piece of additional shooting was done to explain the film's closure with Rick and Rachel in the car. This was shot near Cedar Lake in Big Bear, California.

Version two of the film was screened on 8 May in San Diego. Harrison Ford, busy filming *Return of the Jedi* (Richard Marquand, 1983) at the time, even put in an appearance. Some audience members objected to the voice-over and others were very positive about the wilderness shots that concluded the film on a high note, offering some release from the claustrophobia of the rest of the film's setting. For the filmmakers, the screening was considered a success and suggested that Rick Deckard's voice-over was the right choice to help develop the story. Famously, the voice-over has been eliminated from the Director's Cut of the film as released in 1982.

Warner Brothers were responsible for marketing the film. On 12 January 1982 a teaser trailer was released. On 7 June 1982 a full theatrical trailer hit the screens. On 25 June 1982, *Blade Runner* was released in 1,290 cinemas across North America.

Generally bad reviews and little box office ensued (see **GROSSES**). That same summer *ET: The Extra-Terrestrial* was released and its optimism and sunnier emotions connected better with the mass audience. There is an emotional tone to *Blade Runner* that just is not mass market.

CRITICAL CONDITION: 'A bleak but hypnotic movie that is totally unlike any other science fiction film I've ever seen,' said *Starburst*. The reviewer went on to suggest that the film improved on the book, writing that 'you feel in *Blade Runner* that you are seeing for the first time in a science fiction movie a real city of the future'. The *Monthly Film Bulletin* also noted the difference to the source book: 'Much to its own detriment, *Blade Runner* is so busy emulating the box office trumps played by *Star Wars* and *Raiders of the Lost Ark* – respectively, toytown hardware and explosive violence – that its *raison d'être*, alias Philip K Dick, gets rather lost in the wash.' 'Rubbished on its initial release, director Ridley Scott takes a simple plot . . . and transforms the look of science fiction forever . . . a filmmaker working at the absolute peak of his powers,' felt Ian Freer in *Empire*.

As for the actors, 'Ford is always good when surrounded by amazing visuals, perhaps because he keeps cool and does not seem to notice them,' suggested Roger Ebert in the *Chicago Sun-Times*, though *Screen International* felt they weren't really the main thing a viewer noticed: 'The special effects dominate the film . . .' On the other hand, 'The script has some superb scenes, notably between Ford and femme fatale Young . . . But something has gone badly wrong in its dramatic structure,' complained *Time Out*. The *New Yorker*'s Pauline Kael felt that '*Blade Runner* has nothing to give the audience – not even a second of sorrow for Sebastian. It hasn't been thought out in human terms.'

GROSSES: The film grossed just $27 million on its initial release. On its 1992 re-release The Director's Cut grossed just $3.74 million.

POSTER: The film's poster was an illustration by John Alvin emphasising the more violent and noirish aspect of the story, the film's action and cityscape. It foregrounded the Rick and Rachel story. Deckard's face fills the left side of the image as he clutches a gun at face height; Rachel hangs in the space below and they are engulfed by the cityscape. A photo-based poster was also created during the film's initial release. Drew Struzan, famous for his posters for the *Star Wars*, *Indiana Jones* and *Back to the Future* films among many others, was also commissioned by Warner Brothers to create a poster image. It arranged all of the main characters around the face of an anxious-looking Deckard, and was used as the cover for the source novel when it was reprinted to tie in with *Blade Runner*'s original release in 1982.

HOME ENTERTAINMENT: *Blade Runner* remains available on VHS, either just as a VHS or as part of a more lavish box set featuring photographs, a one-sheet poster and a 35mm frame of film from *Blade Runner*. The Director's Cut is available on DVD but as yet without a Director's Commentary.

DELETED SCENES: Inevitably, every film has scenes that are dropped or never even filmed, often because of scheduling and hence financing. For budgetary reasons all of the scenes involving a replicant named Mary were cut. Hampton Fancher described her as looking like a classic American mum. Had she been in the film, Mary would have been the longest to survive, finally being gunned down by Deckard at the end of the film as she hides in a cupboard at JF Sebastian's.

Another cut scene was when Deckard investigates Leon's apartment. The concept was that when Deckard entered the bathroom Leon would be revealed hanging on the ceiling, unnoticed, ready to attack Rick from above.

An idea that had to go was Zhora's dance, originally designed to combine Claymation (stop-frame animation using clay models; today it would more than likely be rendered using CGI) and a snake. It would have cost about $200,000 to achieve.

Another scene was the discovery of the real Eldon Tyrell, his frozen body encased in a Cryo Crypt, thereby informing us that the Tyrell we have been watching is himself a replicant, who has been able to create replicants.

Other scenes that never made it were an establishing scene that Scott was keen on in order to show the Nexus 6 replicants rebellion. We would have been shown a massive pit excavation with a furnace at one end into which were being dumped bodies. Batty emerges from the bodies and the other replicants join him in killing the workers.

Another abandoned scene, for a possible opening of the film, had been written by Fancher that showed a Midwest farmscape and a massive tractor tilling the soil. A Spinner arrives and Deckard appears. Rick goes towards the farmhouse and explores, looking at photographs and other household items. The farmer asks what Rick is doing there and Rick kills the farmer. Ivor Powell commented in an interview at the time 'this is a real Ridley-ism – [Deckard] just pulls out [the farmer's] bottom jaw bone and sees a number stamped on it'. The farmer is a replicant; the scene was designed to show a blade runner at work.

ALTERNATIVE ENDINGS: There are many versions of *Blade Runner* available, and even upon its original release there was notable concern about the obviously happy ending being so inconsistent with all that has preceded it.

An early idea for the film's ending was built around the premise that all Rick Deckard wants is to be able to afford a real sheep which is why he takes the hunting job to pay for the real sheep. Rick has fallen in love with Rachel. After killing the last replicant he goes home to find Rachel on the roof cradling the real sheep. Deckard and Rachel talk and she compares herself to the feelings of the false sheep, ignored in favour of a real one. She hands the sheep to Rick and she steps off the roof to her 'death'. Deckard subsequently heads out of town in his Spinner and comes to the desert. As he stares at the sand he sees a tortoise and is thrilled by this sign of real life. The tortoise ends up flipped on its shell and Rick does not help, just waits and watches. Finally the tortoise rights itself and carries on, symbolising nature and therefore humanity's capacity for survival and hope.

Scott's idea for an elaborate opening to the film involved Deckard on a train, covered with graffiti but very sleek, as it comes into the city from the desert where Deckard has been on vacation. Rick drives on to a sixteen-lane freeway where the car drives itself. Deckard then gets a message to report to the precinct. He leaves his car to filter off the freeway and he goes up into a freeway tower where he is met by a Spinner at the top.

AWARDS: *Blade Runner*, while not a big hit at the box office, was well recognised at awards time.

At the 1983 Oscars it was nominated for Best Art Direction/Set Decoration, the nomination going to Linda DeScenna, Lawrence

G Paull and David L Snyder. The film was also nominated for Best Visual Effects, the nominees being David Dryer, Douglas Trumbull and Richard Yuricich.

At the BAFTAs in 1983, Jordan Cronenweth won the award for Best Cinematography and Michael Kaplan and Charles Knode won the award for Best Costume Design. *Blade Runner* was also nominated for BAFTAs in the categories of Best Film Editing (Terry Rawlings), Best Make-up (Marvin G Westmore), Best Score (Vangelis), Best Sound (Bud Alper, Graham V Hartstone, Gerry Humphreys and Peter Pennell), Best Special Effects (Douglas Trumbull, David Dryer and Richard Yuricich). At the British Society of Cinematographers Awards Jordan Cronenweth was nominated for Best Cinematography.

In a similar vein, in 1983 *Blade Runner* was voted the Third Most Favourite Science Fiction Film of All Time at the World Science Fiction Convention.

Maybe *Blade Runner*'s most significant accolade was its induction in 1993 into the National Film Registry by the National Film Preservation Board of America.

TRIVIA: As part of the film's solid cult following, novelist KW Jeter has written three spin-off novels (see also **TECH TALK**).

Tyrell's bedroom set was in fact the same set as Tyrell's office but simply redressed. The same set was then used again for the interview room seen at the beginning of the film for the action between Holden and Leon.

For the ice room scene the ceilings were hosed down over five days prior to shooting to create the icicle effect.

The crew on *Blade Runner* got to a point where they nicknamed the movie *Blood Runner*.

The Bradbury Building has previously been a location for an *Outer Limits* episode.

John Alvin who painted the *Blade Runner* release poster revised his design for a *Blade Runner 2000* painting which is similar to the original but markedly different too. The likeness to Harrison Ford is far more accurate and in the top right of the image is Roy Batty's face.

A model from the movie *Dark Star* appears in the *Blade Runner* night skies for just a moment, connecting the film back to Dan O'Bannon, the originator of *Alien*.

GREAT SCOTT: Blade Runner is one of the finest examples of a film that was misunderstood upon initial release only to emerge as a cinematic long-distance runner. *The Shawshank Redemption* (Frank Darabont, 1994) had a similar post-theatrical release trajectory. The Director's Cut of *Blade Runner* did indeed improve much of the material, since it removed Deckard's voice-over, in a way allowing the images more breathing space. In 2003, a souped-up new DVD release of the film is planned. This plays into the hands of the Off World faithful and their understandable enthusiasm for every last grain of information about this dreamy, melancholy and intense film, which, despite its preoccupation with death and gloom, is, deep down, a fairly upbeat story. For all its variations and alterations to the source material the sense of peace that hangs over the end of Dick's text is there in the film too.

Inevitably there are edits, changes and eliminations between the book and the film: Roy Batty in the movie is Ingard Baty in the book; the Tyrell Corporation of the movie is The Rosen Association in the novel and is located in Seattle. The iconic rooftop chase and showdown between Batty and Deckard in *Blade Runner* is a far simpler confrontation in the novel – Deckard finds Baty in a room and shoots him. There is even a replicant, Plokov, not included in the film at all who attempts to kill Rick in his vehicle by strangling him, though Deckard shoots him causing him to thrash around greatly. In fact, one of the most faithful inclusions in the film is the thrashing around of the replicants when they are shot (notably Pris in her death throes); Philip K Dick describes the deaths as kinetic. The theme of salvation that is clearly part of Deckard's emotional journey in the film is in the novel too, notably in his dialogue with Mercer, a cultish, deity figure. Even Sean Young's beautiful eyes as Rachel are faithful realisations of the description of Rachel's eyes in the book.

Blade Runner is a perfect example of how a terrific adaptation can result in a terrific film. The movie does not slavishly and mind numbingly translate the action and plot of the novel to the screen but instead takes the spirit of it and finds a cinematic form for it.

In June 2002 *Wired* Magazine ran a piece about the top twenty science fiction films of all time. While there were some surprising omissions, such as *Forbidden Planet*, testifying perhaps more to readers' ages and sense of film history and nothing more, the film that rolled in at number one was *Blade Runner*. The film probably remains Scott's greatest achievement and certainly his most widely known film. Though it enjoyed a cult following to begin with, *Blade Runner* has resonated with audiences in an age of ever-growing cities and the thrills and fears of genetic engineering. It has established itself as a real classic, endlessly referenced, homaged, debated, analysed and documented, a film that is many different things to many different people. Its range of influence has extended even to architecture, which for Ridley Scott, an architecture fan, is a big satisfaction.

For all the ways in which *Blade Runner* has embedded itself in popular culture so forcefully it is worth taking the time to remind oneself of the film's cinematic achievement: the way it works as a film. Like nearly of all of Scott's films it has a simple premise that is essentially riffed on rather than cluttered with endless plot turns. It adheres to the six 'nonsubmersible units', a term coined by Stanley Kubrick to describe the basic blocks of action or sequences around which you would build a film screenplay. Scott excels at this accumulation of patterns. It is still, perhaps, Scott's greatest film: one of the key films of the 1980s and one of the key science fiction films of all time.

SCOTT FREE: 'My most complete and personal film . . .'

'The elevator door was the perfect ending, but it also felt like a prison, it also felt like the end of the road. And that, I found, maybe just too oppressive for words.'

Legend (1985)

(Colour, 94 minutes)

20th Century Fox (Universal Pix in USA)
A Legend Production
Producer: Arnon Milchan
Screenplay: William Hjortsberg
Cinematographer (Panavision, Fujicolor): Alex Thomson
Editor: Terry Rawlings
Music: Jerry Goldsmith
Special Make-up: Rob Bottin
Costumes: Charles Knode
Special Effects Supervisor: Hugh Harlow

Choreography: Arlene Phillips
1st Assistant Directors: Garth Thomas, Bill Westley
Additional Photography: Max Mowdray, Harry Oakes
Supervising Art Directors: Norman Dorme, Les Dilley
Art Director: Assheton Gorton
Set Decorator: Ann Mollo
Co-Producer: Tim Hampton
The Rob Bottin Crew Production Manager: Richard White
Sculptural Design: Henry Alvarez
Lead Special Make-up Artist: Vince Prentice
Lab Technician Supervisor: John Goodwin
Cosmetic Print Supervisor: Margaret Beserra
Visual Effects – Matte Photography Consultant: Stanley
Sayer, Fotherly Ltd, Peerless Camera Co

CAST: Tom Cruise (*Jack*), Mia Sara (*Princess Lili*), Tim Curry (*Darkness*), David Bennent (*Honeythorn Gump*), Alice Playten (*Blix*), Billy Barty (*Screwball*), Cork Hubbert (*Brown Tom*), Pox (*Peter O'Farrell*), Blunder (*Kiran Shah*), Anabelle Lanyon (*Oona*), Robert Picardo (*Meg Mucklebones*), Tina Martin (*Nell*)

BUDGET: $25 million

MPAA: PG 13

BBFC: PG

TAG LINE: No Good without Evil. No Love without Hate. No Innocence without Lust. I am Darkness.

SUMMARY: In a beautiful, perfect picture book forest filled with animals an unidentified figure moves through the forest and comes to a clearing that reveals a sinister tower and dark skies. The figure is the goblin, Blix, en route to her master Darkness. In Darkness's chamber, a voice says, 'I am the Lord of Darkness. I require the solace of the shadows and the darkness of the night. Sunshine is my destroyer . . . There shall not be another dawn.' Blix arrives and Darkness instructs her to destroy the source of good and hope – these are the unicorns. Blix sets out.

Far from Darkness is the sunny meadow and cottage where Princess Lili goes to visit the humble Nell, who thinks Lili should be searching for her true love. Lili then goes to find her friend Jack

O'the Green, a forest 'spirit' who is flesh and blood. Jack and Lili are clearly attracted to each other and they run through the trees. Jack takes Lili to see the unicorns and Lili approaches them, scaring them away. Jack is angry. Lili then throws her ring away saying that the one who finds it will be her suitor. Jack takes the plunge into the deep pool it has fallen into.

While Jack seeks the ring, Blix and two other goblins hunt down the unicorns. A storm engulfs the forest and Lili is terrified. One unicorn is killed and the horn is taken. Jack rises to the surface, finding it frozen over. He smashes through it. Snow engulfs the forest. Lili runs back to Nell's cottage to hide and Blix and the goblins try and hunt Lili out but fail and head back towards Darkness. Lili is lost in the forest.

Jack sleeps in the snow and is awoken by the forest fairy Honeythorn Gump and his elfin friends. Together they set out to find and protect the remaining unicorn. Jack approaches the surviving unicorn saying he is sorry for what has happened. Jack is then charged by Gump to lead the mission to destroy Darkness. Jack is led to a treasury of armour where he finds a sword waiting. Lili is then captured by Blix and taken to Darkness.

Jack and his fellow adventurers find themselves crossing a swamp, encountering the terrifying Meg Mucklebones whom Jack slays. The heroes then plunge into the bowels of Darkness's lair and Oona the sprite gives assistance, freeing them. Meanwhile, Lili is seduced by Darkness and eventually succumbs. The second unicorn is readied for slaying. Jack and Honeythorn prepare to defeat Darkness, using the simple and logical device of shields as mirrors and some good old-fashioned heroics. Jack finally confronts Darkness in a savage duel and Darkness is dispatched. Lili awakens from her spell and is reunited with Jack. Jack and Lili bid farewell to their friends and the unicorns live again.

THE CONCEPT: *Legend* was part of a run of terrific high-fantasy films in the 1980s such as *The Dark Crystal* (Jim Henson and Frank Oz, 1982), *Labyrinth* (Jim Henson, 1986), *Willow* (Ron Howard, 1988), *Return to Oz* (Walter Murch, 1985) and *Time Bandits* (Terry Gilliam, 1982), all of them shot in Britain.

One of the key influences on the film was the film *Wild Child* (François Truffaut, 1969) which Scott screened for Tom Cruise to inform his performance as a primal forest character. Another vital source for the film was Disney's *Fantasia* (Ben Sharpsteen, 1940), notably the 'Night on Bald Mountain' sequence. Scott wanted to fuse the sensibilities of *Beauty and the Beast* (Jean Cocteau, 1946) with Shakespeare's *A Midsummer Night's Dream*.

Legend, originally titled *Legend of Darkness*, was written by William Hjortsberg, whose novel *Falling Angel* was adapted by Alan Parker into the film *Angel Heart* (1987). Scott had enjoyed Hjortberg's book *Symbiography*.

Scott felt that Hjortsberg, being an American writer, would help make the screenplay accessible to a mainstream audience. Together Scott and Hjortbserg worked on fifteen drafts of the script between 1982 and 1984 and the film was budgeted at $25 million. Typically, Scott turned to art history and illustration for a visual sensibility. One of the key inspirations was the glorious work of British illustrator Arthur Rackham, famous for illustrating fairy tales with his gnarled, whimsical and detailed images. The work of Heath Robinson also helped Scott visualise his film. Illustrator Alan Lee worked on the film for a period and certainly the film's elf designs carry echoes of Brian Froud, a regular Jim Henson collaborator who developed the look for *The Dark Crystal* and *Labyrinth*.

The very simple premise of *Legend* centred on the Lord of Darkness wanting to possess the world. Like *Blade Runner*, the development, creation and reception of the movie was filled with intensity and challenge as the screenplay went through numerous drafts. Initially the script had a more intense approach than Scott wanted: for example, one of the scenes that Hjortsberg had originally written included a scene of Darkness having sex with Lili.

There had been a planned novel of *Legend* which would not only detail the screen narrative but expand on it too. Sadly, the publishing deal came to nothing and there was no such book. Scott's biggest structural issue was in how to begin and end the film. One draft of the screenplay ended with Lili leaving Jack with her ring and the anticipation on Jack's part that she would return to him the next day. This ending suggested something more knowing in Lili and only added to Jack's innocence so that he was really the only innocent in the entire story.

In contrast to the darkness of *Blade Runner* and *Alien*, Scott wanted *Legend* to be a family film and it remains his most family-orientated film, though Darkness is pretty frightening no matter how old you are. In keeping with certain Scott themes,

Legend is his most nature-filled film and may yet be his most personal, deriving as it did from his own initial concept.

The unicorn motif of *Blade Runner* would receive a much fuller workout in *Legend*, a film that synthesises references from the Bible, medieval literature and fairy tale. Scott had at one point considered shooting the film in northern California, where the Ewok scenes had been shot for *Return of the Jedi* (Richard Marquand, 1983), but then opted for an all-interior shoot at Pinewood Studios with a lavish set designed by Assheton Gorton. *Legend* is a beautiful-looking film, the artifice of the set adding to the fantasy. The film is a paean to pantheism. The film was shot by Alex Thomson who had worked with John Boorman on *Excalibur* (1981) and went on to shoot Jim Henson's *Labyrinth*.

Tim Curry is truly unrecognisable as Darkness beneath Bottin's make-up which remains one of the most frightening versions of screen evil make-up ever. Darkness is absolutely the Devil, with his cloven feet and dark horns erupting from his blood red skin.

Scott's initial cut of the film ran over an acceptable length, coming in at 125 minutes. He then cut it down to 113 minutes and the American preview reduced it to about 85 minutes. Originally, *Legend* was to have been released in America in June 1985 but it was then rescheduled for 8 November 1985 and then its release was delayed again. In December 1985 *Legend* was released in the UK and other territories with a running time of 94 minutes but its release was postponed in America until spring 1986 – the film bombed there. Elsewhere the film's reception was similarly muted. More recently, the film's fortunes have revived and it enjoys a cult following.

CASTING: One of the most significant features of *Legend* is that it features one of Tom Cruise's early star performances. By the time of *Legend*, Tom Cruise had begun to make his name, notably with *Taps* (Harold Becker, 1981), *All The Right Moves* (Michael Chapman, 1983) and *Risky Business* (Paul Brickman, 1983). It would be his role as Maverick in *Top Gun* (Tony Scott, 1986) that would see him break out into being a superstar and he went on to star in *The Color of Money* (Martin Scorsese, 1986), *Rain Man* (Barry Levinson, 1988), *Born on the Fourth of July* (Oliver Stone, 1989), *Far and Away (*Ron Howard, 1992), *Interview with the Vampire (*Neil Jordan, 1994), *Jerry Maguire* (Cameron Crowe, 1996), *Eyes Wide Shut* (Stanley Kubrick, 1999), *Magnolia*

(Paul Thomas Anderson, 2000), *Vanilla Sky* (Cameron Crowe, 2001), *Minority Report* (Steven Spielberg, 2002) and *The Last Samurai* (Ed Zwick, 2003).

Starring with him was Mia Sara who would soon be seen in *Ferris Bueller's Day Off* (John Hughes, 1986), one of the classics of the teen comedy cycle of 1980s movies.

Tim Curry was given the role of Darkness after Scott had seen him on film in *The Rocky Horror Picture Show* (Jim Sharman, 1975). At one point Mickey Rooney was to have been in the film as one of the forest folk. Originally, Scott had considered Tim Curry for the role of Meg Mucklebones but that role eventually went to Robert Picardo who has since gone on to star in *Star Trek* on television.

MAKING IT: While Scott had been directing *Blade Runner* he was also mulling over the development of *Legend*, a very personal project which in some ways spun out of his failure to turn *Tristan and Isolde* into a movie (see **Ridley's Unrealised Visions**). Scott acknowledged that such a project might not be mainstream enough. Interestingly *Star Wars: Episode II – Attack of the Clones* (George Lucas, 2002), though, has a similar narrative to *Tristan and Isolde*.

Universal seemed desperate to appeal to a youth market, perhaps encouraged by the massive success of their other fantasy outing, *ET: The Extra-Terrestrial* in 1982. The studio though failed to register the film's own identity and hence failed to market it effectively or respect the director's treatment of the material.

THE SHOOT: On 23 March 1984 shooting on *Legend* began, and lasted for 21 weeks. During the shoot, there was a gas explosion on the set and a fire destroyed much of the forest set. They only lost three days.

As with *Blade Runner*, *Legend* has a cult following due, in part, to the various versions of the film in circulation. Scott had to endure battles with the Hollywood studios in terms of the kind of film he had been given the money to make and the kind of film the studio wanted. The studio feared Cruise's long hair would not appeal to a teen audience and they ensured that Alice Playten dubbed David Bennent's German accent for Honeythorn Gump as they felt audiences would not be able to understand it.

Tim Curry was a full eighteen inches taller once he donned the hooves as part of his costume for Darkness. For Darkness's chair, Scott did all the design work.

Storyboard artist Martin Asbury was drafted in to sketch out the sequence of the film. One of the scenes that notably got axed was to have had Jack battling a two-headed monster called Aberaxas. Only then could Jack get to his armour and sword. The finished film has less hassle for Jack en route to the armour and sword. Of the voluminous number of storyboards created for *Legend* – there were 411 pages generated – key images and sequences mapped out on paper included goblins chasing shafts of light, goblins blowing the Great Horn, Jack fighting Meg Mucklebones, and a thrilling-sounding ending where the unicorn drives its horn through the heart of Darkness (appropriately enough, given Scott's affinity for Joseph Conrad), killing him.

Initially, Richard Edlund suggested a way to make all the characters small. He suggested shooting in 70mm then taking the negative and shrinking the actors to any size. However, this would have been prohibitively expensive.

By the time of the film's completion, after the problems with the changes following the text screenings and the low gross, Scott was wondering if his career as a feature film director might be over.

There were rumours of a Duran Duran project after *Legend* and also a drama about an athlete. The goblin Tic, named in the credits, never appears in the film. In *Legend*, the sound of the unicorns at play was in fact the sound of humpback whales. Famed computer game, *The Legend of Zelda*, according to its creator Shigeru Miyamoto, owes its inspiration to *Legend*.

COLLABORATORS: Cinematographer Alex Thomson has also worked in this capacity on *Hamlet* (Kenneth Branagh, 1996), *The Scarlet Letter* (Roland Joffe, 1995), *Black Beauty* (Caroline Thomson, 1994), *Demolition Man* (Marco Brambilia, 1993), *Cliffhanger* (Renny Harlin, 1993), *Alien³* (David Fincher, 1992) and *The Keep* (Michael Mann, 1983). He had worked as a camera operator on numerous other films early in his career, including *Doctor Zhivago* (David Lean, 1965).

Adding to Scott's vision was make-up ace Rob Bottin who had excelled himself with John Carpenter's intense and strangely beautiful effects for *The Thing* (John Carpenter, 1982) and also on the movies *The Howling* (Joe Dante, 1980) and *Explorers* (Joe Dante, 1985). Bottin would go on to Dante's sadly forgotten *Explorers* and the thunderous movie *Total Recall* (Paul Verhoeven, 1990).

The costumes were designed by Charles Knode who had performed the same duties on *Blade Runner*, and who went on to work on *1492: Conquest of Paradise* and *Braveheart* (Mel Gibson, 1995).

Composer Jerry Goldsmith worked with Scott for the second time, having had the same position on *Alien*, and editor Terry Rawlings for the third, after *Alien* and *Blade Runner*. Les Dilley returned as supervising art director after working with Scott on *Alien*.

MUSIC: Jerry Goldsmith's lush score, drawing on Impressionistic and Romantic traditions, was composed over three months in London but was replaced by a more contemporary-styled synth score by Tangerine Dream, who had scored Cruise's film *Risky Business*. Tangerine Dream composed their alternative soundtrack in about three weeks for use on the American release print. Bryan Ferry recorded a song to tie in with the film and a promo: 'Is Your Love Strong Enough?' Tragically, in the painful aftermath of the film's release, Jerry Goldsmith's score session master-tape and written score were lost. Mike Ross-Trevor of the Hit Factory in London is the hero of the hour, though – he kept a two-track digital copy mixed down from an eight-track session master of the scoring session. Some of the score was composed prior to the shoot in order for choreographed dance elements to be developed by Arlene Philips. The *Legend* music is lyrical and sweeping, notable for its Dress Waltz theme. The Goldsmith score is a cult favourite today.

THE OPENING: Red titles on a black screen emphasise the name Ridley Scott and then a magical forest at night appears. This is obviously already a very different film to Scott's other, frequently more frantic films, notably *The Duellists*, *Alien* and *Blade Runner*.

ON THE SCREEN: To its credit *Legend* feels more like a poem than a conventional dramatic movie playing out as a series of riffs on a fantasy theme of nature, darkness and light. There is a picture book artifice to the entire film. When it was made there was a street realism even to the more fantastic movies such as the underrated *Big Trouble in Little China* (John Carpenter, 1986) and the not so hot *The Golden Child* (Michael Ritchie, 1986) and the incredible *Back to the Future* (Robert Zemeckis, 1985).

For Alex Thomson the project was a real challenge to imbue the material with a real fantasy world feeling. One of the key approaches he and Scott took was to change the diffusion shot to shot.

Perhaps the film's single most astonishing shot is one of its simplest. In the scene, Jack approaches the surviving unicorn in an act of apology. The unicorn appears to glow with an appropriate magic. This effect was achieved on the set by shining reflective light from down on the snow. There was also a bank of fake snow just beyond where Tom Cruise stood and by backlighting the scene very strongly the light was bounced back up on to the horse. Talking about the film at the time of its release, Alex Thomson added that 'the way that Tom's arms were outstretched in this quasi-religious pose . . .' enhanced the power of the scene.

Legend's poetic feel, its looseness, is no doubt one reason it did not fare well when first released in the fast times of popular movies. A film released at about the same time was the adaptation of Angela Carter's novel *Company of Wolves*, directed by Neil Jordan, and that was received far more positively for its weaving of sensuality, fantasy and intensity.

Meg Mucklebones is a borrowing from the epic poem *Beowulf* where it is the assumed name of Grendel's mother. Epic themes run through the film, notably the development of Jack's courage and sense of mission. There is also the theme of faith being played out, such as when Oona frees Jack and his friends, thereby proving that her love for Jack endures.

Since 1985, *Legend* has built up a fervent cult following, not perhaps at *Blade Runner*, *Alien* or *Thelma & Louise* levels but significant nonetheless. *Legend* is one of Scott's best films and utterly beautiful to look at. Scott's affinity for the wilderness and the power of natural and elemental forces, notably fire and ice, is all over this film. Darkness is established as decadent from the start with his wine glasses as well as the ornate design of his lair as seen in the end phase of the film. Scott contrasts between the blood red decadence of Darkness's lair and the bright blue skies and greens of the meadow. Lili is dressed in white at all times with one key exception late in the film when she wears a very ornate black dress as she is seduced by Darkness. The film draws on Classical, Romantic and folklore ideas and images and Jerry Goldsmith's score evokes the sound of British composing ace Ralph Vaughan Williams.

HEROES AND VILLAINS: Jack O'the Green is primal and cocks his head like an inquisitive animal much of the time. Cruise is frequently shown crouching playfully, turning his head abruptly, alert to the sights and sounds of the forest. He is so connected with it that in one shot we see him cradle a fox that reinforces his connection to nature. Jack is pure and childlike, an innocent who must go through a trial. *Legend* is in many ways the most undiluted Scott film ever with its images of the wilderness, innocence and experience. Darkness says to Jack when they confront one another, 'What have we here? A little boy?'

Jack's companion Oona the fairy is very much like Tinkerbell to Jack's Peter Pan in her fidelity to him and her pint-sized feistiness. Scott encourages the audience to use its imagination regarding Darkness's appearance as it is withheld until very late in the film. There is a melancholy to Darkness's evil just as there is to Roy Batty's (see **Blade Runner**). For example, Darkness recalls Batty in his charge at Jack near the end of the film. Darkness is quite a lonely figure who just wants Lili to sit and talk with him.

PICTURE PERFECT: Scott punctuates the big shots with neat little inserts that express his themes, notably of the wooden clock in the cottage. The clock has a carving of death hunting a young woman; in the film Darkness hunts Lili and eventually ensnares her. The dance scene in which Lili is seduced by Darkness recalls the work of the great filmmakers of the 1940s Michael Powell and Emeric Pressburger, cinema fantasists like Scott but of a different kind. The huge pillars that we see in Darkness's lair during Lili's dance in rags recall those seen in *Blade Runner*. In Scott films, the architecture is as threatening as the characters on many occasions.

One of the film's greatest shots is of Jack visiting a unicorn at night. The unicorn seems to be emanating soft blue light. In some Scott films such as *Someone* to *Watch Over Me*, *Blade Runner* and *G.I. Jane*, the use of blue light suggests menace. In *Legend* blue light represents good. Lili represents beauty and innocence (she wears white almost throughout) and Scott repeatedly frames and lights her with rim lighting from the sun. Scott uses a long lens for the scene of goblins in their camp. This makes us feel we are hiding in our observation of them, keeping a safe distance from these dangerous characters.

Scott's subtle use of sound runs throughout the film such as when we hear a heartbeat as Jack swims to find the ring. The sound adds a real intensity to an already charged moment. One of the most powerful sequences is when the unicorn is killed. A storm rages and pink blossom swirls wildly. It is a beautiful but dark moment.

Blix's playful and sinister rhymes recall the words of the Witches in *Macbeth*. 'Mortal world turned to ice. Here be goblin paradise,' Blix says.

The scene of Lili running through Darkness's lair in rags has no sync sound, just music, and it demonstrates Scott's flair for the simply achieved effect. Scott cannot help but add a flourish so that a statue comes to life as Lili dances.

Note too Scott's use of intercutting as Lili sings and unicorns approach, while Blix prepares to take aim at the unicorns.

The swamp monster Meg Mucklebones is a classic Rob Bottin creature, terrifying and a little funny too. And, back in the early 1980s, this was a physical, not a digital effect. *Legend*, like the other 1980s movies, is a pre-digital fantasy; the world has a real weight to it. The dissolve from Oona's face to Lili's would be a morph effect today but might lose the sense of psychology, the blurring of lines.

A shot of Jack and Honeythorn peering over a rock at the imperilled unicorn about to be put into the furnace recalls a shot in *Indiana Jones and the Temple of Doom* (Steven Spielberg, 1984).

The final shot of *Legend* is clearly a real forest with the fairy-folk waving goodbye. The shot is very believable, almost like a documentary – it does not have an all-out triumphal feeling to its ending.

TECH TALK: The film uses sound as much as image to create reality. The film was shot almost entirely on a soundstage though. Scott had considered filming among the redwoods of northern California. The dialogue is not so much naturalistic as choral. The cottage at the beginning of the film is the epitome of good and innocence with the sunlight streaming through its windows.

Fifty builders took fourteen weeks to construct the forest set. For the winter scenes, 1,500 icicles were made. The columns in Darkness's lair reached twenty-five feet high and were nine feet in diameter. Nick Gillard, famous now for his Jedi choreography on George Lucas's *Star Wars* three prequels, was Tom Cruise's stunt double on *Legend*. Vic Armstrong doubled for Tim Curry as Darkness and was also his stand-in.

MOVIE TALK:

Darkness: 'I am the Lord of Darkness. I require the solace of the shadows and the darkness of the night. Sunshine is my destroyer. There shall never be another dawn.'

Nell: 'Magic is a very wonderful thing.'

Honeythorn Gump (to Jack): 'Do you think you can upset the order of the universe and not pay the price?'

Darkness: 'Beneath the skin we are already one.'

Darkness: 'We are all animals, my lady.'

Darkness: 'The dreams of youth are the regrets of maturity.'

THE BIG IDEA: The influence of *La Belle et la Bête* (Jean Cocteau, 1946) connects *Legend* to *Blade Runner* and also *Hannibal*. The attraction of great evil to great good predates Hannibal's attraction to Clarice so that even that later film functions as a fairy tale of sorts. 'If life is a dream, many dread the waking,' Honeythorn Gump says.

Legend has a classic apocalyptic ending, just as so many of Scott's other films do. The connection to nature that is seen as a sign of goodness in *Legend* is continued through to *White Squall* and *Gladiator* and, by 1985, had already been played out in *Blade Runner,* most obviously the woods and unicorn dream. In Scott's films, what ensures humanity's survival is some sense of the wild.

CRITICAL CONDITION: '. . . like *Blade Runner* before it, the film suffers so much from an over emphasis on details it becomes a plodding bore,' complained the *Monthly Film Bulletin*. Others preferred to dwell on the technical side of *Legend*: 'Let it be said that Legend is an impressive technical achievement. Scott is a perfectionist who takes infinite pains to make things look right,' wrote Roger Ebert in the *Chicago Sun-Times*; 'And, lo, it came to pass that the enchanted forest was filled up to here with all manner of backlighting and slow motion and starburst filters . . .' confirmed *Time Out*. However, Ebert, in the *Chicago Sun-Times*, continued: 'It is so effective in rendering evil . . . that it's too dreary and gloomy for its own good.'

GROSSES: The film cost $25 million to produce and grossed around $15 million at the North American box office. There was a range of artwork created to promote the film. In London, Selfridges ran a store display of costumes from the film over Christmas 1985.

HOME ENTERTAINMENT: Part of *Legend*'s cult following, thanks to the home video market, is not just due to its status as an undiscovered gem but because various edits of the film exist, only adding to its mystery and intrigue. In Britain, the film is available on VHS and on Region 2 DVD. This disc features just the film's trailer (which is actually quite terrifying); the Region 1 Director's Edition disc, released in May 2002, features an incredible range of extras which will hopefully one day be available on the Region 2 format. These extras are: a feature-length Ridley Scott commentary, trailers, the Bryan Ferry music promo, publicity stills, production photographs, both the 113-minute and 89-minute cuts of the film, the documentary 'Creating A Myth: The Making of Legend', the isolated score and several 'lost' scenes, an alternative opening and The Faerie Dance. There are also storyboards for sequences entitled Lili and the Unicorn, Jack's Challenge and Downfall of Darkness. The current DVD cover for both regions features Darkness sneering as he holds an apple in his hand. Within the apple are the faces of Jack and Lili.

DELETED SCENES: Given the film's variations it is worth going through some of the differences that have done and do exist. The film opened the 1985 Venice Film Festival. The versions of the film that were released were a European cinema version that ran to 94 minutes and which is available in Britain at this length on DVD (see **HOME ENTERTAINMENT**), an American cinema version of 86 minutes and finally a TV version which also ran 94 minutes. Terry Rawlings again worked with Scott in editing the film and at the time of the film's American release said, 'The studio wanted to play around with it. They wanted it to go faster . . . Many of the lingering moments were lost . . .'

Examples of differences between the American and European versions of *Legend* include the following:

In the USA version someone is tortured by demons at the start of the film and Darkness is on his throne – he is blue with yellow fingernails. In the European cut there is only Darkness's arm and no torture scene.

In the European cut, Lili is referred to as a Princess but in the American version she is called a Lady.

In the USA version Lili has a vision of the future where she is briefly encased in ice; in the European version, Lili is not encased in ice.

In the American version, when Darkness plunges to his doom, three shooting stars appear.

In the USA edition, lightning strikes a tree before the unicorn falls.

AWARDS: Unsurprisingly, *Legend* was Oscar nominated for Best Make-up in 1987 with the nomination going to Rob Bottin and Peter Robb-King. At the BAFTAS a nomination for Best Costume Design was made to Charles Knode as were nominations for Best Make-up and Best Visual Effects. David Bennent also received a nomination at the Young Artist Awards. At the British Cinematography Society Awards, Alex Thomson won the award for Best Cinematography in 1985 (at the time of the film's British release).

GREAT SCOTT: While not at a *Blade Runner* cult fever pitch, *Legend* is, however, the other Ridley Scott film that time has helped to increase in stature. Compared to other high-fantasy films made around the same time, *Legend* has an intensity not seen elsewhere. Nor do those other movies have anything like the beautiful aura of Scott's *Legend* – can you imagine something as ambient and darkly seductive as Lili's dance for Darkness in any other big-budget fantasy? In commercial terms Scott possibly paid the price at the time for stopping the simple narrative of his movie simply to enjoy (some might say indulge) the undistilled power of a well-crafted image. In the film's favour is the physicality of its effects and environment. Would *Legend* feel quite as believable in the CGI world of today?

And, of course, the film is one of Tom Cruise's forgotten efforts: it demonstrates the athleticism he would bring to bear on future starring roles and this film is certainly one of his best. His early career facility for creating appealingly simple characters is perfect for the character of Jack. Obviously, *Legend* is the most all-out summation of Ridley Scott's fairy-tale leanings, but in an age where machismo action seems to prevail in the broadest of fantasy cinema, perhaps the cult following of *Legend* will always remain small but passionate.

Legend has taken time to gather appreciation. Snubbed on release, perhaps because it lacked the whiz-bang pace of the most popular fantasy movies of the time, the film is finally getting acknowledgement that is its due. Even by today's fantasy movie standards *Legend* is luxurious and may well be far too slow for today's children. The film does drift at certain points but why can't cinema still be about the unforgettable image? Old-time drama is not the be all and end all. The film does accumulate more interest when grouped with Scott's other all-out fantasies, *Alien* and *Blade Runner*. There is a genuine menace to the story. *Legend* belongs with *Alien*, *Blade Runner*, *Thelma & Louise*, *Gladiator* and *Black Hawk Down* as a definitive Ridley Scott movie.

SCOTT FREE: In an interview with *Starburst* magazine at the time of the film's release Scott laid out his reasons for making the film and offered up a surprising source of visual inspiration: 'It is not a film of the future or the past. It is not even a story of now. The conflict between darkness and light has been with us since the creation . . . and will remain with us throughout eternity.' He went on to explain that 'I wanted to give *Legend* a more contemporary movement rather than getting bogged down in a too classical retelling'. Perhaps surprisingly, 'It was primarily Disney animation that influenced me.' He stated that, 'I made *Legend* primarily for children, my children to be precise.'

Someone to Watch Over Me (1987)

(Colour, 103 minutes)

Columbia Pictures
Producers: Thierry Ganay and Harold Schneider
Executive Producer: Ridley Scott
Associate Producer: Mimi Polk
Screenplay: Howard Franklin
Cinematographer (Deluxe, Color): Steven Poster
Editor: Claire Simpson
Music: Michael Kamen
Sound (Dolby): Gene Cantamessa
Production Designer: James D Bissell

Set Decorator: Linda de Scenna, Steven J Jordan
Art Direction: Christopher Burian Mohr, Jay Moore
1st Assistant Director: Joseph P Reidy
Production Manager: Max Stein, Bill Gerrity
Costume Design: Colleen Atwood
Stunt Co-ordinator: Glenn Wilder, Ronnie Ronell
Casting: Joy Todd

CAST: Tom Berenger (*Mike Keegan*), Mimi Rogers (*Claire Gregory*), Lorraine Bracco (*Ellie Keegan*), Jerry Orbach (*Lt Garber*), John Rubinstein (*Neil Steinhart*), Andreas Katsulas (*Joey Venza*), Tony DiBenedetto (*TJ*), James Moriarty (*Koontz*), Mark Moses (*Win Hockings*), Daniel High Kelly (*Scotty*), Haley Cross (*Tommy*), Joanne Baron (*Helen Greening*)

BUDGET: $12 million

MPAA: R

BBFC: 15

SUMMARY: New York City, the late 1980s. Mike and Ellie Keegan are celebrating their wedding anniversary in their small and homely Queens suburban house, far beyond the bright lights of Manhattan. Mike and Ellie are clearly in love and enjoy the friendship of their police force buddies: Mike is a detective and Ellie is a former police officer. They have a young son, Tommy.

Across town at a swanky nightclub a splashy, high-society party is in full flow. In attendance is socialite Claire with her boyfriend, Neil. Claire bumps into hotshot thirty-something Wynn, who jokes about Claire's choice of men and then invites her to meet him in a downstairs room. Claire smilingly accepts and takes the elevator down. As Wynn waits for Claire, he is visited by a menacing figure named Joe Venza, who has a grievance against Wynn's business practice. Wynn goes to explain but his mouth is not as fast as Venza's hand. Just as Claire enters the room, Venza rams a knife through Wynn's throat, killing him instantly. Claire is spotted by Venza and he realises that she has witnessed the murder. Claire leaps into the lift and Venza pursues her, attempting to prise the doors apart to get to the witness. Claire gets away and is put under police protection but Venza is well connected and might be able to get to Claire easily.

Mike Keegan is part of the team assigned to protect Claire around the clock. At home, Mike and Ellie talk about how lonely the marriage becomes for Ellie once Mike is on a case. Mike begins the process of protecting Claire and upon first arriving at Claire's apartment he is intrigued and clearly in awe of such opulence. Mike explains that part of the protection is that Claire must always be accompanied by a cop. Claire is uneasy with this but soon enough Mike is accompanying Claire to a function at the Guggenheim Museum. Mike is again aware that he is dealing with a different kind of social circle. Claire and Mike talk and there is some connection and attraction between them. Claire goes to the bathroom and Mike does not accompany her. Venza tracks Claire down and threatens her with murder if she identifies him in the police line-up that must surely follow. Mike realises someone has been in the bathroom and rushes to see if Claire is safe. Sure enough Mike realises Venza has attacked and swiftly spots him running from the reception. Mike pursues, and emerges outside. Venza offers himself up for arrest.

Mike and Ellie look for a new house and Claire is relieved that her term of imprisonment in her own home is finally over. Claire and Mike go out for a drink on his last night bodyguarding her. Mike gets some good-humoured knocks from his colleagues at work about being seen out with Claire. Claire identifies Venza in the line-up and soon after trouble rears its head again when a technicality means Venza can go free.

Mike stays with Claire after switching his duty rota to days. As he and Claire lie together Venza's hitman enters the house in an attempt to kill Claire. Mike engages in a cat and mouse gun hunt around the apartment, eventually killing the hitman. Claire is incensed at Mike for the violence that unfolded in her home yet still their romantic attraction unfolds. Mike's anxieties are compounded when Ellie kicks him out of their home.

Venza strikes one more time to seek revenge on Mike. He takes Tommy and Ellie hostage and Mike must rescue them. Venza is finally eliminated in a shootout in Mike's house and Claire leaves Mike's life. Mike and Ellie reunite.

THE CONCEPT: Scott had been told the story for *Someone to Watch Over Me* by Howard Franklin in 1985 during the aftermath of the frustrations of *Legend* in terms of its editing, music changes and finally critical and commercial reception. At the time Scott had been involved in the development of a film called *Johnny Utah*, which eventually became the terrific *Point Break* (Kathryn Bigelow, 1991), again demonstrating that what a director chooses to pass on is as illuminating as what they commit to. One of the most appealing aspects of *Someone to Watch Over Me* appears to have been the chance to foreground the actors within the romantic thriller genre. Scott particularly liked the way the story focused on the disruption of a marriage. Sadly the film was poorly marketed and failed to register greatly with the public.

CASTING: Tom Berenger had begun to make a name for himself in films that included *The Big Chill* (Lawrence Kasdan, 1983) and *Platoon* (Oliver Stone, 1986). He cameoed in *Born on the Fourth of July* (Oliver Stone, 1989) as the marine recruitment officer who visits Ron Kovic's high school. Berenger also starred in the epic TV movie *Gettysburg* (Ronald F Maxwell, 1993).

Mimi Rogers had been married to Tom Cruise for a period of time. Since this film, Mimi Rogers has continued to carve out a successful movie career in films such as *White Sands* (Roger Donaldson, 1991), *The Rapture* (Michael Tolkien, 1991) *Desperate Hours* (Michael Cimino, 1990) and *Lost in Space* (Stephen Hopkins, 1998). She had a cameo in *Austin Powers: International Man of Mystery* (Jay Roach, 1997).

Lorraine Bracco went on to shine in *GoodFellas* (Martin Scorsese, 1990) and television's *The Sopranos* among others.

MAKING IT: Where Scott had made several lavish fantasies in the broadest sense in the first phase of his career, in the late 1980s he made two small-scale dramas, each of them suffused with visual dynamism. The first of these was *Someone to Watch Over Me*, a combination of Scott's visual acuity and also a very welcome warmth and down-to-earth quality. The strength of the film's performances reminds the viewer of how powerful Scott's casting skill has been in all his work, especially his more fanciful pieces. The film is perhaps more a job-for-hire project than any of Scott's preceding movies had been. The film was made during David Puttnam's time as head of Columbia Pictures.

THE SHOOT: The film was shot in the second half of 1986 in Manhattan, Queens and LA (where Wynn's murder was filmed on board the *Queen Mary*, moored at Long Beach). More specifically, the locations included New York's Upper East Side, Rex II Ristorante and Lake View Hospital in Los Angeles, Harbor View Restaurant, Central Park and Center Street.

COLLABORATORS: Steven B Poster the cinematographer on *Someone to Watch Over Me* has also shot the ace kids' fantasy film *The Boy Who Could Fly* (Nick Castle, 1986), *Rocky V* (John G Avildsen, 1990) and *Big Top Pee-wee* (Randal Kleiser, 1988) as well as providing additional photography on *Close Encounters of the Third Kind* (Steven Spielberg, 1977) and *Blade Runner*.

Michael Kamen began in film music in the early 1980s and continues to score successfully and widely today on films such as the *Lethal Weapon* series (Richard Donner, 1987, 1989, 1992 and 1998), the *Die Hard* movies (John McTiernan, 1988; Renny Harlin, 1990; John McTiernan, 1995), *What Dreams May Come* (Vincent Ward, 1997), *Robin Hood: Prince of Thieves* (Kevin Reynolds, 1991) and the epic war series produced by Steven Spielberg and Tom Hanks, *Band of Brothers* (2001).

MUSIC: To enhance the majesty and class of Claire's home, in contrast to the party scene at Mike's at the opening of the film, Scott laces classical music over the images. 'O Mio Bambino Caro' from Puccini's *Gianni Schicchi* is also used in *G.I. Jane*.

For *Someone to Watch Over Me,* British composer Michael Kamen wrote the score. Vangelis supplied a song 'Memories of Green' (also used in **Blade Runner**) and Sting's credits rendition of the Gershwin title tune appears on a compilation of Sting songs. Sting performs the song at the beginning of the film and Roberta Flack sings it at the end.

THE OPENING: The film's opening shot recalls the opening wide shot of *Blade Runner*. The visuals alone carry us from the grandiosity of Manhattan to the very close but culturally distant suburb of Queens.

ON THE SCREEN: Scott's treatment of a fairly routine story is what elevates *Someone to Watch Over Me*, a healthy sign of a strong director organising and transforming the written word on to the screen. The film is one of Scott's warmest and is certainly ripe for rediscovery. Scott's skill with actors is central to the film's success and Tom Berenger, Mimi Rogers and Lorraine Bracco are outstanding. The character of Mike Keegan (Tom Berenger) feels guilt at his clandestine romance. The implication earlier in the film that he is Irish Catholic matches with Ellie's Italian Catholic – note the crucifix on the chain that she wears. Keegan is a by-the-book cop who clearly finds straying from the code and convention testing and wearing just as Deckard does in *Blade Runner* and Starling does in *Hannibal*. Scott's casting is excellent and the faces he has chosen do so much. Berenger conveys Keegan's weariness and intensity through the film's noir-like situation. He journeys through a shadowy urban environment that contrasts with the apparent simplicity and openness of home. For Scott, cities are always a place to emphasise claustrophobia.

HEROES AND VILLAINS: Mike's domestic life is richly and economically described in the performances and, to adopt a Scott approach, the performance given by the set design. Contrasting with Claire's sharp and angular, highly polished world, Mike's home is certainly humble, everyday and rustic even. When Mike and Ellie check out a possible new home, Scott keeps in frame a round stained glass window of a little house in the country; perhaps an ideal retreat for this family. The kitchen is lit only by the sunlight streaming through the windows. Similarly, Ellie's rough and ready, jeans and sweatshirt look contrasts immediately and vividly with Claire's always neat and angular clothing. Claire evokes memories of Joan Crawford in film noir such as *Mildred Pierce* (Michael Curtiz, 1945). Clearly, Scott is moving in the same slightly noirish world as previously, in *Blade Runner*.

When the audience first meet Mike, Scott frames him repeatedly in doorways, the straight lines and sturdiness of the simple Queens clapboard house reinforcing Keegan's character – his simplicity, strength and reliability. 'It's nice to have somebody you can count on,' Claire says of her boyfriend, Neil, early in the film but he is ultimately revealed to be an ineffectual moaner. Mike says of Claire, 'She's my responsibility.' This film is along similar lines to *The Bodyguard* (Mick Jackson, 1992), which had been kicking around Hollywood as a script since the mid-1970s, though Scott's film is the stronger. Scott's hero is a classic and stoic American figure.

Venza's attempt to open the lift doors recalls Roy Batty's unrelenting pursuit and superstrength in *Blade Runner*.

One of the rewarding subtleties of the film is its reference to, and the inherent humour in, the tensions of class difference. Berenger has a subtle accent and there is a funny scene which emphasises the disparity between his and Claire's backgrounds when he mispronounces aperitif as 'appertif'. There is an amusing and touching motif around Mike's choice of tie and suit, though, at home, Mike then suddenly complains about Ellie's constant swearing – Ellie is one of the strong and gutsy Scott women of this picture.

Scott's direction of the actors is confident, emphasising the glances and gestures of Mike and Claire that say so much more than dialogue: at one point there is a jokey scene based around their body language as they share a lift together. Scott has always been able to evoke the sensuality of movement and shapes such as the shot of Ellie in profile as she lies in bed.

Scott goes for powerful effects in simple ways too, such as Ellie in tears when taken hostage.

Mike is a maverick in taking his relationship further with Claire. This relationship works for Scott because it gives him the space to dramatise the conflict between the civil and the more wild. Mike has a rough diamond quality but it is the villain Venza who represents the wild and violent. Mike and Claire's relationship has a refreshing gentility to it: 'You look rather elegant,' Claire says to Mike. 'We're causing quite a scandal,' she adds later on, like someone from another time, when they go to the Guggenheim Museum. This film has the most natural dialogue of all Scott's films. Mike is tough faced but sensitive and thoughtful, just like Slocombe in *Thelma & Louise*.

Like Ellie, Claire is a typical Ridley Scott woman, determined not to have her life compromised by a threat. Claire is very much the innocent in the film, engulfed in a world of darkness, just like Lili in *Legend* and Clarice in *Hannibal*. Claire is an innocent who grows up regarding the violence of the world: 'I never saw anybody killed before'; Mike is an innocent in the duplicity of relationships and cannot handle it. He's set up as something of a little boy such as when we see him throwing paper balls into light fittings and playing football with little fruits on the kitchen table. In *Someone to Watch Over Me*, Tom Berenger, as Harrison Ford has frequently done, brings something believable to his performance allowing it to transcend the demands of the genre.

PICTURE PERFECT: Throughout the film, figures cut through bright lights, notably in the nightclub scene, and for silhouettes and close-ups in the final shootout scene. As in his other films, Scott suggests menace and danger by using harsh, cold blue rim lighting on men's faces. However, Scott also uses rim lighting for a loving shot of Claire in profile towards the end of the film. Scott again uses blue light and smoke, backlit, though in this film his images are not as dense, or maybe not as cluttered, as in his previous films.

Scott uses intercutting to create tension. The best example of this is near the beginning of the film where Claire is in the lift on her way to see Wynn. Her journey below ground is intercut with Wynn being confronted by Venza. The intercutting allows the audience to fear for Claire because they are aware of the danger that she could be in.

Already known for his big pictures and fantastic situations and worlds, this film gave Scott the chance to go 'normal' and he confidently makes the transition. This film is like Ridley Scott Unplugged. For example, near the start of the film there is a warm, low-key and humorous scene in the bedroom between Mike and Ellie.

When Mike goes to the nightclub to commence his investigation, Scott shoots it handheld, adding a real uneasiness to Mike's experience as he journeys into foreign territory. Film noir is a genre famous for charting modern men and women's unease with the urban life. As in *Blade Runner*, Ridley Scott draws on film noir-styled visuals to build a melancholy, subdued atmosphere. The silhouette of Claire at her apartment window at night as the rain falls is hyper-noirish. The stillness of this shot neatly matches the shot of Mike watching over Tommy as Tommy sleeps.

Scott's old *Alien* trick of building tension and putting the viewer in the victim's shoes shines through during Venza's attack on Claire in the bathroom at the Guggenheim function. The shot is handheld as Claire enters the bathroom and then there is a shot of Venza's feet, which Claire does not see. Then there is Venza's attack as the camera looms up behind Claire. An ominous, low-level rumbling sound accompanies the attack.

Scott's other flourish in building tension and visual interest is in the cat and mouse shootout in Claire's apartment (see **Top Shots**) where Mike confronts one of Venza's hitmen. Claire's apartment is a mass of mirrors and mazelike corridors, just like a labyrinth. Mike uses the mirrors to catch his opponent in what might be a reference to Orson Welles's film noir classic *Lady from Shanghai* (1948).

As in all his work, Scott uses décor in *Someone to Watch Over Me* to emphasise an emotional and dramatic situation. The sterility of the hospital corridor plays up the coldness of Mike and Ellie's relationship at this point. The distance at which they stand only underlines the point.

Scott uses a long lens during the cocktail discussion scene to provide an intimate framing which is not intrusive.

The majesty and exotic quality of Claire's apartment is expressed best through the graceful tracking shots that contrast to the far simpler and sometimes handheld camera work for the scenes at Mike's home. Like Peter Weir's magnificent film *Witness* (1985), *Someone to Watch Over Me* contrasts cultures around a doomed love story where professional and personal interests cannot be reconciled.

TECH TALK: The swanky party scene which kicks the picture off was shot not in New York but at the Los Angeles Mayan Theater – Scott filmed this shot himself from a helicopter. It was his opportunity to rhapsodise one of his favourite pieces of architecture – the Chrysler Building in Manhattan. Claire's apartment was a set built at Culver City studios.

MOVIE TALK:
Claire (to Mike): 'Let me watch over you tonight.'

THE BIG IDEA: Scott's taste for romance must have been a huge appeal of this film. Like the romance of Rick and Rachel (see **Blade Runner**), Mike and Claire's relationship is fairly charged. There is no more romantic exchange in the film than when Claire says, 'I'm going to miss you. It's been nice having you watch over me', to which Mike humbly replies, 'It's been nice being around you, Claire.' The scene of the two of them just looking at one another in the lift is warm. At their moment of farewell, an exchange of smiles says more than words.

Even on such a relatively small-scale film as this, Scott finds a way to point up the story's fairy-tale quality. One of the film's lines has the abstract quality of a fairy tale when Venza sees Claire and says to her, as though casting a spell, 'If you ever see me again, you never saw me before.'

Someone to Watch Over Me is not a film that extensively explores the familiar Scott motif of the primal. Instead it features occasionally as the source of a particular scene or an image. One way in which Scott expresses it in this film is through the importance of the family unit under threat so that one of the closing images is of Mike, Ellie and Tommy all huddled together amidst the carnage of a shootout in their own home.

One of the central themes revolves around Mike and Ellie in terms of whether he will be forgiven for his indiscretion. Like a kid, Mike says to Ellie, 'I want to come home. I do love you, Ellie', to which she replies, 'I love you too, Michael.' They are innocents who have been challenged by the sometimes cruel and ugly world.

CRITICAL CONDITION: Many of the reviews stressed the visual in *Someone to Watch Over Me*: 'The final image . . . is a remarkably potent tableau,' said *Monthly Film Bulletin*; 'A cliché maybe, but when Ridley shoots New York, it's something special,' enthused *Empire*; and 'With its stunning cityscapes and Chanel-ad like surreality, *Someone to Watch Over Me* shows off director Ridley Scott's extraordinary visual artistry,' agreed the *Washington Post*. The *Chicago Sun-Times* picked on another element within the film: '. . . *Someone to Watch Over Me* does contain one element of extraordinary interest. That is the character of the cop's wife.' *Time Out*, however, summed up the plotline as 'Scott's gleaming fusion of eternal triangle and killer-on-the-loose'. The *New Yorker* review was that 'Ridley Scott's thriller *Someone to Watch Over Me* is all moods. Prodigious planning and editing have gone into them, along with a lot of smoke, Gothic lighting and interior decoration.' In hindsight *A Biographical Dictionary of Film* commented, '*Someone to Watch Over Me* is far richer than reputation suggests.'

GROSSES: *Someone to Watch Over Me* grossed just over $10 million when it was released in North America in autumn 1987.

POSTER: The film's poster is simple: Mike on the left of frame standing strong, Claire lies at his side. In the background we can make out the face of Venza. A European version of the poster emphasised Venza pulling apart the doors of the lift – this formed the central element of the advert which also featured the New York skyline.

HOME ENTERTAINMENT: *Someone to Watch Over Me* is available on both VHS and DVD, both Region 1 and Region 2. The DVDs include the film trailer.

AWARDS: *Someone to Watch Over Me* was nominated for an American Society of Cinematographers Award for Outstanding Achievement in a Theatrical Release and was also nominated for an International Fantasy Film Award in the category of Best Film for Ridley Scott.

GREAT SCOTT: This is one of Scott's least well-known movies. While he does charge it with cinematic flourishes and terrific performances, it is not essential Ridley and you'd be forgiven for finding it routine at times. It does deserve more recognition than it gets, however, especially for the warmth with which the characters are drawn. Just as a director such as Steven Spielberg has his smaller, often stronger, efforts overlooked in the shadow of dinosaurs and war stories, so too Ridley Scott's smaller movies have to fight to be heard against the roar of his big canvas pictures. Like *Legend*, *Someone to Watch Over Me* is a movie that will be rediscovered and newly appreciated. It is certainly preferable to the thunderous and empty *G.I. Jane* and the freakish *Hannibal*.

As with all Scott's films, *Someone to Watch Over Me* reflects Scott's skill at suggesting an environment and immersing us within it so that is becomes a character in itself. The film is refreshing for its concentration on characters rather than hysteria or trauma. This means that, when the jumps and shivers do come, they have more impact and the audience really feels for the doomed lovers at the heart of the story. Along with the ending of *Gladiator*, *Someone to Watch Over Me*'s ending is Ridley Scott's most melancholy. The film is a triumph of characterisation and mood over the familiar mechanics of an urban thriller. The film combines the requirements of the detective genre with a universally moving story of doomed love. It remains refreshing in the Scott scheme of things, especially at the stage in his career when it was made, for its smaller scale. It helped pave the way for Scott's successful treatment of the *Thelma & Louise* screenplay four years later. It also brought an end to Scott's high-level fantasy filmmaking of the previous few years.

SCOTT FREE: 'I figured I'd better go down a route of being normal after what had happened with *Legend* and *Blade Runner*.'

Black Rain (1989)

(Colour, 126 minutes)

A Paramount Picture release of a Jaffe/Lansing production
in association with Michael Douglas
Producers: Stanley R Jaffe, Sherry Lansing
Executive Producers: Craig Bolotin, Julie Kirkham
Screenplay: Craig Bolotin and Warren Lewis
Cinematographer (Super 35, Technicolor): Jan De Bont
Editor: Tony Rolf
Music: Hans Zimmer
Sound Recordist: Donald O'Mitchell
Sound Editor: Richard Adams
Sound (Dolby): Keith A Wester, James A Sabat
Production Design: Norris Spencer
Art Direction: John J Moore, Herman F Zimmerman, Kazuo Takenaka
Set Design: Alan S Kaye, Robert Maddy, James R Bayliss
Set Decoration: John Alan Hicks, Leslie Bloom, Richard C Goddard, John M Dwyer, Kyoji Sasaki
Costume Design: Ellen Mirojnick
Special Effects Supervisor: Stan Parks
Second Unit Director: Bobby Bass
Additional Photography: Howard Atherton
Aerial Photography: David Nowell
Additional Editing: William Gordean, Jacqueline Cambas
Line Producer (Japan): Yosuke Mizuno
Associate Producer: Alan Poul
Assistant Directors: Aldric La'auli Porter, Benjamin Rosenberg, Masayuki Taniguchi, Dennis Maguire
Casting: Diane Crittenden, Nobuaki Murooka
Additional Casting: Melissa Skoff

CAST: Michael Douglas (*Nick Conklin*), Andy Garcia (*Charlie Vincent*), Ken Takakura (*Masamoto*), Kate Capshaw (*Joyce*), Yusaku Matsuda (*Sato*), Shigeru Koyama (*Ohashi*), John Spencer (*Oliver*), Guts Ishimatsu (*Katayama*), Yuya Uchida (*Nashida*), Tomisaburo Wakayama (*Sugai*), Miyuki Ono (*Miyuki*)

BUDGET: $14 million

MPAA: R

BBFC: 15

TAG LINE: An American cop in Japan. Their country. Their laws. Their game. His rules.

SUMMARY: New York, the late 1980s. Nick Conklin races his motorbike under the Brooklyn Bridge in a madcap bet that he wins. Back at work, Conklin, a detective with the NYPD, is brought before Internal Affairs for corrupt policing involving stolen money. Conklin's career is under real threat but he refuses to comply with the bureaucracy.

With his 28-year-old partner, Charlie Vincent, Nick, who is said to be in his late 30s, goes for lunch at a diner. In the diner, Nick and Charlie witness a violent murder by a Japanese yakuza (gangster). Conklin and Vincent pursue the criminals and Nick confronts the main one, Sato, in a meat warehouse where he is almost suffocated to death. Charlie saves him just in time and the criminal is taken back to the police house for questioning. Conklin's job is on the line and his problems are further complicated by his marital and financial problems, all of which have left him strapped for cash. Clearly considered a loose cannon, Conklin is charged with the job of taking the yakuza back to Osaka, thereby getting Conklin out of the way. Conklin is furious but can do nothing except take the job. He and Charlie escort Sato to Osaka.

Arriving in Osaka, Conklin and Charlie hand over Sato only to realise they have handed him over to fake cops, set up by Sato. Conklin and Vincent spend time with the Japanese police, and are just about tolerated as observers of local police practice. Conklin cannot help but get involved and finds it very difficult to integrate and tolerate the Japanese ethic. Vincent is far more pliable.

In a nightclub, Conklin meets the owner, an American named Joyce who is able to offer Nick some clues as to the nature of the crimes going on. Conklin registers the nature of the crime before the authorities do. The crime going down is the counterfeiting of American dollars. Police detective Masamoto is assigned to chaperon Conklin and Vincent during their stay, which creates tension. Conklin and Vincent break the rules and go along with a SWAT team to raid Sato's hideout. Relations do begin to warm up, though, when Charlie and Nick go out drinking, encouraging Masamoto to join them.

Returning to their hotel, Nick and Charlie are lured into a trap. Charlie is killed by Sato's thugs and the need to nail Sato suddenly becomes personal for Nick. He tries to get Masamoto to join him in getting Sato but Masamoto refuses and he must go it alone. Nick goes to Sato's new meeting place, an Osaka steelworks, where Nick observes a yakuza meeting. Nick tries to gun Sato down but fails. Sato gets away.

The yakuza clan heads meet at a vineyard and Conklin goes in to finish the job himself. Masamoto comes to his aid. Nick races Sato on motorbike after a tense shootout. Conklin and Sato fight and finally Nick and Masamoto bring Sato in to the police. Nick says goodbye to American nightclub-owner Joyce (see **HEROES AND VILLAINS**) and then says farewell to Masamoto at the airport. In a final gesture, Nick's maverick streak remains strong until the end and he returns to New York.

THE CONCEPT: The film's producers, Stanley R Jaffe and Sherry Lansing, were enjoying much success at the time of *Black Rain*. Having recently produced *The Accused* and also *Fatal Attraction* they were known for taking on melodramatic subjects that emphasised a social milieu. As with *Someone to Watch Over Me*, *Black Rain* represented another real-world film for Scott, obviously different to his earliest features. By the late 1980s, the success of *Beverly Hills Cop* (Martin Brest, 1984), *Lethal Weapon* (Richard Donner, 1987), *Die Hard* (John McTiernan, 1988) and *Sea of Love* (Harold Becker, 1989) and a cluster of other police action movies had created a whole subgenre which marked the continuation of the Western genre, albeit in a new guise.

CASTING: *Black Rain* stars Michael Douglas, who was riding very high at that point after *Romancing the Stone* (Robert

Zemeckis, 1984), *Fatal Attraction* (Adrian Lyne, 1987) and his Oscar-winning role in *Wall Street* (Oliver Stone, 1987). He went on to star in a number of well-written features, frequently with a social reference point, such as *Falling Down* (Joel Schumacher, 1993), *Disclosure* (Barry Levinson, 1996), *Traffic* (Steven Soderbergh, 2000) and *The Wonder Boys* (Curtis Hanson, 2001). Back in the 1970s Douglas had starred in *The China Syndrome* (James Bridges, 1979) and produced *One Flew Over the Cuckoo's Nest* (Milos Forman, 1976). In an early draft of the screenplay, the action begins with Conklin gambling and his age is put at late 30s, though Douglas was in his mid-40s by the time he played the part. Douglas has always had a taste for roles which fire social issue sparks.

Ken Takakura who played Masamoto was a huge star in Japan, easily overshadowing Hollywood star Michael Douglas during the Japanese phase of the shoot. Takakura had appeared in the film *The Yakuza* (Sydney Pollack, 1975).

Andy Garcia was hot off *The Untouchables* (Brian De Palma, 1987) when *Black Rain* was made and most recently has starred in *Ocean's Eleven* (Steven Soderbergh, 2001) and the year after *Black Rain* he had a main role in *The Godfather: Part III* (Francis Ford Coppola, 1990).

Yusaka Matsuda, the actor playing Sato, was known as a comedian in Japan. He died of cancer just after the film was released.

Jackie Chan had been approached to appear in *Black Rain* but he declined. He did not want to play a bad guy.

MAKING IT: *Black Rain* remains unique in Scott's output as it is the one time he worked as a director for hire on a feature film. As with *Someone to Watch Over Me* this is a fairly routine thriller made more interesting by the culture clash at its centre. In *Someone to Watch Over Me* the most interesting conflict was not between the good guy and the bad guy but between class. In *Black Rain*, the good guy/bad guy element is predictable; it is the sparks given off by nationalities mixing that saves the film. This was part of a cycle of mid- and late-1980s cop films where the cop was something of a 'fish out of water' (see **THE CONCEPT**). For Scott one of the most appealing aspects of the project was the chance to explore the look of contemporary urban Japan. In an article in *Premiere* movie magazine at the time, Steve Pond wrote: 'Any way you look at it, the Orient clearly haunts this British director.' For example, *Blade Runner* has an undercurrent of the Oriental in its design and some of its supporting characters.

THE SHOOT: Filming on *Black Rain* began on 28 October 1988 in Osaka until 8 December 1988. The shoot then returned to America where it wrapped on 14 March 1989. Among its locations was The Ennis Brown House in Los Angeles, where Scott had also filmed on *Blade Runner*. In *Black Rain*, the house was a location for the Osaka police station.

The shoot began in Japan, and then moved to New York, followed by Los Angeles. Finally, the unit went up to the wine country in northern California.

The nightclub location was the production's biggest set, measuring 150 feet long and standing three storeys high.

COLLABORATORS: Hans Zimmer has also contributed scores to *Driving Miss Daisy* (Bruce Beresford, 1988), *Backdraft* (Ron Howard, 1991), *Rain Man* (Barry Levinson, 1988), *Regarding Henry* (Mike Nichols, 1991), *Pearl Harbor* (Michael Bay, 2001), *The Peacemaker* (Mimi Leder, 1997), *The Prince of Egypt* (Brenda Chapman, Steve Hickner, Simon Wells, 1997) and *The Thin Red Line* (Terrence Malick, 1997). He has worked on a number of other Scott films: *White Squall*, *Thelma & Louise*, *Gladiator*, *Hannibal* and *Black Hawk Down*.

Jan De Bont also served in the capacity of director of photography on *Flesh and Bone* (Paul Verhoeven, 1985), *All the Right Moves* (Paul Brickman, 1983) and *Die Hard* (John McTiernan, 1988). Subsequently, he has directed *Speed* (1994), *Twister* (1996) and *The Haunting* (2000).

MUSIC: This soundtrack is significant as it marks the first time Hans Zimmer worked with Ridley Scott (see also **Thelma & Louise**, **Gladiator**, **Hannibal** and **Black Hawk Down**). The score combines late 80s Western sounds with traces of an older, more traditional Japanese sound.

THE OPENING: We see a red screen and opening credits in white. The red pulls back to reveal itself as a red disc, a rising sun which then dissolves to a globe sculpture in New York. Scott fuses the central drama and conflict in one shot, where the East meets

RIDLEY SCOTT Black Rain

the West. Zimmer's music comes in at this early point, tinged with an Eastern sensibility.

A song plays on the soundtrack, the lyrics emphasising the failure and desperation that define Nick's character, situation and the drama that will unfold.

HEROES AND VILLAINS: Nick is a burned-out and unconventional cop. He is another of Scott's maverick heroes. Nick rides a bike rather than a car and the way he dresses physicalises his maverick attitude. He is not clean cut, contrasting readily with his much younger partner, Charlie. The film is a police procedural in the tradition of *The French Connection* (William Friedkin, 1971) and shares with *Witness* (Peter Weir, 1985) the culture clash dynamic. Like *Gladiator*, *Black Hawk Down*, *White Squall* and *G.I. Jane* it is in the very masculine world of tough talk and action. But this is not always what makes things work. It is Charlie who successfully integrates into Osaka – he wins the crowd by being a little more conventional. Nick's punk ethic is challenged when he has to dress smartly for his Internal Affairs meeting. 'Suits, man,' Conklin says disparagingly during the meeting, but at the end of the film he again wears a jacket and tie, without being told to – he has taken on board some of the Japanese codes of order.

Nick subscribes to a simple code that is challenged. 'I caught him, my case,' he says to his captain, but Conklin will not be given that opportunity this time and so the unfolding drama is a chance for Conklin to rescue his professional standing, his honour. Nick is a tense man who thinks he is cool; Charlie is the cool one. On the plane Charlie relaxes but Nick constantly flips cards in a game of patience, which he has a serious lack of. Nick is in fact a control freak right up there with Keegan and Sheldon and Urgayle in *Someone to Watch Over Me*, *White Squall* and *G.I. Jane* respectively. Nick is out of his small world and his racism and ignorance define him. In one scene where Nick is being shown a page of headshots of suspects at the Osaka police offices, Conklin dismisses them as 'identical strangers'. Conklin's sense of duty is both a blessing and a curse, as it is for so many Ridley Scott heroes. 'I can't go back without him,' Nick says of Charlie.

There is comic mileage in little details such as Nick being unable to get to grips with chopsticks and noodles. The scene of Vincent and Masamoto singing in the club is warm and juxtaposed neatly with the sequence where Charlie is killed. This scene is the turning point in the middle of the film. It is also unexpected that the sidekick character gets killed that early. Nick trashes Sato's hideaway, in a personal note of revenge and anger prompted by Charlie's murder – he cannot control himself or his situation any longer. Nick is relentless. He does not have anything else to live for in a way that mirrors Maximus (see **Gladiator**) and Deckard (see **Blade Runner**).

Masamoto is a more obvious control freak and he learns to loosen up during his time spent with the American cops. Charlie swaps ties with Masamoto in an effort to loosen Masamoto up. In *Someone to Watch Over Me*, Claire jokes about Mike's tie. Throughout the film Masamoto speaks about code, in a way that would make Maximus proud. The order and restraint of Masamoto is in obvious contrast to the Americans who are perceived as negligent. Masamoto is the guide through the adventure, he is wise and calm. Conklin is like a spoiled kid who goes from ignorance, rather than innocence, to a kind of experience.

Joyce the nightclub owner delights in Nick and Vincent's evident failings: 'Americans who are less than perfect,' she says. Joyce is a tough-talking, strong woman, who in the film seems to be underwritten or rather underdeveloped on screen. There is the sense that some of her scenes have been dropped. Her farewell to Nick suggests more of a relationship had developed than was shown in the final cut.

The film ends with a conciliatory farewell scene between Conklin and Masamoto. The tone is one of warmth but, as always, Scott avoids anything too sentimental. Conklin is revived by the experience and has had his opinions challenged.

PICTURE PERFECT: Scott cannot help but romance New York with his camera, the first shot of the skyline revealing the city tinged with golden sunlight. Even the steam and towering skyscrapers are things of beauty for Scott, whose framing and use of the cities in the film recalls *Blade Runner*, albeit less pumped up. This is a more naturalistic film. Like *Blade Runner*, the detective comes to find his own better self and humanity through a culture clash, whether with policemen or replicants.

The bike chase that starts the film is staged with a foreground element, in this case the row of parked cars that add visual interest and depth to the tracking shot. At the end of the film the vineyard fences do the same job and the aerial shots add real urgency and sweep to the closing bike chase action.

Conklin's spacious apartment is somewhat empty, reflecting his life. It is not a very homely place. This contrasts with the comfortable, slightly rustic, warmth of Mike Keegan's home in *Someone to Watch Over Me*.

As with Scott's other films, small gestures and moments gain significance as the film develops. Like Maximus rubbing the earth in his hands or Mike Keegan fussing about his tie, Charlie's matador joke with his jacket starts out as a laugh and later in the film is the source of great danger (see **Top Shots**). In *G.I. Jane* the ringing of the bell is a routine way to back out of the training but for Jordan it is a way to vent her anger at the system she is in and make clear her wish to defeat rather than give in to it. In *Black Rain*, Scott's skill at using a look rather than a line of dialogue remains as true as ever. Masamoto and Nick simply exchange an uneasy look after the steelworks shootout, both knowing what will ensue.

The Internal Affairs meeting is in a dark room into which sunlight cuts through the blinds, rather like in *Blade Runner* during the questioning session at the beginning of the film with Leon. It is a noirish device that hints at corruption and the urban.

Scott trades on the audience's genre familiarity, as he always has done. The yakuza murder in the diner at the beginning of the film is framed and carried out rather like a Western, notably in a shot of Charlie's hands flexing for the gun in his holster. Scott's typically strong choice and placement of music is evident here as Conklin and Vincent give chase.

Scott portrays the city as a steely blue environment. This is a cold-looking film, about harsh behaviour and the corruption of cities. Scott layers the frame with smoke and traffic, lending everything a sense of realism. Scott's affinity for visual atmosphere is shown in the chase through the meat warehouse with the strips of light and the sense of cold.

As Sato is questioned he seems able to see Conklin through the two-way mirror in a moment that recalls *Someone to Watch Over Me* when Claire sees Venza in the line-up of suspects. Sato is a perfect supercriminal for whom traditional codes do not matter – this will prove his real undoing.

The establishing shot of Osaka emphasises its industrial might. It is a shot that comes across as a more laidback version of the establishing shot at the beginning of *Blade Runner*. Once the film gets down to street level, Scott emphasises its otherworldliness to the Westerner with its neon, colour and noise.

Scott's skilful use of sound to enhance tension and fear is exemplified when Charlie is attacked and surrounded by the yakuza heavies on their bikes. The neon light enhances the alien feel of the environment, giving the scene a fairy-tale quality that makes it feel like Nick and Charlie are lost in the woods and will perish. The bikers all have banners on their bikes which evidently and powerfully recall samurai images. There is a gladiator-like aspect to this, fitting with the matador allusions when we first meet Charlie. The film is very much a Western on Japanese soil. Sugai says, 'I'm bound by duty and honour,' and he reprimands Sato saying, 'You must learn to honour our yakuza code.' The movie is really an urban Western as so many cop movies have been since the demise of the Western itself.

The scene of Nick at Joyce's apartment is all hard lines and block-like organisation. Nick grieves for Charlie there. Masamoto shows up with a box of Charlie's things and Nick can't handle it so Masamoto takes care of Charlie's funeral arrangements. Masamoto presents Nick with a box and Nick takes Charlie's gun; Masamoto takes Charlie's NYPD badge. This scene is shot in shadow, emphasising the downbeat nature of the moment.

Sato is associated with furnaces and fire when Nick hunts him down. Sato taunts Nick in the steelworks like *Blade Runner*'s Batty might do. Like Roy Batty, Sato is a strong and determined character.

TECH TALK: As director of photography, Jan De Bont had a crew of about 350 people at key occasions. In an interview at the time of the film's release, De Bont said, 'We didn't want a *Godfather*-type look, but a similar feeling.' The footage of the Osaka steel mill was partially shot in California. Scott's famous backlight had a certain kind of artifice that was not as highly favoured by De Bont. Filming in Japan was very expensive because of location costs and so the production relocated to America.

While much of the film had a harsh and realistic quality to the lighting, for those scenes with Joyce De Bont and Scott opted for a diffused light. The club set was notable for integrating light sources as elements of the design, such as the spotlights on scaffolding. This was an extension of Scott's approach in *Blade Runner* where the illuminated umbrella handles lit the faces of extras passing by the camera.

Another huge interior for the film was the fish market where there was a serious time restriction because of the enormous fee imposed for shooting on location there. The crew had just a weekend to film and Scott and the crew worked non-stop over a 22-hour stretch. Filming at the fishmarket would originally have cost $1 million for the weekend but that figure was eventually negotiated down by the producers.

For the bike chase across the vineyard at the end the crew filmed in the Napa Valley. This is also where they built the Japanese temple that the winery owners wanted to keep erected for use as a restaurant. For some shots of the Osaka streets, downtown LA was used. A total of 700,000 feet of footage was shot on *Black Rain*.

MOVIE TALK:
Internal Affairs guy: 'I don't like heroes, Conklin. They think the rules don't apply.'

Nick: 'Sometimes you gotta choose a side.'
Joyce: 'I did. I'm on my side.'

Masamoto: 'Perhaps you should think less of yourself and more of your group.'

Masamoto: 'You've dishonoured me and our department.'

Masamoto: 'You cannot fix everything.'

THE BIG IDEA: *Black Rain* addresses cultural imperialism rather like *1492: Conquest of Paradise* did a few years later. This is especially evident when Sugai speaks with Nick explaining what the Black Rain is – the Black Rain is defined as the fallout from the B29 bomb dropped on Hiroshima – 'The heat brought black rain. You shoved your values down our throat. You created Sato and thousands like him.' Interestingly, a 1990 film from Japan also entitled *Black Rain* was released exploring the effects on the lives of a Japanese family of the dropping of the bomb on Hiroshima. This film was directed by Shohei Imamura.

There are classic elemental associations in the film, reflecting Scott's taste for the archetypal narrative and character. Sato occupies a moral hell of corruption where he has abandoned even the concept of honour amongst thieves. Even the yakuza boss Sugai talks of Sato saying, 'He knows nothing of loyalty and respect.' They teach Sato a lesson at the vineyard by getting him to cut off one of his fingers for messing them around. Scott likes to show the physical pain of violence.

Scott originally had Sato impaled on a fencepost after the chase and fight at the end but the producers felt it did not carry enough sense of justice and that Conklin remained immoral. So, instead it was reshot with Conklin and Masamoto bringing Sato in.

CRITICAL CONDITION: Many of the reviews the film received were not overly complimentary: 'Is Ridley Scott the new Fritz Lang? . . . the cultural payoffs and any cross-cultural bonding between Conklin and Sato are not worked through in any psychological or dramatic sense,' suggested the *Monthly Film Bulletin*; 'Scott distracts us with overwrought visuals,' wrote Roger Ebert in the *Chicago Sun-Times*; and 'Obvious stuff . . .' confirmed *Time Out*. *Empire* thought Scott an odd choice of director and harked back to a previous film: '[He] tries to portray contemporary Japan as an alien wonderland . . . The result is something like *Blade Runner 2*, but without depth and resonance,' while *USA Today* connected to it real life: 'Don't expect to see this at the UN.' '[Scott] approaches this prickly action thriller with the gusto of a sushi chef in a fish storm . . . It's a gorgeous, erratic movie,' wrote the *Washington Post*, with at least a glimpse of the positive.

GROSSES: The film opened on 22 September 1989 and grossed $45 million.

POSTER: With Michael Douglas's career on the up at the time perhaps the most important element on the advert was his face. The poster features him with his shades on looking directly at us. There is some indication of the Japanese setting in the background.

HOME ENTERTAINMENT: *Black Rain* is available on VHS and on Region 1 and 2 DVDs. As yet they do not include any special features.

AWARDS: Few gongs were handed out to this film, other than Oscars for Best Sound Effects Editing to Milton C Burrow and William L Manger and the Oscar for Best Sound Recording which went to Donald O Mitchell, Kevin O'Connell, Greg P Russell and Keith A Wester.

GREAT SCOTT: There is a familiar Scott melancholy beneath the pizzazz and filmmaking flair in this story about two lonely men looking to prove their worth. The film, though, is anonymous as a Ridley Scott film. It came at a time of transition for the director from the high fantasy he began with to movies that were more obviously rooted in reality. The texture of the culture clash is what saves this movie from being mundane. The performances, as always in Scott's films, are strong and believeable. Of Charlie's death, Ridley Scott commented that, 'Nick suddenly realises his impotence.'

The film really sparkles whenever Andy Garcia is on screen. The rest of the movie is fairly glum and certainly lacks the richer drama of *Someone to Watch Over Me*, which elevated that film beyond any cliché it could have fallen into. *Black Rain* is like an impoverished real-world *Blade Runner*, without the poetry of fantasy – it once again demonstrates just how skilled Ridley Scott is at utilising the gifts of science fiction and fantasy to enhance the drama.

Despite the film's success, *Black Rain* remains a fairly routine outing for Scott and could not be considered essential Ridley viewing. In the bigger picture, the film was part of the big wave of cop movies to hit Hollywood in the late 1980s, particularly those following a 'fish out of water' narrative line (see **THE CONCEPT** and **MAKING IT**).

SCOTT FREE: 'It's strangers in a strange land.'

Thelma & Louise (1991)

(Colour, 128 minutes)

A Pathe Entertainment presentation of a Percy Main
Production
Producers: Ridley Scott, Mimi Polk
Screenplay: Callie Khouri

Cinematographer (Color): Adrian Biddle
Editor: Thom Noble
Music: Hans Zimmer
Sound: Keith A Wester
Production Design: Norris Spencer
Art Direction: Lisa Dean
Set Decoration: Anne Ahrens
Set Design: Alan Kaye
Assistant Director: Steve Danton
2nd Unit Director-Stunt Co-Ordinator: Bobby Bass
Co-Producer: Dean O'Brien

CAST: Susan Sarandon (*Louise Sawyer*), Geena Davis (*Thelma Dickenson*), Harvey Keitel (*Hal Slocombe*), Michael Madsen (*Jimmy*), Christopher McDonald (*Darryl*), Brad Pitt (*JD*), Stephen Tobolowsky (*Max*), Timothy Carhart (*Harlan*), Lucinda Jenney (*Lena, the waitress*), Jason Beghe (*State Trooper Policeman*), Marco St John (*Truck Driver*), Sonny Carl Davis (*Albert*), Ken Swofford (*Major*), Shelly De Sal (*East Indian Motel Clerk*), Carol Mansell (*Witness*), Stephen Polk (*Surveillance Man*), Rob Roy Fitzgerald (*Plainclothes Cop*), Jack Lindine (*ID Tech*), Michael Delman (*Silver Bullet dancer*), Kristel L Rose (*Girl smoker*), Noel Walcott (*Mountain bike rider*)

BUDGET: $16 million

MPAA: R

BBFC: 15

TAG LINE: Somebody said get a life . . . so they did.

SUMMARY: In Arkansas, Louise is a diner waitress. She calls her best friend Thelma about the camping trip they have planned for the weekend. Thelma cannot talk freely with her husband Darryl around as he prepares for work so she calls Louise back later and they arrange to set out in Louise's T-Bird that afternoon for the cabin that belongs to a friend of Louise's. Thelma has still not told Darryl and brings almost everything but the kitchen sink, even a gun.

They make a stop at a bar and Thelma and Louise's weekend takes an abrupt and unexpected turn. A bar regular, Harlan, dances with Thelma who gets swept up in her new-found freedom, though Louise is a little more circumspect. Thelma and Harlan go outside and Harlan attempts to rape her. Louise shoots Harlan dead with Thelma's gun. Suddenly, everything changes. Thelma and Louise drive off, unseen by anybody. Neither woman knows what to do and Thelma is especially freaked. Louise insists on some kind of calm. They stop off and attempt to make a plan.

Harlan's dead body is bagged and Hal Slocombe, a cop, questions one of the bar's waitresses. Hal Slocombe is advised to put out a call for the capture of the two women. In a motel, Thelma and Louise argue about what to do. Louise calls up her boyfriend Jimmy and asks him to wire her savings of several thousand dollars to her. Jimmy agrees and Louise asks if Jimmy still loves her, though she cannot tell him what she has done.

Thelma and Louise drive on into the Western landscape. Louise tells Thelma not to tell Darryl what has happened if she calls him. Louise's plan is to go to Mexico but she needs to know if Thelma is going to go with her. Louise calls Jimmy again and he tells her he has the money. Thelma calls Darryl who berates her.

Coming out of the phonebooth, Thelma trips over a young guy named JD who is looking for a ride. Louise refuses to give him a lift and then decides they will only use secondary roads and not the interstate. She wants a route to Mexico that will not take them through Texas. On the open road, Thelma and Louise spot JD and this time give him a lift.

In Arkansas, Slocombe tells Darryl what has happened and Darryl can't handle it. The police begin to pick up the trail. Louise goes to pick up the money wired by Jimmy and finds that Jimmy is there too. In their motel room Louise says she will not tell Jimmy what has happened. Louise goes to Jimmy's room and they talk.

Thelma is visited by JD they have sex. The next morning, Thelma is revived by her night with JD but they discover he has stolen Louise's savings. Thelma and Louise find themselves in an ever-worsening situation as Thelma robs a convenience store of its cash.

In Arkansas, Slocombe snoops around Louise's apartment, and focuses on her photographs, then goes and questions Louise's employer. Slocombe and Darryl watch the CCTV footage of the robbery. The FBI are eager to track down and catch Thelma and Louise. They get JD, who tells the cops where Thelma and Louise are heading. At Thelma's house, the phones are tapped in case she phones Darryl and they can trace their location. Thelma calls and then Louise speaks to Slocombe who says he wants to help.

Way out west, Thelma and Louise drive throughout the night through the mesas. They are taunted by an abusive truck driver and are then pursued by a policeman whom they lock up in the boot of his police car. The FBI agent wants to put an end to Thelma and Louise but Hal stresses caution. Thelma and Louise come across the lorry driver again and this time teach him not to be so impolite. The police close in and there is a tense chase across country until Thelma and Louise reach the edge of the Grand Canyon. As police marksmen prepare to shoot at them, Hal prevents them. Thelma and Louise drive towards and over the canyon edge with Hal chasing after them.

THE CONCEPT: The idea for the film came to screenwriter Callie Khouri in what sounds like a lightning bolt moment while she was sitting in her car. Khouri had been in Los Angeles since 1982, starting out as an actress and then moving into production in music videos. So the legend goes, she wrote the *Thelma & Louise* screenplay, her first, after work, referring to a couple of other scripts to get the formatting down. *Thelma & Louise* kick-started a revival of women's pictures in Hollywood. In the years that followed the studios produced *Stepmom* (Chris Columbus, 1998), *How to Make an American Quilt* (Jocelyn Moorhouse, 1995), *To Wong Foo, Thanks for Everything, Julie Newmar* (Beeban Kidron, 1995) and *Waiting to Exhale* (Forest Whitaker, 1995) among others. As with *Blade Runner*, Alan Ladd Jr, a real Hollywood angel, was the executive overseeing the movie during his tenure at MGM.

CASTING: Geena Davis was still a relatively new actress at this point and had lobbied for around a year to be considered for the role of Thelma prior to being cast. Davis had been very strong in two movies prior to *Thelma & Louise*. The first was David Cronenberg's *The Fly* (1986) and the second was the fabulous *The Accidental Tourist* (Lawrence Kasdan, 1988).

Susan Sarandon made her breakthrough with *The Rocky Horror Picture Show* (Jim Sharman, 1975) and she went on to appear in *The Great Waldo Pepper* (George Roy Hill, 1975), *Atlantic City* (Louis Malle, 1980), *The Hunger* (Tony Scott, 1983), *The Witches of Eastwick* (George Miller, 1987) and *Bull*

Durham (Ron Shelton, 1988). Sarandon's profile continues to ride high and more recently she has starred opposite Goldie Hawn in *The Banger Sisters* (Bob Dolman, 2002).

As with other Scott films, *Thelma & Louise* introduced a someday soon movie star, Brad Pitt, who went on to star in films including *Legends of the Fall* (Ed Zwick, 1994), *Interview with the Vampire* (Neil Jordan, 1994), *Se7en* (David Fincher, 1995) *Ocean's Eleven* (Steven Soderbergh, 2001) and *The Mexican* (Gore Verbinski, 2001).

Upcoming actor Michael Madsen also appeared. He followed up *Thelma & Louise* with a starring role in Quentin Tarantino's debut feature, *Reservoir Dogs* (1992). Ridley Scott's brother, Tony, went on to direct a Tarantino screenplay, *True Romance*.

Harvey Keitel returned to work with Scott again (see **The Duellists**). Since this film he has starred in *Reservoir Dogs* (Quentin Tarantino, 1992), *The Piano* (Jane Campion, 1993), *Pulp Fiction* (Quentin Tarantino, 1994), *Holy Smoke* (Jane Campion, 1999) and *Red Dragon* (Brett Ratner, 2002); see **Ridley Scott: Filmography as Producer**.

Before Susan Sarandon and Geena Davis got behind the wheel on *Thelma & Louise*, Jodie Foster and Michelle Pfeiffer were in consideration. Meryl Streep and Goldie Hawn had also taken a look at the script as they were keen to appear in a film together. They instead went on to team up on the Gothic horror comedy *Death Becomes Her* (Robert Zemeckis, 1992).

MAKING IT: Callie Khouri's script was sent through to Scott's company, called Percy Main at the time. At one point Khouri had considered raising the financing to shoot it herself super low budget. Like *Black Rain* and *Someone to Watch Over Me*, *Thelma & Louise* was a fairly small-scale drama, this time set against the expansive and beautiful backdrop of the American desert. Scott read the material and considered he would be best placed to produce the film, though he was busy shooting commercials. Scott read the script and never considered it to be a male-bashing story. Scott began interviewing potential directors for the project, none of whom seemed able to grasp the basic idea of the material. Eventually, Scott decided that maybe he was the man for the job.

THE SHOOT: *Thelma & Louise* began shooting on 11 June 1990 and wrapped on 31 August 1990. From all accounts it was a very straightforward and uncomplicated production, ranging across 54 locations, which saw a rewarding collaboration between Scott and his cast. Unusually for a feature film, the last day of filming was of the last scene in the film. The Caravan Motor Inn where Thelma and Louise stop first after the murder of Harlan was a favoured hangout for 1970s TV legends such as Jamie Farr (*M*A*S*H*) and Michael Landon (*Little House on the Prairie*). At the end of each day the costumes for Thelma and Louise would be washed and cleaned, as standard wardrobe practice. Sarandon and Davis would then dirty them up the next morning. The guy with whom Louise trades her watch for his hat was one of only very few people actually living in the former mining town where the scene was shot.

LOCATION: Locations included Bakersfield for much of the first part of the film and then Gorman in California and Utah Arches National Park and Canyonlands National Park (Utah) stood in for Arizona and New Mexico. For those who want to get even more specific, DuPar's Restaurant was the location for Louise's coffee shop; Tarzana doubled for an Arkansas suburb, and the Silver Bullet Saloon was the bar. The film was not shot along the route the characters take. The location where they drive over the edge was not at the Grand Canyon; it was a spot appropriately named Dead Horse Point.

COLLABORATORS: Hans Zimmer and Ridley Scott teamed up for the second time with this film (see **Black Rain**), and Adrian Biddle (see **Alien**) came on board as the Director of Photography. Scott had worked with Adrian Biddle as an assistant camera operator many times before on commercials, several of which had been shot in the American desert. Biddle has been with Scott since the early 1970s.

Screenwriter Callie Khouri has gone on to make her debut as a feature film director with the film *Divine Secrets of the Ya-Ya Sisterhood* (2002) adapted from Rebecca Wells's novel about relationships between mothers and daughters. The film stars Sandra Bullock, Ellen Burstyn, Ashley Judd and Maggie Smith.

MUSIC: As with *White Squall*, *Thelma & Louise* contains the most source music of Ridley Scott's films, whether it is country music being played in a bar or music on the radio. Hans Zimmer's steel guitar theme, with its more contemporary beat, weaves in and out of the film. It recalls the legacy of Ry Cooder's score for Wim Wenders's *Paris, Texas* (1984). Like that film, *Thelma & Louise* was filmed by a European, bringing a sense of wonder to the American landscape and the shapes within it. The use of upbeat gospel-inflected music over the start of the end credits adds to the celebratory feel as do images from different parts of the film as the end credits roll.

INFLUENCES: One of Scott's key movie references for *Thelma & Louise* was the film *Badlands* (1973), directed by the great Terrence Malick, who was, like Scott, very much at home filming the great outdoors though treating it with an even more intense sense of the mystic. That film tells about a young man and woman on the run across wild America. Like Thelma and Louise, the characters at the centre of Malick's movie gain our sympathy and, like *Thelma & Louise*, *Badlands* is very aware of the road movie tradition it is both part, and a revision, of.

Typically, Scott also turned to other visual references for the film, notably the paintings of John Register, whose classically American subjects include highways and diners.

THE OPENING: The first shot of the film is of the desert highway, starting in black and white and then coming up into colour. The camera pans left to right to reveal the expanse of land. It is vast and wonderful and contrasts with where we first see the film's heroines.

ON THE SCREEN: As a Ridley Scott film, *Thelma & Louise* contains all the director's trademarks beyond just the big pictures and lush images. Significantly, it is also Scott's most obviously funny film in terms of dialogue and situation and notably the range of caricatured men in the film. Apparently, Scott and the male actors pumped up the comedy of their characters compared to what was in the screenplay.

Just as he fused film noir with science fiction in *Blade Runner* and horror with science fiction in *Alien,* placing strong women at the centre of both those films, in *Thelma & Louise* two women are at the centre of a typically male genre, the outlaw road film.

This is a film about outlaw women, tough individuals who honour the bond of friendship. As outlaws, Thelma and Louise are amongst Scott's most obvious maverick figures, especially in the setting of the American West, though maybe someday Scott will make a traditional, historically set Western.

There is a realistic look to the film in keeping with Scott's work on *Someone to Watch Over Me* and *Black Rain*. The naturalism of the film starts with the establishing scenes where we meet Thelma and Louise in their separate places. With the expanse of the American desert, though, Scott has a rich and fascinating landscape to present and he contrasts this with the rain of Arkansas where the story begins. Towards the end of the film, as events become more intense and dangerous, the landscape has a greyer pall to it. It is not as warm looking as it had been. Thelma and Louise become progressively dusty and tanned and so begin to appear wilder and less civilised.

For Scott the overriding visual drive was to suggest the glory of a last journey. He is in his element in the late part of the film as the women drive though the mesas of the West and there is a terrific and dreamy sequence set at night.

HEROES AND VILLAINS: Clearly both Thelma and Louise are mavericks in a classic maverick setting, the American West. Hal Slocombe is a maverick too in the sense that he doesn't want to close the net too tight on Thelma and Louise; he is not a caricature and he is sensitive and patient – in the shot of the policemen watching the unidentified romantic movie on the TV in Thelma and Darryl's house the viewer gets the sense it is Hal's choice of what to watch.

WOMEN: Scott's movies have always featured strong women, but *Thelma & Louise* was the first to focus exclusively on two female protagonists.

When Louise phones Thelma, the first question she asks is very telling and sets up a lot of what will follow: 'How're you doing, little housewife?' When Thelma says she has to ask Darryl if she can go away for the weekend the audience realise Thelma is perhaps not very happily situated. Scott adds to this by showing us Thelma early in the morning in her very cluttered kitchen as Darryl gets ready for work and she munches on a chocolate bar. *Thelma & Louise* is refreshing in part because it shows us working-class women. Originally Callie Khouri conceived of Louise working on the reception desk of a huge, Texas-based oil company.

Scott introduces his heroines as much through art direction as dialogue and character conflicts. Thelma is shown rushing around in her nightie in complete disarray. Her clothing and movement is clumsy. By contrast, Louise moves confidently and dresses neatly. When they hit the road, Louise is in jeans, boots and a short denim jacket. She looks like a cowgirl. Thelma wears a big flouncy summer dress. Much later in the film they will be swapping clothes, signifying how the characters have changed, become one another and truly intermingled. Thelma wears Louise's jacket and Louise wears Thelma's.

Louise is the lynchpin to start with. She holds things together and is like a big sister for Thelma. From the start of the film Louise is established as a tidy and ordered person, a statement never better made than in the quiet but powerful shot of the glass washed and dried on the sideboard of Louise's apartment. Like other Scott heroes, Louise comes to realise she cannot always be in control and has to cope with chaos, starting with Thelma's slightly bumbling and gawky behaviour. Thelma gets into Louise's car and says, 'Louise, will you take care of this gun?' as she holds it in her fingertips.

Louise is a control person who finds her life wildly out of control and much of the film's drama comes out of Louise grappling with this loss of control. Soon after the attack on Thelma in the car park, Louise says, 'I'm gonna stop some place for a coffee and I'm gonna get it together.' A little later Louise says, 'Now's not the time to panic', and insists that 'I'll figure out what to do.' Later in the movie, when JD has taken Louise's savings, she breaks down and it is Thelma who kicks into gear as the strong one.

When Louise's backstory comes out towards the end of the film it throws everything that has gone before into a new light. Women are strong; they want the respect of men. All through the film they speak on behalf of all women for politeness etc. Scott's direction is subtle in places, as in the uneasy glance Louise throws Harlan when he lands at their table. She then puffs smoke in his face. Conversely, Thelma scrunches her face up with delight. For Geena Davis the appeal of the project was the equality of the female leads and for Susan Sarandon it was the debate it might spark. It certainly did that, to a degree they had not anticipated (see **RELEASE**).

As the story unfolds, Thelma emerges as a wild child finally released so that by the end of the film she sports a T-shirt that reads DRIVIN' MY LIFE AWAY. Early on she checks herself in the wing mirror and you can see her creating a new identity for herself. She pretends to smoke and pouts with her sunglasses on. She finds herself in the wilderness that she and Louise race across. Louise says to Thelma, 'You're usually so sedate,' to which Thelma replies, 'I've had it up to my ass with sedate.'

As in all his films, Scott embellishes the main action of *Thelma & Louise* with short but pointed images that have a documentary feel, such as the women jostling for mirror space in the ladies' toilets.

It was a year of strong female characters at the movies, notably in *Terminator 2: Judgment Day* (James Cameron, 1991), *La Femme Nikita* (Luc Besson, 1990) and *Sleeping with the Enemy* (Joseph Ruben, 1991).

Scott not only cast locations, even the choice of Louise's car – a green T-bird – is important. It is virtually a character in the film, reflecting Louise's personality. Callie Khouri's script played up Louise's bond with her car even more than the film does and it included a line where Thelma complained that Louise cares 'more about that car than you do about most people'. With its strong-willed, determined women the film built on the hints at Scott's interest in strong female protagonists apparent since *Alien*.

MEN: All the men in the film represent specific things. Some behave childishly; others are lovers while others are thieves. There is a shot late in the film where Darryl is in the foreground waiting for Thelma to call while in the background, out of focus, some of the FBI men play on the pinball machine in the living room.

Darryl ultimately comes across as a vain, insensitive and incompetent man whose lack of appeal is emphasised in his dress sense – just look at that awful shirt and hair. He is a goof who even has a pinball machine in his living room. Like a spoiled brat he says to Thelma, 'Haven't I told you I can't stand it when you holler in the morning?' When Thelma calls him much later in the film to tell him how she is, Darryl's concern only continues until he is distracted by a sports game on TV. Thelma says of Darryl, 'He prides himself on being infantile,' and also adds that 'He is an asshole. Most of the time I let it slide.' When Thelma explains to him in a phonecall where she is all he can say is 'You get your butt back here now.' Thelma rebels and says 'You're my husband not my father.'

In developing the characters, Scott had not originally planned for Darryl or the truck driver to be such broadly comic characters (see **ON THE SCREEN**). Michael Madsen was cast because Scott really responded to his look.

There is an intensity to the pivotal rape scene and Scott makes Harlan an unsettling presence from the moment he first meets Thelma and Louise. Harlan, like the other men in the film, feels threatened by the women.

Hal Slocombe, played by Harvey Keitel, is a quiet and thoughtful man, rather like Captain Tanner in the film *The Sugarland Express* (Steven Spielberg, 1974). Slocombe sees Thelma and Louise as people, especially after seeing pictures of Louise as a child and being aware of her past in Texas. Hal says, 'There's two girls out there who had a chance.' He has a conversation with Louise and his first question is to ask about their welfare. Hal says he wants to help. In one of the film's deleted scenes, Hal's sensitivity and desire to understand what Thelma and Louise are doing is strengthened as he lies in bed asking his wife what it would take to make her shoot somebody. Hal is not a traditional tough guy cop – he is wearing pastel blue pyjamas.

Late in the film, Thelma and Louise encounter a different sort of state trooper in the desert who is a figure to be mocked for his intensity, his glasses, his perfect presentation.

Scott pushes the menacing force of the police. Max the FBI guy is certainly dedicated but goofy too. At the end of the film any humour in the forces that pursue Thelma and Louise are gone. Scott makes the helicopter hideous as it rises like a monster at the edge of the canyon. Scott then uses extreme close-ups of the fingers on triggers and Thelma says that the police 'looks like the army'. To extend and intensify the critical moment, the audience watch Hal run in slow motion after Thelma and Louise as they race towards the edge of the canyon. Scott goes for powerful close-ups in the final shots of Thelma and Louise as they clasp hands. The freeze frame makes them immortal and the fade to white does not suggest doom or death. For the screenwriter, the ending of the film is symbolic.

PICTURE PERFECT: Scott's eye for the American desert landscape of rock, sand, sky, drive-ins and parking lots is evident throughout the film in the way he makes the most of the shapes and forms of the landscape and also of the classic locations of highways, gas stations and diners. *Thelma & Louise* is a compendium of Americana. The signs and adverts and the heat and dust of the West are lovingly shot by the director nowhere more so than in a shot of the car passing by cowboys in a swirl of dust. He takes the classic Western drama of the conflict that exists when civilisation and the wilderness collide. A preoccupation of American culture is a preoccupation of Ridley Scott's too.

As with all his films, Scott uses décor and environments to add to the meaning and situation of the characters. At the very beginning of the film the hard, regular lines of the diner are what Louise is first associated with. For Thelma, she is initially associated with very cluttered and chintzy décor. JD is an idealised character in Thelma's eyes but he emerges as a liar and a thief.

To amplify the moment when Thelma and Louise first sight the grandeur of the West, Scott chooses to cut the sync sound for a moment. Like other Scott films the drama charts a path from innocence to experience in the wilderness. Thelma says to Louise's boyfriend, 'You know me, Jimmy, I'm just a wild woman.' Thelma also talks about the 'call of the wild' later in the film. Thelma becomes a real outlaw and then later admits that 'Something's crossed over in me. I can't go back.' She goes on to explain how 'I feel awake. Wide awake. Everything looks different.'

Neat images fill the film like little flourishes such as the shot of the FBI cars all pulling up in order outside Darryl and Thelma's home or of the police cars racing in a wave across the desert at the end of the film. Or Thelma, soon after the rape scene, accidentally knocking the coffee cup to floor in the diner as she gets up to go. The sound of the glass smashing punctuates the scene's anxious tone. Louise just wants some peace and quiet; the glass shatters as Thelma and Louise's dream of a weekend away shatters.

TECH TALK: As Scott's career developed he began filming with two cameras as part of an effort to capture the spontaneity of the actors. It was rare for more than four takes on any given shot.

When we watch Thelma and Louise react to the tanker blowing up after they have fired at it, Scott had to film their reactions separately to the event as, in the initial take, they were apparently underwhelmed by the moment.

For the scene of Thelma and Louise by the railroad looking at the map, there is no train passing by just off camera. It is instead a sound effect, with a wind machine in place to suggest the train's effect on their hair.

MOVIE TALK:

Louise: 'You get what you settle for.'

Louise (to Harlan): 'Looks like you got a real fucked-up idea of fun.'

Thelma: 'You're a real live outlaw.'
JD: 'You're the one who's stealing my heart.'

Louise: 'We're fugitives now? Right? Let's start behaving like that.'

Thelma: 'You're not going to give up on me, are you?'

Thelma: 'No matter what happens I'm glad I came with you . . . Let's not get caught . . . Let's keep going.'

THE BIG IDEA: The question around which the drama is built is: can the heroes break out of their typical world? Can they meet the challenge, just as Scott's other heroes do? On his commentary to the DVD release of the film, Scott explains how he wanted the landscape to become bigger and more expansive as Thelma and Louise 'become more heroic'.

Thelma & Louise proved once and for all that Scott could make very warm and human films yet there is still his familiar sense of melancholy amongst the energy and frequent high spirits. This comes across best in the storyline between Louise and Jimmy: 'We both got what we settled for,' she says to him. This is a love that will not be able to run the distance because of larger forces, just like the doomed love of Mike and Claire in Someone to Watch Over Me. Forget about aliens, future cities, unicorns, gladiators and duellists, the whole motel room segment of the film with Thelma and JD and Louise and Jimmy is enough evidence in all of Scott's output that he can direct compelling human drama.

In her book about the film, entitled Thelma & Louise, Marita Sturken comments that the drama plays with contrasts: 'Thelma & Louise is a film about space, both the wide open space of the American West and the coninuing space of the home.'

RELEASE: The film certainly made an impact as a feminist tale of female empowerment while also being an all-out road-trip movie. Others saw the movie as the latest in a fine American tradition of wilderness adventures which goes way back in American history to Huckleberry Finn and Tom Sawyer and before, though it is probably just coincidence that Louise's surname is Sawyer. *Thelma & Louise* even made the cover of *Time* magazine with Susan Sarandon and Geena Davis on the cover and an article inside titled 'Gender Bender' by Richard Schickel. It became the film that everyone was talking about; a watercooler movie. Speaking in retrospect in *Premiere* movie magazine in June 2001, Susan Sarandon said that the power of the film came from 'a primal threat – a woman with a gun'. Geena Davis added: 'I'd never been in a movie that touched a nerve like that.'

The film surprised audiences when released. It was a sleeper hit but it impacted massively on the pop culture landscape and over the summer of 1991 a lot of newspapers and magazines covered it. Some reviews and responses to the film praised it and others were pretty damning – one review even suggested that no responsible adult should take an impressionable daughter to see it. Since the film's release, women have taken the road trip that Thelma and Louise make in tribute to the characters and what they represent. With this film, Ridley Scott made a movie anthem; the film's opening shot of the American desert and a road stretching to the mountain on the horizon symbolises the film's main concern, visualising both a dead end and a possibility.

The film prompted a lot of discussion about what it said regarding the place of contemporary women. Other debates developed around the ways in which the film represents women more generally. *Thelma & Louise* is nirvana for the student of pop culture. For the more critical, the film was filled with contradictions. Was it a feminist film or was it not? In what ways did the film raise issues of the way women are represented inside and outside of the movies? Did it condone gals and guns? Did men get a bad ride in the film? Scott had apparently stirred up a storm in the summer of 1991, but the film endures today as one of the finest Hollywood films of the 1990s and certainly of the last thirty years, a genuine classic addition to the road movie genre.

CRITICAL CONDITION: 'While it falls short of masterpiece, this . . . is a must see, both for Ridley Scott's breathless, epic realisation of a smart, funny script and bravura performances from its eponymous leads,' said Angie Errigo in *Empire*, while *Sight and Sound* thought it 'reinvented sisterhood for the American screen'. The ending also caused comment: '*Thelma &*

Louise begins like an episode of *I Love Lucy* and ends with the impact of *Easy Rider*,' felt *Rolling Stone*, and the *Guardian* thought, 'Scott's film is exhilaratingly accomplished . . . the apocalyptic ending seems more fabricated than inevitable.' Other choice responses to the film's issues when it was released included 'degrading to men' (*New York Daily News*), 'a PMS movie, plain and simple' (*Time*), 'a recruiting film for the NRA [the National Rifle Association]' (*People*) and 'a fascist version of feminism' (*US News and World Reporter*).

In an article entitled 'Lay off *Thelma & Louise*', the *New York Times* came readily to the film's defence, not that it really needed it.

GROSSES: With a budget of $16 million the film grossed around $45 million at the box office.

POSTER: The original release poster emphasised the landscape with a blue sky over a desert highway leading to rose red terrain. Over the top of the poster was a 'Polaroid' of Thelma and Louise *à la* the moment early in the film when they take a snapshot of themselves just before setting out on their adventure. For the Region 2 DVD release a new image makes the cover of the disc. It emphasises the outlaw aspect of the movie with Thelma and Louise in the T-Bird being pursued by the police.

HOME ENTERTAINMENT: *Thelma & Louise* is available on VHS on the MGM Movie Time label. It is also available on Region 1 and 2 DVDs with commentaries by Ridley Scott, Callie Khouri, Susan Sarandon and Geena Davis. The disc also features out-takes, a behind-the-scenes featurette and a retrospective documentary. It is very well packaged (see **POSTER**).

DELETED SCENES: A fair number of scenes were deleted from the theatrical release, primarily, it seems, in order to favour the pace of the story. The scenes that never made it are:

A scene where Thelma talks to Louise about how good looking JD is after they have first encountered him.

A scene where Thelma, Louise and JD talk about his education, which he lies about.

A scene where Hal is in bed with his wife, their two daughters down the hallway, and he asks what would have to occur for her to shoot somebody (see **MEN**).

A scene of Thelma and Louise at night talking about God as they drive.

A scene of Thelma and Louise driving in the day and Thelma complaining about what they have to eat and drink.

A scene where Thelma and Louise talk about changing the T-Bird for another car.

A scene of Louise checking a map that Thelma has mauled.

A scene of JD being picked up by a cop at a gas station.

A scene of Jimmy being questioned at the police station by Hal.

A scene of Thelma and Louise being chased by two police cars.

A scene of Hal in the chopper sighting Thelma and Louise.

A scene of JD arriving at the police station.

As part of the process of finding the best ending for the film, Scott shot material for a different ending to the final cut: after the car zooms off the cliff it drops through the canyon as Keitel's character watches. We then see the car racing down the highway towards the horizon accompanied on the soundtrack by BB King singing 'Better Not Look Down'.

AWARDS: After a drought of awards for *Legend*, *Someone to Watch Over Me* and *Black Rain*, Scott and his colleagues were inundated with this film. The film won an Oscar for Best Screenplay for Callie Khouri and was nominated for Best Actress in a Leading Role (had this won, it would have been unique as it would have been shared by Geena Davis and Susan Sarandon). The film also won Oscars for Best Cinematography and Best Film Editing. Ridley Scott was nominated for a Best Director Oscar.

At the British Society of Cinematographers Awards in 1992, Adrian Biddle was nominated. At the Boston Society of Film Critics Awards, the film grabbed Best Actress Award for Geena Davis and at the BAFTAS nominations were up for Best Actress, Best Cinematography, Best Editing and Best Film Score.

At the Golden Globes the film was nominated for Best Picture and Best Performance by an Actress. Susan Sarandon won Actress of the Year at the London Film Critics Circle Awards and at the MTV Movie Awards Davis and Sarandon won that most traditional of accolades, Best Screen Duo. Harvey Keitel picked up an award at the National Society of Film Critics Awards in the Best Supporting Actor category. And Callie Khouri's screenplay won Best Screenplay at the Writers' Guild of America Awards.

The British Academy of Film and Television Awards 1992 awarded the film Best Direction and Best Film.

At the César Awards, France 1992, the film was nominated for a César in the category of Best Foreign Film.

GREAT SCOTT: Alongside *Alien*, *Blade Runner* and *Gladiator*, *Thelma & Louise* remains Scott's biggest film. It came at just the right time for him, after the modest success of *Someone to Watch Over Me* and *Black Rain*. The film combines Scott's sweet visuals with strong characters; it is both intimate and epic. How could anyone deny Scott's skill with actors when this film includes such powerful acting, such as when Thelma cries in the car after Harlan's attack on her?

This film showed a new and warmer Ridley Scott. Prior to *Thelma & Louise,* Scott was not known for the comedy quotient in his films. This film has its share of funny scenes, such as the one where Thelma and Louise are confronted by the policeman and end up shooting up his car and locking him in its boot. The subsequent moment with the cyclist stopping by the car is also amusing. For all the humour in the scene with the cop though, there is a seriousness to it when Thelma says to him, 'My husband wasn't sweet to me, look how I turned out.'

Thelma & Louise is further proof (see also **The Duellists**) that Ridley really, really wants to make a Western someday. Here's hoping. The film captured something of the zeitgeist when it was released in the summer of 1991; not the first time in Scott's career (see **Alien** and **Blade Runner**; also **Gladiator**).

SCOTT FREE: 'I think the movie is really about "you get what you settle for".'

1492: Conquest of Paradise (1992)

(Colour, 153 minutes)

A Paramount Release of a Percy Main/Legende/Cyrk
Production
Screenplay: Roselyne Bosch
Producers: Ridley Scott, Alain Goldman

Executive Producers: Mimi Polk, Iain Smith
Co-Producers: Marc Boyman, Roselyne Bosch, Pere Fages
Associate Producer: Garth Thomas
Director of Photography: Adrian Biddle
Editors: William Anderson, Françoise Bonnot, Leslie Healey
Art Director: Martin Hitchcock, Antonio Paton, Kevin Phipps, Luke Scott
Music: Vangelis
Assistant Director: Javier Chinchilla
Stunt Co-ordinator: Greg Powell
Sound: Pierre Gamet
Special Effects: Nick Brook, Reyes Abades
Unit Production Manager: Jose Luis Escolar
Production Design: Norman Spencer
Superivising Art Directors: Benjamin Fernandez, Leslie Tomkins
Art Direction: Raul Antonio Paton, Kevin Phipps, Martin Hitchcock, Luke Scott
Set Decoration: Ann Mollo
Costume Design: Charles Knode, Barbara Rutter
Assistant Director: Terry Needham
Special Effects Supervisor: Kit West
2nd Assistant Director: Hugh Johnson
Casting: Louis Digiamo, Dan Parada

CAST: Gérard Depardieu (*Christopher Columbus*), Armand Assante (*Sanchez*), Sigourney Weaver (*Queen Isabel*), Loren Dean (*Older Fernando*), Angela Molina (*Beatrix*), Fernando Rey (*Marchena*), Michael Wincott (*Moxica*), Tcheky Karyo (*Pinzon*), Kevin Dunn (*Captain Mendez*), Frank Langella (*Santangel*), Mark Margolis (*Bobadilla*), Kario Salem (*Árojaz*), Billy Sullivan (*Younger Fernando*), John Heffernan (*Brother Buyl*), Arnold Vosloo (*Guevara*), Steven Waddington (*Bartolome*), Fernando G Cuervo (*Giacomo*), Jose Louis Ferrer (*Alonso*), Bercelio Moya (*Utapan*)

BUDGET: $44 million

MPAA: PG 13

BBFC: 15

TAG LINE: Centuries before the exploration of space, there was another voyage into the unknown.

Above Feraud (Harvey Keitel) displays lethal accuracy in *The Duellists*

Below Lambert (Veronica Cartwright) is confronted by the Alien

Above JF Sebastian (William Sanderson), Pris (Daryl Hannah) and Roy Batty (Rutger Hauer) together in JF's apartment in *Blade Runner*

Below 'A real city of the future,' as one reviewer called it. Rick Deckard (Harrison Ford) holds on in Ridley Scott's spectacular cityscape

Above Jack O'the Green (Tom Cruise), Lili (Mia Sara) and their beloved unicorn in *Legend*, a lesser-known but definitive Ridley Scott movie

Below The romantic triangle of *Someone to Watch Over Me*: Claire (Mimi Rogers), Mike (Tom Berenger) and Ellie (Lorraine Bracco)

Left Charlie (Andy Garcia) and Nick (Michael Douglas) walk the noirish streets of Osaka

Below Thelma (Geena Davis) and Louise (Susan Sarandon) prepare to make their last run for freedom

Above *1492: Conquest of Paradise*: Columbus (Gérard Depardieu) looks to his destiny as he arrives in the New World

Below Christopher Sheldon (Jeff Bridges) charts a course to discovery with Chuck Gieg (Scott Wolf) and his wife (Caroline Goodall) at his side

Above Jordan O'Neill (Demi Moore) presses on with her mission to succeed in *G.I. Jane*

Below Maximus (Russell Crowe) fights for survival, for the crowd and for freedom

Above Hannibal Lecter (Anthony Hopkins) confronts Pazzi (Giancarlo Giannini) with civilised brutality

Below *Black Hawk Down*: light and shadow intensify the fight for survival in Somalia

Ridley Scott looks to new filmmaking horizons

SUMMARY: It is 1491 and 39-year-old Christopher Columbus, an Italian living in a Spanish monastery, believes that he can find a new, third route to the East from Spain. Sitting by the sea with his young son Fernando, Columbus watches a ship disappear beyond the horizon.

Columbus talks with his monk friend about his ambition but the monk warns him to be cautious – Spain is a nation 'gripped by fear and superstition' which 'persecuted men for daring to dream'. Columbus is determined and talks to his wife Beatrix about the possibility. He presents his project to the University of Salamanca where he is mocked though he says his travels will help make Spain an empire, but he is accused of having Messianic, Chosen One leanings. Columbus is made to serve a penance for an outburst at the monastery but still he cannot and will not quit his obsession.

A shipowner named Pinzon approaches Columbus offering the possibility of support. Columbus is granted an audience with Queen Isabel and she decides to fund his voyage. The Treasurer, Sanchez, draws up a contract for Columbus but he is not happy with it, because the document does not grant him certain rights and titles. This irks Sanchez who begins to find Columbus's lack of humility frustrating.

Columbus sets sail. Weeks later the crew come to the verge of mutiny as they have not seen land. Columbus only succeeds in rallying the crew at the last moment. Sitting on deck one night, Columbus smacks a bug on his neck and realises that land is near. When the Spanish finally step ashore they are confronted by an indigenous tribe. Columbus and his people interact peacefully with them. When Pinzon falls ill with a fever, Columbus returns him to Spain. Thirty-nine men are left on the island. This is not the mainland route Columbus had hoped to find. Nonetheless, he is greeted as a hero when he returns to Spain with a handful of island tribesmen and various artefacts, including cigars and gold. However, Sanchez is unconvinced of Columbus's success and some dissent towards the expedition builds.

Columbus enlists the support of his two brothers and begins to gather a new crew for a return journey. One of these includes military man Moxica. Returning to the islands, Columbus and his crew find the 39 men murdered and tensions develop. A church is built and a huge bell raised. Moxica challenges Columbus's leadership and an inherent racism and imperialism creates a huge culture clash. A battle is fought and the working community and infrastructure Columbus has introduced is destroyed. Moxica kills himself and the church is burned to the ground. Columbus is left to return to Spain, penniless and without stature.

Soon after, the University of Salamanca takes great delight, as Columbus anonymously watches, in announcing that Amerigo Vespucci has found the mainland route East. Sanchez is present but he is silent and doesn't speak up for Columbus. Outside, however, Sanchez alludes to Columbus's greatness. Columbus is imprisoned for his 'failure' and for treating the peoples of the New World with equality, though he is finally set free.

It would have taken Columbus just another week's sailing to have made the same discovery. Still, Columbus wants to return. He goes to the Queen and she permits him to return but Columbus's eldest son Diego goes instead and Columbus remains in Spain. His youngest son, Fernando, asks his father to narrate his adventures for a biography to restore his father's name.

THE CONCEPT: The idea for *1492: Conquest of Paradise* arose in 1987 when journalist Roselyne Bosch was researching an article about the 500th anniversary celebrations of the discovery of America to go in *La Pointe* magazine. Bosch visited the archives in Seville and came to the conclusion that there were many conflicting stories about Christopher Columbus. For Bosch, Columbus was primarily a rebel figure. She took her story to producer Alain Goldman and they both agreed that Ridley Scott would be the best director for the film. Ironically and tellingly, Scott had been considering his own project about Columbus. As several Scott projects show (see **The Duellists** and **Gladiator** for example), he is well aware of what a rich seam history provides for stories.

CASTING: Scott's one absolute was that Gérard Depardieu be cast as Columbus. At the time, Depardieu was at a real career high point and, thanks to *Cyrano de Bergerac* (Jean-Paul Rappeneau, 1990) and *Green Card* (Peter Weir, 1990), had somewhat broken through to audiences outside France. His other notable films also include art-house blockbusters *The Return of Martin Guerre* (Daniel Vigne, 1982) and *Jean de Florette* (Claude Berri, 1986).

Armand Assante (Sanchez) had appeared in numerous TV and film projects before *1492*, including *Private Benjamin* (Howard

Zieff, 1980), *The Marrying Man* (Jerry Rees, 1991) and *The Mambo Kings* (Arne Glimcher, 1992). He went on to appear in *Fatal Instinct* (Carl Reiner, 1993) and *After the Storm* (Guy Ferland, 2001).

Anjelica Huston, star of *Prizzi's Honor* (John Huston, 1985), *The Grifters* (Stephen Frears, 1990) and *The Addams Family* (Barry Sonnenfeld, 1991) was approached for the role of Queen Isabel but ultimately was unable to commit and so the part went to Sigourney Weaver who had starred in Scott's second feature *Alien*.

MAKING IT: Funding was raised from Paramount for American rights ($10 million), $11 million came from French distributor Gaumont, and some more from territory by territory sales at the Cannes Film Festival. In contrast to the small-scale drama of the iconic *Thelma & Louise*, Scott's follow-up once again emphasised his taste for working across a range of genres. In each project he finds ways to transform a screenplay into what is distinctly a Ridley Scott movie. *1492* gives Scott's wilderness versus civilisation theme a full workout, even in the film's subtitle *Conquest of Paradise*. Some posters for the release of the film emphasised the danger of the journey with the ship barely discernible amidst a raging sea, tinged with the golden glow of promise. Other posters emphasised Columbus's moment of discovery.

THE SHOOT: Shooting on *1492: Conquest of Paradise* began on 2 December 1991 and continued for about eighty days. Interiors were shot at Pinewood Studios in England. Exterior footage (the majority of the film) was shot in Spain, the Dominican Republic and Costa Rica, the primary location for the New World part of the film because of its pristine beaches, islands and jungles. The shoot in Spain and Costa Rica lasted about two months with several weeks then spent aboard the replica ships.

The majority of the time, the action was shot using two cameras, one for the master shot and the other on either a close-up or a two-shot. In all his films, Scott's obvious delight in shooting on location adds believability to the drama and often 'larger than life' action on screen.

The location crew constructed the new mission and the belltower. The scene of the burning of the heretics took seventeen hours to shoot, and culminated in a near revolt by the performers in that scene.

COLLABORATORS: Scott reunited with Director of Photography Adrian Biddle (**Alien, Thelma & Louise**) as they enjoyed the success of their previous collaboration, *Thelma & Louise*. Vangelis teamed up with Scott again (**Blade Runner, Someone to Watch Over Me**) for the creation of the film's score.

MUSIC: In the film, Vangelis's music is not triumphal in the way you might expect; instead it emphasises mystery, unease and certainly solemnity. The opening sequence of the film shows various engravings and pictures documenting Columbus's voyage and this is shot with a blood-red filter. The music here is far from fanfare-like. Throughout the film there is a religiosity to much of Vangelis's music. Scott has a career-long skill in not taking the most obvious route with his use of music and sound. Whether this is partly an issue of nationality and also of creative sensibility is open to question. The moment when land is sighted is not a big joyous moment. Instead it is the opposite. The mist clears like a curtain pulling aside to reveal a new scene and an island is seen for the first time. There is no fanfare of music. Vangelis's score remains something of a cult favourite because of its strength as a stand-alone album (see **Soundtrack Listing**). Hans Zimmer (**Black Rain, Thelma & Louise**) had originally been due to write the score but had other scoring commitments. Vangelis's soundtrack serves not just the film but is a strong stand-alone soundtrack with its combination of choral and synthesiser elements.

INFLUENCES: To enhance the sense of period, a lot of scenes involved practically lit sets using candlelight. For Director of Photography Adrian Biddle the paintings of the Old Masters inspired his work – he went after a theatricality to the film's look.

THE OPENING: A series of images of engravings and drawings suggesting the fifteenth century fill the screen. A blood-red filter colours what the viewer sees and 'mournful' music plays. This is not a celebratory opening for such a famous story of adventure. Evidently the filmmakers intended a revisionist approach to a key event in European exploration beyond the Atlantic.

ON THE SCREEN: Throughout his career Scott has been notable for not shying away from a graphic portrayal of violence and, in order to give some sense of the barbarism of the Inquisition in fifteenth-century Spain, he shows people being burned at the stake. It is not a gross-out sequence but there is a definite intensity to it and it shows what kind of a world it is that Columbus has chosen to challenge. Like the most skilful of storytellers, Scott knows that it is always better to show than tell.

Certainly in Scott's films since *1492*, the director has taken on stories that emphasise the drama of the unit working together and fracturing. *1492*, like *Gladiator*, portrays a world of men, though both have women wielding power and influence back home: Queen Isabel in Spain and Lucilla in Rome. In *1492*, the bonhomie of men is captured briefly and quietly in an exchange between Captain Mendez and Columbus. Scott's films always benefit from such quiet moments amidst the more large-scale scheme of things.

Colours and emotions are part of the drama in any Scott film. The graphic design and emphasis on colour and bold shapes that is such a hallmark of Scott's visual sense is especially evident in that moment when the Spanish first arrive on land, carrying triangular banners in bold colours that contrast with the muted greens of the island. Then too there's the golden sunlight filtering through the sides of the ship throughout its sea voyage. This creates a sense not of fear, danger or the unknown but of glory. Colours are emotions in Ridley Scott's cinema. The shots of the ships sailing are always beautiful, and they have a sense of promise of the exotic, and of the grandiose. They are romantic images to create a feeling of the mindset of Columbus.

HEROES AND VILLAINS: Like all Scott protagonists, Columbus is a maverick and a dreamer. 'I want to get behind the weather,' he says early on, committing himself to an almost superhuman task. There is an elemental quality to Columbus in Scott's film as he challenges the basic laws of the universe and the earth, just like Jack O'the Green does in *Legend*. Columbus also challenges the institutions of the state, the church and the university. He foreshadows Maximus in *Gladiator* and Jordan O'Neill in *G.I. Jane*. Columbus is shown as a man who has great faith in himself, in his own resolve and ability. Maximus in *Gladiator* is very much in the same mould, regardless of the alleged realities of history, as is Christopher Sheldon in *White Squall*. Columbus must confront the monolith of the state; even in an apparently very different film like *Hannibal*, Scott's hero, Clarice Starling, has to maintain her confidence in the face of a menacing and all-powerful institution, the FBI.

1492 also hooks into the same idea that plays a big part in *Black Hawk Down* where a mighty force go in and are not prepared for the indigenous power and resolve they are confronted by.

Columbus displays Godlike tendencies in the segment of the story after discovering the New World: 'We will not harm these people even though we have the power to do it.' A little later, Columbus says to his arch-enemy on the second voyage, Moxica, 'In one act of brutality you have created chaos . . . your criminal savagery.'

The love of his family is what ultimately saves Columbus in this film and this brings the story full circle. The first image of Columbus is of him with his son Fernando looking out to sea. The last image is of a spot of ink as Fernando starts writing, with he and his father in a room looking out to sea. Like Sheldon in *White Squall*, Columbus finds solace in his sons.

Scott makes Columbus something of a 'saint'. He is predominantly shown wearing a white shirt on his adventures, contrasting with the black of Moxica. He is frequently framed with sunlight or candles in shot, suggesting his character as a source of light and illumination. Late in the film, Columbus is framed with a crucifix in shot, suggesting not only his earlier hints of Messianic tendencies but also his purity and inevitable and unjust 'punishment'. Early in the film, Columbus is ordered to serve penance for trashing a monastic library and is made to lie with his arms outstretched on the floor of the church.

Then there is the evil Moxica who functions primarily as the Devil figure in Eden. Moxica hates the natives and does nothing to understand them. Moxica's sharp features contrast with Columbus's soft and round face. Where Columbus is democratic, saying that even the nobles should work, Moxica just sits around, happy for the indigenous people to serve him.

PICTURE PERFECT: Having arrived on the New World island Scott changes tack with his camera style. Where much of what preceded was composed of wide shots and elegant camera moves, the director uses a handheld camera for that sequence where the explorers push through the all-encompassing forest upon arrival. This lends the action some uncertainty and there is something simultaneously threatening and beautiful about this 'new world'. We are in unknown territory and there is a reportage quality to the film as though we are really there with the explorers. Even though the forest is unknown, Scott and Adrian Biddle cannot help but make it look terrific and beautiful. This truly is shown as a paradise with sunlight streaming through the rich greens and tree canopies. When the crew are on their first island in *1492*, the initial handheld camerawork gives way to a graceful fluid track through the trees, showing the voyagers and the islanders peacefully together. The shot is perfect and graceful which corresponds with the voice-over and the action being shown.

In the sequence where Columbus returns, the landing is far more military with drums and guns all to hand. Scott goes for the dreamlike, the unknown and the mysterious. A close-up reveals Columbus's relief at this point. Scott extends and amplifies the moment of Columbus arriving on land, using slow motion as his feet slam on to the sand and it glistens with golden sunlight.

TECH TALK: The dialogue in *1492: Conquest of Paradise* is non-naturalistic, in keeping with a lot of the dialogue in Scott's films. There is something compressed and symbolic about the lines; it is often as designed and heightened as the images. It's as though the dialogue serves more as a statement of the film's ideas than of characters' psychology. This is an approach that Scott also takes in his characterisation of Roy Batty in *Blade Runner* and some of his other films, notably *Gladiator* and *G.I. Jane*.

MOVIE TALK:

Columbus (telling Queen Isabel about the people of the New World): 'Nature is their God . . . They see him in a leaf, in a stone, in a shell.'

Columbus: 'We have returned to Eden.'

Brother Buyl (to Columbus): 'You must learn to control your passion.'

Columbus: 'Reality was beyond my expectations.'

THE BIG IDEA: All of Scott's films build their drama around the conflict between the wild and the civilised. In this film there is a shot of the two opposing forces: one in the forest, the other out in the open of the river. Kevin Costner's *Dances with Wolves* (based on the novel by Michael Blake) in 1990 had created a taste for the wilderness movie again. *1492* was released at the same time as *The Last of the Mohicans* (Michael Mann, 1992) and, like that film, is about the violent encounter between European and native people. In *1492*, Columbus says that 'Paradise and Hell can both be earthly. We carry them both wherever we go'. It is the kind of remark that you could imagine Darkness saying in *Legend*.

The sense of invasion that Columbus's journey creates is made vivid so that we can anticipate something dubious in this conquest of Paradise. In this segment of the story, Scott invokes classic lost Eden, fallen Paradise associations, notably in the shot of a snake on a branch. When Alonzo is bitten by a snake, Columbus kills it, though the islander with them watches and does not step forward to help. The invaders will be duly punished for not respecting their new environment.

Scott's taste for apocalyptic images rounds out *1492* with a huge storm bringing rain, fire and destruction to the world that has been forced upon nature. Columbus is shown buffeted and blasted by the elements and ultimately defeated by them, alone in the dark. This apocalyptic swirl is handled a lot like the storm in *White Squall* where that film's dreamer and schemer is able to control all else, except nature. In a humorous cutaway, as Columbus's world has fallen, there is a shot of invincible ants working away carrying leaves. They have survived the destruction and endured in a way that human actions have not.

Scott has always found vivid ways to associate characters with their surroundings so that the meanings of their characters are amplified. When we first see Columbus he is sitting on a rock beside the sea. A close-up on his profile focus-pulls to the shore and water behind him. He is immediately associated with natural forces and power.

In the scene where Columbus notices gold on a native's necklace the film is able to allude to the source of much bigger trouble to come. At this point, Columbus's folly has really been set in motion and the film goes on to dramatise the dangers of imperialism and too much ambition, rather like Roland Joffe's 1986 film *The Mission* did. Other films that deal with some of the same dramas are *The Emerald Forest* (John Boorman, 1985), *The Mosquito Coast* (Peter Weir, 1986) and *The Thin Red Line*

(Terrence Malick, 1998). *1492*'s culture clash drama also recalls the story of *Black Robe* (Bruce Beresford, 1991) based on the novel by Brian Moore and Scott's own earlier *Black Rain*. The closing words of the film are: 'Life has more imagination than we carry in our dreams.'

RELEASE: In some ways *1492: Conquest of Paradise* helped pave the way for the more narratively compelling and dramatic *Gladiator*, almost a decade later but with an equally broad, land-spanning canvas and period setting.

Soon after production began it was announced in the media that Alexander and Ilya Salkind, producers of *Superman: The Movie* (Richard Donner, 1978) and *The Three Musketeers* (Richard Lester, 1974), were also making a Columbus movie, *Christopher Columbus: The Discovery* (John Glen, 1992). That version starred Marlon Brando, Tom Selleck, George Corraface, Rachel Ward, Robert Davi, Benicio Del Toro and Catherine Zeta-Jones. The Salkind version, released ahead of Scott's, depicts Columbus as a cheery fellow. Brando's role is basically a cameo as Spanish Inquistor Tomas de Torquemada, Tom Selleck plays King Ferdinand and Corraface is Columbus. The one-two punch on audiences of the Salkind and the Scott versions may have damaged both at the box office. It also recalled the previous year's two Robin Hood movies, released within months of one another (*Robin Hood: Prince of Thieves*, Kevin Reynolds and *Robin Hood*, John Irvin). The filmmaking community is a small town.

CRITICAL CONDITION: 'Ridley Scott's *1492: Conquest of Paradise* sees Christopher Columbus as more complex and humane than in any other screen treatments of the character,' wrote Roger Ebert of the *Chicago Sun-Times*. 'Scott's manipulative technique . . . is applied with a piercing accuracy and grace to anything from massive crowd scenes to the detail of shipboard routine,' was Philip Strick's assessment in *Sight and Sound*.

GROSSES: *1492: Conquest of Paradise* was released in North America on 2 October 1992. It had a budget of around $44 million and grossed around $7 million at the North American box office.

POSTER: One promotional image was a piece of artwork that depicted a tiny ship on a gold-tinged but stormy sea beneath the starry sky. This is the cover of the CD soundtrack. The other promotional image showed Columbus landing on the shore of the New World – it is an image that suggests joy.

HOME ENTERTAINMENT: In America, *1492: Conquest of Paradise* is available on VHS video. In the UK, the film is available on VHS and also DVD. The disc's one extra is the film trailer.

AWARDS: After *Thelma & Louise*'s massive awards success anything would have looked slim compared to it. At the British Society of Cinematographer Awards, Adrian Biddle was again a nominee.

GREAT SCOTT: *1492: Conquest of Paradise* was Scott's second historically based film, following on from *The Duellists* (1977), though this film was on a far more epic scale (see **Gladiator**). However, for all its scale, expanse and ambition, *1492* feels like one of Scott's minor movies. It is beautiful and astonishing in parts but as a whole is less satisfying than many of his other films.

There is a lack of emphasis on what would seem to be the most compelling and dramatic parts of the story, notably the time spent on the islands. The conflict between Columbus and Moxica could have been the source of the entire film. *1492* sloshes around in an effort to cover everything. Did we need to see all the preparations and attempts to raise financing for the expedition? Maybe Scott was reminded of securing funding for a film. Depardieu certainly has the physical presence but lacks menace or arrogance. He is too gentle.

In *1492*, Scott once more gets strong performances but they are in the service of a slightly shapeless story. The film is most fluid once land is discovered. The film is not that celebratory, rightly so, and perhaps that is one reason why it did not prove that popular. While it praises the maverick and the dreamer it can only condemn European imperialism. It is a melancholy film.

SCOTT FREE: 'I think [Columbus] can be forgiven. His elaborations convinced both the church and the crown to take this giant leap for mankind.'

'You have to understand the times to really understand the man and his actions.'

White Squall (1996)

(Colour, 127 minutes)

A Buena Vista Pictures Release of a Hollywood Pictures
presentation in association with Largo Entertainment of a
Scott Free Production
Producers: Mimi Polk Gitlin, Rocky Lang
Executive Producer: Ridley Scott
Co-Producers: Nigel Wool, Todd Robinson
Screenplay: Todd Robinson
Cinematographer (Technicolor color): Hugh Johnson
Editor: Gerry Hambling
Music: Jeff Rona
Production Design: Peter J Hampton, Leslie Tomkins
Art Direction: Joseph P Lucky
Set Decorator: Rand Sagers
Costume Design: Judianna Makovsky
Sound (Dolby): Ken Weston
Associate Producer: Terry Needham
Assistant Director: Terry Needham
Second Unit Director: David Tringham
Unit Production Manager: Nigel Wooll
Special Effects: Joss Williams, Walt Conti, David Fuhrer
Casting: Louis Di Giaimo

CAST: Jeff Bridges (*Sheldon*), Caroline Goodall (*Dr Alice
Sheldon*), John Savage (*McCrae*), Scott Wolf (*Chuck Gieg*),
Jeremy Sisto (*Frank Beaumont*), Ryan Phillipe (*Gil Martin*), David
Lascer (*Robert March*), Eric Michael Cole (*Dean Preston*), Jason
Marsden (*Shay Jennings*), David Selby (*Francis Beaumont*), Julio
Mechoso (*Girard Pascal*), Zeljiko Ivanek (*Sanders*), Balthazar
Getty (*Todd Johnstone*), Ethan Embry (*Tracy Lapchick*), Jordan
Clarke (*Charles Gieg*), Lizbeth MacKay (*Middy Gieg*), Jill Larson
(*Peggy Beaumont*), James Medina (*Cuban Commander*), James
Rebhorn (*Tyler*), Camilla Overbye Roos (*Bregitta*)

BUDGET: $38 million

MPAA: PG 13

BBFC: 12

TAG LINE: When a freak of nature turns adventure to disaster your only hope is the will to survive.

SUMMARY: Mystic, Connecticut, 1961. Young Chuck Gieg leaves home for a year of education on board the ship *The Albatross* despite his father's reservations. Boarding a plane, Chuck meets a couple of other teenage boys also bound for life on the ocean for the academic year. On board the ship are the English teacher, McCrae, the ship's doctor and science and maths teacher, Alice, and finally the taciturn skipper, Sheldon.

Sheldon is a tough teacher yet compassionate. The boys are soon being turned into men, learning how to run a ship and are getting ready for departure. As the educational process unfolds, each of the boys' frailties emerge. There are tensions on board the ship and Chuck finds himself solving everybody's concerns. Chuck gets caught in a noose as he attempts to climb the mast and Sheldon compels Shay to break his fear of heights to save him since Chuck was up the mast on Shay's behalf. Sheldon emphasises the need for discipline and interdependence. Sheldon announces that they are going to host a cruise for a group of Danish students. The boys flip when they realise they are all teenage girls. Frank is pulled out of the corps by his parents when they arrive on the island to see how he is. Family tensions explode and Frank and his father fight; Frank then runs. Chuck calms him down.

During an English lesson about Homer dolphins are sighted. While most of the boys are in thrall to the scene, Frank shoots a dolphin with a little dart gun. The boys bring the dolphin on to the deck. Sheldon presents Frank with a mallet with which to finish killing the animal. Frank is unable to and so Sheldon kills it. Chuck and Shay go to the captain to try and defend Frank and Sheldon asks if Frank knows how much they care about his welfare. Frank is then expelled from the ship and returns to Florida. As he leaves, Shay salutes Frank from atop the mast he had been so afraid of climbing early on.

A Cuban boat approaches and Sheldon lets the Cubans aboard. The boys are sent to get their passports to prove they are not Cuban stowaways. There is a tense showdown during which Sheldon's concern leads him to courageously protect the boys. The Cuban ship leaves and *The Albatross* continues on its way.

The ship moors and the boys go on land and run wild with spears and face paint. They reach the top of a mountain and uncover an old metal box containing a book in which they inscribe their names. They then return to the ship and continue on the return part of their journey. The boys receive their exam results and Dean happily passes with flying colours.

And then the ship is hit by a white squall which destroys the ship and kills some of the crew. A tribunal is then held at which Sheldon's career hangs in the balance. He is saved by the boys who speak up for him and appeal to the Captain's sense of what is right.

THE CONCEPT: *White Squall* is based on a true story. Screenwriter Todd Robinson was holidaying in Hawaii when he was introduced to Chuck Gieg, who told him the story of his time on *The Albatross* thirty years before. Robinson recognised the story would make a compelling screenplay and so developed one.

The screenplay generated some Hollywood interest. Around this time Scott was considering directing *Mulholland Falls* (see **Ridlley's Unrealised Visions**). However, when the *White Squall* script was passed on to him he apparently shut himself away for ninety minutes, read the material and then re-emerged stating he would make the movie. Speaking to the *Trojan*, the USC campus newspaper, at the time of the film's release, Scott said, 'The script touched me, in terms of context, the subtext, the rite of passage. And it was very earnest, in a good way, and very honest, in a good way. And I think it was worthwhile.' For Scott, part of the project was to honour the memory of those crew members who died, rather as he honoured the soldiers with *Black Hawk Down*.

The lessons learned by the young men converge and climax when the ship is the victim of an extreme weather front called a white squall. Despite the appeal of the performers and the effectiveness of the storytelling, the film failed to make much of a wave at the box office. Like *Someone to Watch Over Me*, it is something of a forgotten Ridley Scott picture. As always, Scott referred to previous feature films to guide his thought processes: *Mutiny on the Bounty* (Frank Lloyd, 1935) and John Huston's 1956 adaptation of *Moby Dick* were key references.

The screenplay for *White Squall* was inspired by the book *The Last Voyage of The Albatross* written by Chuck Gieg and Felix Sutton. This is the first of Scott's movies based on a real-life event.

CASTING: Jeff Bridges was already a well-known acting talent, having been seen in *The Last Picture Show* (Peter Bogdanovich,

1971), *Jagged Edge* (Richard Marquand, 1985) and *Fearless* (Peter Weir, 1993); he went on to star in *The Big Lebowski* (Joel Coen, 1998) and *K-PAX* (Iain Softley, 2001).

Caroline Goodall, who plays Sheldon's wife in *White Squall*, had also played the wife to the main characters in Steven Spielberg's *Hook* (1991) and *Schindler's List* (1993).

The film is primarily a rites of passage story set in an unusual milieu and, despite the casting of these two established actors, it also featured a cast of emerging Hollywood acting talent. Scott Wolf (Chuck) had starred in the TV series *Party of Five* and went on to appear in *Go* (Doug Liman, 1999); Balthazar Getty (Todd) went on to star in David Lynch's *Lost Highway* (1997); and Ryan Phillipe has appeared in a number of movies since *White Squall*, including *I Know What You Did Last Summer* (Jim Gillespie, 1997), *Cruel Intentions* (Roger Kumble, 1999) and *Gosford Park* (Robert Altman, 2001). Of Jeff Bridges's performance in the film, Scott said, 'Jeff . . . has the gestures . . . I needed someone who was kind of heroic but who was real.'

MAKING IT: After *1492*, the prospect of another sea-set story was not the first thing on Ridley Scott's mind. He had been involved with another project as an executive producer, *Monkey Trouble*, about a nine-year-old and her pet monkey. Scott also served as a hands-on producer on *The Browning Version*, directed by fellow northeasterner Mike Figgis.

In 1995, Scott also headed up a consortium to buy Shepperton Studios (see **Ridley Scott's Business Ventures**) and Percy Main was redubbed Scott Free.

THE SHOOT: The film had an expansive location shoot, taking in the Caribbean Islands of Grenada, St Lucia and St Vincent before moving inland to Georgia and South Carolina. Those parts of the film that occur after the storm were shot in a converted warehouse. The squall sequence itself was shot in Malta at Mediterranean Film Studios over a four-week period. For a shot of *The Albatross* on high seas, early in the film, the unit travelled to the Cape of Good Hope off the coast of South Africa.

One problem the production encountered was finding coastlines not spoiled by the tourist trade. For the scene of the boys climbing the mountain Scott shot the scene on Mount Soufriere on St Lucia.

One of the primary locations for the film was Young Island, part of St Vincent.

The ship that *White Squall* was filmed on was named *Eye of the Wind*. It was built in 1911 and has featured in the films *The Blue Lagoon* (Randal Kleiser, 1980), *Savage Islands* (Ferdinand Fairfax, 1983) and the TV mini series *Tai-Pan*.

Chuck Gieg and the real Captain Christopher Sheldon advised on the film during its location shoot and it marked the first time they had met since the events depicted in the film.

With *White Squall*, Scott and his director of photography Hugh Johnson did not want any kind of cosmetic look; they were content for a certain roughness to carry into the images to emphasise the believability of the situation. Therefore, a Steadicam was not used. Instead just a handheld camera was favoured and this meant that the uneven roll of the ship was always a factor in what the shots would look like. Scott and Johnson also went for a very clean hard light which makes *White Squall* one of Scott's least artificial-looking movies. In this it anticipates much of *Black Hawk Down*.

COLLABORATORS: For production designer Peter Hampton (**The Duellists, Blade Runner**) the courtroom set was a challenge as the production could not find an appropriate courtroom and so ended up building one. The upside of this was that they could have windows as big as they wanted. Producer Mimi Polk had worked with Scott previously on *Someone to Watch Over Me* and *Thelma & Louise* and Hans Zimmer returned after *Black Rain* and *Thelma & Louise*.

MUSIC: After *Thelma & Louise*, this is the Scott film with the most source music, in this case early 60s rock and roll. Like the film, the music is something of a gem. Composed by Jeff Rona, who has written themes for stacks of TV shows such as *Chicago Hope*, *High Incident* and *Homicide: Life on the Street*, the score combines a poetic and ambient sensibility with inventive use of shells and percussive elements. Hans Zimmer produced the album (Jeff Rona is part of Zimmer's Media Ventures outfit).

A song written and performed by Sting closes the film. It is a melancholy tune called 'Valparaiso'. Images from the film run over the first part of the end titles as we watch the boys write their names in the book. This is the film's key sequence. There is no music used on the squall sequence which enhances its believability. Scott lets the terror speak for itself. The sequence where the boys raise the sail with McCrae is scored with percussive and compelling music with an up feel to it.

THE OPENING: The film's opening credits are dark and watery. (When it was released the film was dubbed *Dead Poets Society* on water and it makes a good companion piece to Peter Weir's 1989 film – both of them are about imposing father figures who their 'sons' must break away from.)

ON THE SCREEN: The dialogue is more choral than naturalistic, in keeping with some of Scott's other films, notably *Blade Runner* and *Legend*. Again, the film has the quality of a fairy tale with its characters being taken away from normal life into a far more vivid experience that compels them to grow up.

HEROES AND VILLAINS: Sheldon is a man of nature, rather like Columbus is (**1492**), and he is given to grand statements about the natural world. There is a sense of the epic beneath the surface of this story and it reflects Scott's literary leanings in its references to Homer. The other story that the film is akin to is *Captains Courageous*, the Rudyard Kipling tale that became a 1937 film starring Spencer Tracy and directed by Victor Fleming. At one point in *White Squall* the English teacher quotes from Kipling's 'If'. The marine setting with young men and story of honour and loss of innocence is strongly linked to Scott's Joseph Conrad interest. Conrad's novel *Billy Budd* grapples with themes of honour and redemption, and Herman Melville of *Moby Dick* fame wrote a short story called 'Benito Cereno', in which the setting of a ship served as a microcosm of society. The boat in *White Squall* is like a microcosm of the world at large as well as being a place removed from everyday routine in which the boys' adventure unfolds before returning them to the everyday at the conclusion.

The skipper Sheldon is first seen simply in a quiet cutaway of him watching McCrae. Sheldon is a quiet contained man, a control-orientated person, like many other Scott heroes and heroines. The shot of Sheldon is, like him, contained and understated. Form is content. Sheldon is initially framed against the straight lines and curve of the wheel, and these lines reinforce his rigidity and stability. 'Don't test me. Not even a little,' Sheldon says to the boys. Sheldon speaks with respect about the elements: 'Behold the power of the wind,' he says. He is attuned to the elements like Jack O'the Green is in *Legend*.

Sheldon is a man of deeds like Maximus in *Gladiator*, but so is Chuck in the way that he holds everyone together, even the skipper at the film's end. 'It takes discipline to make it out here,' Sheldon comments – these kind of elemental announcements make him a titan in chinos. 'And remember sooner or later we all have to face it,' Sheldon says, referring to the challenges and uncertainties of growing up. Like many Scott heroes, Sheldon must come to terms with the fact that he cannot always control everything and in the courtroom scene this is a central theme. Sheldon is stoic and tacit just like other Scott characters, for example Maximus.

Even though a script is the work of a writer or a writing team, when a director with a strong cinematic sense comes on board they will inevitably refine and develop the material further, emphasising focus and arrangement of theme, character, setting. Through the English teacher character McCrae, who most notably quotes from Shakespeare's *The Tempest* at one point, the film makes a series of connections to literary heritage.

Sheldon gets primal with Shay, compelling him to climb the mast. The boys go primal later. Civilisation versus culture is a key motif in the film and there is a very military strain to the 'philosophy' of the film. With this film begins Scott's interest in military movies which continues with *G.I. Jane*, *Gladiator* and *Black Hawk Down*.

Sheldon is more than human. His wife picks up on this: 'I am halfway human,' Sheldon says to Alice as they dance. His hubris and nemesis-delusions of grandeur are like those of Columbus in *1492: Conquest of Paradise*. Sheldon is a control freak. In the aftermath of Frank shooting the dolphin, Sheldon says to Alice, 'He lost control out there,' and Alice can only reply, 'And what's so important about control?'

Sheldon is also a protecting figure, nowhere more so than when the Cuban soldiers board the boat and Sheldon literally forms a human shield between one of the boys and a soldier. And at the end the boys protect Sheldon in return.

Chuck keeps a diary which becomes a voice-over in the film, amplifying the onscreen drama: 'Today the adventure begins. Today I leave the path that he had chosen for me.'

Chuck admires Sheldon who has the masculinity and physicality his own father lacks. 'He's strong, tough and won't take no for an answer,' Chuck writes of Sheldon. Chuck helps Shay overcome bad dreams by saying, '1, 2, 3 wake up'. Dean calls Chuck the glue and Chuck realises that this will be his role in life and that life is not determined by his exam results. The boys throw their results into the sea and the next shot is of the eternal sea, sun and cloud and there is the sound of thunder as the image cuts to a thunderstorm and the beginning of the squall. Scott really captures the frustration of anger and trying to control it as a teenager when Frank cuts his steak. Neat details in a world of epic vistas make the small shots all the more effective.

There is Dean who feels intellectually inferior; there is Shay who is afraid of heights and there is Frank who cannot break out from his father's expectations. Sheldon gets Shay to conquer his fear of heights. The character of Dean is fragile and one of the best scenes of the film is where he confesses he does not understand English and some of the other boys say they will help him. Unity and friendship are what endure for these boys, just as unity will bind the soldiers in *Black Hawk Down*.

PICTURE PERFECT: Scott's film is a relaxed one and, in those key moments where urgency and tension come into play, fast cuts are used, such as in the scene of Chuck hanging from a noose. For the squall sequence there is a slowness to it, almost a real-time quality. As the journey begins, Scott emphasises the grand scale of nature against the puny efforts of man, for example the bus seems minute as it travels towards the dock. There is also promise of adventure suggested by the incredible sunset sky.

When the squall hits there is a vérité feel to the sequence and it is another of Scott's apocalyptic moments in all its blue light menace. At a certain point in the sequence the sync sound drops down and a mournful and elegaic tune comes in in honour of the crew who really died.

Scott contrasts the stillness of the squall's aftermath with the chaos of media coverage as the survivors return to land in St Petersburg, Florida. The first image of the survivors is of them walking in deathly silhouette. Scott emphasises the trauma soon after when Chuck has a flashback in a changing room and echoes and sounds rise on the soundtrack.

When Shay and Chuck sit on the harbour and drink Cokes they are rim lit by the setting sun. The tribunal is a place of light and shadow quite in contrast with the open skies and honesty of life on the ship. In the courtroom only Sheldon gets the golden sunlight on his face. The camera zooms in slowly on Sheldon listening to the prosecution. His answers in his defence are brief and cool, and he takes full responsibility. He is lit low key and the sunlight valorises him. Chuck challenges Sheldon not just to walk out once he hands his ticket in to the judge: 'Bad things happen and there's nothing you can do.' For all Sheldon's fatherly qualities, it is the 'sons' who save him at the end and Chuck reminds him that that ship is 'something that's inside of us'. Frank stands and rings the bell that Shay had rung for him. The boys gather around Sheldon whom, at the end of the film, we see alone outside the courthouse with Chuck watching.

TECH TALK: For the squall sequence two tanks were used. One tank held six million gallons of water and was forty feet deep. The other tank held three million gallons and was eight feet deep. For this part of the film, *The Albatross* was reconstructed in cross section. There were also huge tip tanks that could hold up to five tons of water. Wave machines and even a Navy jet were used to enliven the water and sense of storm.

A mechanical dolphin was designed for the scene where Sheldon clubs one to death. Peerless Effects created an effects shot where a lightning bolt strikes the sea and a part of the water boils.

MOVIE TALK:
Sheldon: 'Each one of you is responsible for the rest.'

Chuck: 'I don't want to be what I was when I left. Anonymous.'

Dean (to Chuck): 'You're the glue.'

Sheldon: 'I lost control, maybe just for an instant . . . it got away from me, the whole thing.'

Sheldon: 'You're young and strong. Everything's ahead of you.'

Chuck: 'In the end you can't run from the wind.'

THE BIG IDEA: *White Squall* is a classic story about the loss of innocence to experience and also of Paradise Lost, notably when one of the boys, Frank, shoots a dolphin with a harpoon. The good side of this savagery and wild child aspect is when Sheldon lets the boys go ashore and they put face paint on and run up the hillside. On the boat, Sheldon's wife Alice asks, 'What are they doing?' to which Sheldon replies, 'Claiming their place in the world.' 'Like Darwin himself we would see blessed nature,' Chuck narrates as the boys go running on the island bare chested and a tribal drumbeat can be heard on the soundtrack. 'I finally understood Homer. The journey's the thing.'

In the squall sequence all the lessons the boys have learned are tested, especially their sense of the unit. It has a mythical and odyssey-like feeling. Even Sheldon has to shout out for help at this point.

More than any other character the one who has the most vivid experience is Chuck. The film starts with him having to leave home and begin his adventure. His dad says it will 'all be here when you come back'. Chuck is the family maverick who says, 'I'm not my brother. I just don't care about that stuff.' His father does not agree with Chuck's decision to take the boat trip. 'Make us proud, son,' Chuck's parents say as he leaves.

Scott uses the motif of the bell. It survives the squall and it clangs as it floats on the surface. It is then held up by the boys in the courtroom. In the shot of the survivors afloat it is almost as if they are alive out of space and time because of the way Scott shoots the faces in shallow focus so that the water spangles and glistens in a hyper-real way.

The ship is a very masculine place where honour, unity and courage reign. When two boys dive into the sea off the mast Scott shoots it in slow motion, glorifying the moment as the film celebrates youth and growing up.

CRITICAL CONDITION: Though *USA Today* felt 'far too much of this handsomely mounted adventure is devoted to routinely dramatised adolescent minutiae', and Roger Ebert of the *Chicago Sun-Times* that, 'Scott has manned his crew with muscular, bronzed young types with keen haircuts, who look as if they hang out in Calvin Klein ads', *Empire*'s review said, 'Director Ridley Scott has fashioned a curiously compulsive drama that for all its inevitable Dead Sailors' Society trappings is still highly entertaining.' Barbara Shulgasser in the *SF Examiner*, meanwhile, commented on Jeff Bridges's portrayal of Sheldon: 'Bridges keeps his smiling to a minimum, and that's pretty much the performance.'

GROSSES: *White Squall* had a budget of around $38 million. When it was released the film failed to make much of an impact with the moviegoing public grossing only around $10 million in North America.

POSTER: A simple photo montage of Jeff Bridges and the faces of the boys. In the bottom part of the image the ship is caught in the squall. A straightforward campaign for a straightforward, no-frills film.

HOME ENTERTAINMENT: *White Squall* is available as a VHS in both America and Britain. In Britain the film is not available yet on DVD. In America the DVD of the film includes a featurette, trailer and chapter search facility.

AWARDS: Just the one award for this movie: at the Motion Picture Sound Editors Awards, the Golden Reel award went to Gerard McCain for Best Sound Editing.

GREAT SCOTT: *White Squall* is (with *Someone to Watch Over Me*) one of Scott's two often-forgotten films. Like the earlier movie, *White Squall*'s commercial failure disguises its interest and sincere emotions. On the surface it is probably the least Ridley Scott-style film yet made but, as is often the case, it is one of the Scott films that most comprehensively dramatises his interests as a filmmaker. The film certainly feels more personal than *G.I. Jane*, *Hannibal* or *Black Rain* and its courtroom conclusion, while echoing the close of *Dead Poets Society* (Peter Weir, 1989), is one of the most emotionally unfettered of Scott's output to date. The courtroom scene has been regarded as unnecessary but it provides the necessary emotional catharsis after the trauma of the storm and demonstrates just how powerfully Sheldon's lessons have stayed with the boys. *White Squall* is a very well-structured story about young people and it is one of Scott's best, though not well known. The film remains the one time Scott has focused on such young protagonists and his direction of the actors confirms his skill with the human side of filmmaking, again reminding us of the inadequacy of the complaint that Scott's movies are all style and no substance. Scott's preferred running time for the film was 2 hours and 34 minutes. Pretty much ignored on its initial release, the film is worth revisiting for the clear way it lays out so many typical Scott ideas and images but also because it is perhaps his most atypical film to date – neither fantasy, nor military drama, nor thriller.

SCOTT FREE: 'Though Sheldon is quite a tough man on the surface you gradually begin to realise that he's Dad. In fact, he is more than Dad. He can say all the things that Dad can't.'

'The rite of passage has evaporated today, so I felt it was worth refreshing people's minds that this did once exist.'

'If there are seven characters in a film, I treat the environment as the eighth character – or the first.'

G.I. Jane (1997)

(Colour, 124 minutes)

A Buena Vista release of a Hollywood Pictures Presentation
in association with Scott Free and Largo Entertainment of a
Roger Birnbaum/Scott Free/Moving Pictures production
Producers: Roger Birnbaum, Demi Moore, Suzanne Todd
Executive Producers: Danielle Alexandra, Julie Bergman
Sender, Chris Zarpas
Co-Producer: Nigel Wooll
Associate Producers: Terry Needham, Diane Minter Lewis,
Tim McBride
Screenplay: David Twohy
Story by: Danielle Alexandra
Cinematographer (Technicolor, Panavision widescreen):
Hugh Johnson
Editor: Pietro Scalia
Music: Trevor Jones
Production Designer: Arthur Max
Supervising Art Director: Bill Hiney
Art Direction: Richard Johnson
Set Design: Thomas Minton
Set Decoration: Cindy Carr
Costume Designer: Marilyn Vance
Sound (Dolby): Keith A Wester
Stunt Co-ordinator: Phil Neilson
Assistant Director: Terry Needham
Casting: Louis DiGiaimo, Brett Goldstein

CAST: Demi Moore (*Lt Jordan O'Neill*), Viggo Mortensen (*Master Chief John Urgayle*), Anne Bancroft (*Senator Lillian DeHaven*), Jason Beghe (*Royce*), Daniel von Bargen (*Theodore Hayes*), John Michael Higgins (*Chief of Staff*), Kevin Gage (*Instructor Max Pyro*), David Warshofsky (*Instructor Johns*), David Vadim Morris (*Sergeant Cortez*), Maris Chestnut (*McCool*), Josh Hopkins (*Ensign F Lee 'Flea' Montgomery*), James Cavaziel (*'Slov' Slovnik*), Boyd Kestner (*'Wick' Wickwire*), Lucinda Jenney (*Lt Blondell*), Joseph Makkar (*Libyan Sentry*)

BUDGET: $50 million

MPAA: R

BBFC: 15

TAG LINE: Failure is not an option.

SUMMARY: Washington, the late 1990s. At a Senate Arms Committee meeting, a male senator outlines the place of women in the modern American military. Senator DeHaven speaks up on behalf of women at the session. Soon after, the Senator is presented with a document outlining a better way to integrate women into the military. The government want to do a PR job and show that women can have a place in frontline military manoeuvres and so look for a test case woman.

At the Naval Intelligence Center, Lieutenant Jordan O'Neill monitors a military operation and challenges the male order with her own tactic. It is to prove the right thing to do and is a success. Unknown to Jordan she is submitted for the test case and is selected. Her partner and colleague, Chris, expresses reservations; Jordan explains she was passed over for Gulf War duties because of a lack of experience and she wants to take this chance to prove herself.

Jordan finds herself despatched to Catalano Navy Base in Florida to train as an elite Navy SEAL. She is exposed to a lot of male chauvinism and Master Chief John Urgayle becomes her great challenge: supportive, damning and also often uncomfortable around her. O'Neill becomes something of a media celebrity, much to the annoyance of the Commanding Officer. A series of intense training manoeuvres highlight Jordan's determination. On one early under-fire exercise, Urgayle watches as a candidate for the SEAL operation chooses not to help Jordan through her exercise and Urgayle makes his displeasure known. O'Neill makes it clear she wants no special favours. To prove her point she even shaves off her hair and goes to sleep in the men's barracks, away from the room that had been provided for her.

The training process culminates in a manoeuvre that ends with a savage assault on O'Neill by Urgayle. O'Neill is then photographed in a set-up to remove her from the training. She is ordered off the camp and returns to her boyfriend. She challenges Senator DeHaven who, it emerges, never thought O'Neill would get as far as she did in the training. O'Neill says she will expose the Senator's corruption and the Senator agrees to have O'Neill reinstated at the camp.

Soon, the unit, including O'Neill, are on an exercise in the Mediterranean Sea. Unexpectedly, they are called in to rescue a Ranger unit in the Libyan desert near the coastline. A US satellite has fallen out of orbit, landed in Libya and US soldiers have been sent to recover it. Led by Urgayle, the unit go into action. When Urgayle is shot, O'Neill leads the unit, successfully escorting the Rangers to safety. O'Neill and the other trainees attain SEAL status.

THE CONCEPT: The original concept for *G.I. Jane* came from screenwriter and executive producer Danielle Alexandra who had been intrigued by the 'women in combat' news stories of the mid-1990s. Eight months of research preceded the writing of a first draft screenplay. David Twohy was brought in to develop and refine the action elements of the script, his reputation for character-driven action being made with his work for *The Fugitive* (Andrew Davis, 1993) feature and also on the underrated *Waterworld* (Kevin Reynolds, 1995). Imagine if Scott had directed that movie!

Prior to it being released as *G.I. Jane*, the film had several other possible titles that included *In Pursuit of Honor*, *A Matter of Honor*, *Navy Cross*, *Pursuit of Honour* and *Undisclosed*.

CASTING: Alexandra always envisioned Demi Moore in the role and Moore was looking for a challenge. On previous occasions, Moore had played strong women characters notably in *Disclosure* (Barry Levinson, 1994) and *A Few Good Men* (Rob Reiner, 1992). Moore had established her can-do credentials in

Hollywood beyond the roles she had played, though – she is notable for having lobbied studios for equal pay for female movie stars. Ridley Scott had also been keen to work with Moore who has always displayed a strength and femininity, rather in the way that Sigourney Weaver always has.

Scott's facility with casting shone through again. Notably he cast Viggo Mortensen, later to achieve fame in Peter Jackson's *Lord of the Rings* (2001–2003) film adaptation, as Master Chief John Urgayle. Scott had been impressed by Mortensen in Sean Penn's strong directorial debut, *The Indian Runner* (1990), and felt the actor was a piece of surprising casting. It was Mortensen who suggested that Urgayle enjoy reading the poetry of DH Lawrence; in doing so suggesting an unexpected sensitivity to the character.

Anne Bancroft most famously starred in *The Graduate* (Mike Reynolds, 1968) with newcomer Dustin Hoffman. She has also appeared in *Silent Movie* (1976), where she starred with the director of the film, her husband Mel Brooks. Bancroft also appeared in a cameo performance in David Lynch's astonishing *The Elephant Man* (1980) as the actress Madge Kendall.

Jason Beghe, who played the State Trooper in *Thelma & Louise*, reappears and Lucinda Jenney, who portrayed a waitress in *Thelma & Louise,* returns in *G.I. Jane* as the doctor who tends to Jordan.

MAKING IT: Two weeks of boot camp awaited the actors, including Moore, and the subsequent promotion for the film centred on Moore's commitment to the film, including this boot camp stint. The Navy and the Department of Defense decided not to offer the film support, so access to working camps did not happen. Instead, the crew used a National Guard camp in Florida at Camp Blanding.

The training shown in the film is not identical to SEAL training, instead it is comprised of different sections' training programmes. Many of the film's extras had military backgrounds. During the boot camp training period prior to filming, many thought that Demi Moore was actually the stunt double for herself, so committed was she to cutting it with all of the physical requirements of the role.

THE SHOOT: For those shots of the submarine at the end of the film, Scott used material from *Crimson Tide*, directed by his brother Tony Scott.

Having ascertained what real-world training involved, Scott and his team embellished it in the interests of exciting drama.

LOCATIONS: For the beach location an inland beach was 'built' by bringing in truckloads of sand. The real beach, also seen in the film, was about an hour away from the camp location. Hunting Island was the location for the POW camp training scene and developed from an initial image Scott had of native huts. The Libya footage was shot in Lone Pine, California. O'Neill's modest house was filmed on the banks of the Potomac River and DeHaven's home was shot at a Maryland mansion. For the US Capitol footage, the crew had to go to the Virginia Capitol Building which bears a fairly close resemblance to the real thing.

COLLABORATORS: The production designer Arthur Max, in his first collaboration with Scott, devised a series of obstacles for the training camp that would be both physically and psychologically testing. Because the production was unable to access official designs for Intelligence Headquarters, Max had to be a little more inventive, tipping his hat to the James Bond approach to intelligence gathering, with an emphasis on the cool and intriguing rather than the more mundane realities of such a place. Arthur Max began his career as a stage and live concert designer doing design and projection for artists such as Pink Floyd and Genesis. He worked as art director on *Cal* (1983), and *Insignificance* (1985) with director Nic Roeg. He was a new Scott recruit but has remained part of the core Scott team, working on *Gladiator* and *Black Hawk Down*.

The director of photography, Hugh Johnson, had been a camera assistant on *The Duellists*, Tony Scott's *The Hunger* (1983) and directed second unit on *1492: Conquest of Paradise*.

The film's editor was Pietro Scalia who had worked as an assistant editor on *The Doors* (Oliver Stone, 1990), *JFK* (Oliver Stone, 1991), *Wall Street* (Oliver Stone, 1987) and *Born on the Fourth of July* (Oliver Stone, 1989). With this film a major Scott collaborator came on board and stayed with him for his following three films.

MUSIC: Trevor Jones supplied the film score, having worked previously on *Excalibur* (John Boorman, 1981), *The Dark Crystal* (Jim Henson, Frank Oz, 1982), *Runaway Train* (Andrei

Konchalovsky, 1985), *Angel Heart* (Alan Parker, 1987) and
Mississippi Burning (Alan Parker, 1988), among many others.
Scott uses a piece of classical music, 'O Mio Bambino Caro' from
Puccini's *Gianni Schicchi*, in *G.I. Jane* during the classroom
lights-out scene. It is also heard in *Someone to Watch Over Me*.
The delicacy of the music contrasts and heightens the barbarism
of the training programme but also muddies it slightly.

THE OPENING: Pulsing music comes in over the film's opening
credits in an urgent drum snare which establishes the military
world of the movie. An aerial shot begins the film as the camera
flies in along the Potomac River towards Washington, as though
hunting it out. The first interior seen is the old-world classicism of
the Congressional Building where a Senate Arms Committee
meeting is in progress. Within these first few shots the film
establishes in all its monumental glory the environment the drama
will begin to unfold in.

ON THE SCREEN: *G.I. Jane*'s most obvious connections are
with *Gladiator* and *Black Hawk Down*, both of them stories with
strong military elements and where the spirit of the unit is central.
Scott uses a documentary technique in much of the film to sell the
illusion the film creates of a tough training camp.

HEROES AND VILLAINS: Other than its hero, *G.I. Jane*'s other
strong, though corrupt, woman is Senator DeHaven. Like O'Neill
she is sure and certain, operating in what is predominantly a
man's world, while also shown maintaining her womanliness. 'I'm
concerned over the Navy's seemingly incontrovertible attitude
towards women in the military,' DeHaven states, establishing the
film's premise. The camera frames DeHaven with the horizontal
and vertical lines of the bookcase behind her reinforcing her
strength of character.

The Senator is a tough-talking maverick, somewhere up the
ladder from someone like Nick Conklin in *Black Rain*. The
Senator is always ready with a quick quip such as, 'How strong do
you have to be to pull a trigger?' when she is challenged about her
wanting more women in the military. 'I like pissed off,' the
Senator tells Jordan early on.

The Senator has a sinister aspect, akin to the shady politicos in
Gladiator. In both these films, the powerless go up against the

all-powerful and win. The heroes are democratic figures who are shown to represent freedom and a punkish disobedience towards the rest of the world.

Throughout the film Scott's camera emphasises the monolithic traditionalism of Washington DC. He gets a particularly effective shot of the male administration standing between the pillars, as they plot to engineer O'Neill's failure.

G.I. Jane is something of a sequel to *Thelma & Louise*, with its female protagonist and, maybe even more importantly, its placing of a woman at the heart of a man's world and movie genre, in this case the war movie; in *Thelma & Louise* it was the outlaw road movie. *Courage Under Fire* (Edward Zwick, 1995) is a similarly themed film that was released in 1995. Zwick's movie dramatised the role of a woman soldier in the Gulf War and her subsequent death. In keeping with its being similar to *Thelma & Louise*, *G.I. Jane* paints gender politics, albeit in a broad way, about partners and fidelity if a woman goes off to war. Jordan's boyfriend Chris says ironically, 'Will I wait if you go off to war?' He is a little like Jimmy in *Thelma & Louise*, sensitive and willing to do whatever it takes to remain with the woman he loves.

The 'bad guys' in *G.I. Jane* are the upholders of tradition and male chauvinism – they don't want women in the military. They select training to be a Navy SEAL as the test case environment for women because it is the toughest training the American military have. The film follows in Oliver Stone (for example, *Platoon*, 1986) and *Full Metal Jacket* (Stanley Kubrick, 1987) territory with its emphasis on military training.

In the lights-out scene, O'Neill's survival instinct is shown. Intensifying the moment is the storm outside – when the lightning flashes across her face we see her munching on a scrap of food that she shares with a fellow trooper.

If Urgayle is such a brute, how can he also be familiar with the more delicate charms of classical music and reading poetry? This is the same conundrum that Clarice has to face with Hannibal Lecter in *Hannibal*. It is the sophisticated monster embodied by Feraud in *The Duellists* and even Commodus in *Gladiator*. Urgayle is a demonic figure, all the scarier for being both physically threatening and mentally alert and educated. Like Roy Batty (**Blade Runner**) he is a thuggish character with a poetic sensibility and turn of phrase. Just recall the scene where O'Neill, all the recruits and the audience first meet him as he inspects the troops. He is Scott's classic figure, the wild and civilised man all rolled into one. Scott's use of slow motion for Urgayle's first appearance emphasises his animal-like aspect and we do not see his eyes; they are almost permanently behind glasses. Urgayle seems to both like and hate O'Neill being there. Scott cast well: not just a strong performer but a strong face, in this case the hard lines and thinness of Viggo Mortensen. 'I never saw a wild thing sorry for itself,' Urgayle asserts as he talks about nature, in the same way that Sheldon does on board *The Albatross* in *White Squall*. Urgayle reads DH Lawrence poetry and his farewell gesture to Jordan acknowledges that he is not all heartless machine as he leaves her his medal for bravery tucked away in the pages of his DH Lawrence book. Inside the book he has ringed the poem 'Self Pity'. Urgayle says something that Roy Batty could easily have spouted to Rick Deckard in *Blade Runner*: 'Pain is your friend, your ally.' Other choice musings include: 'The best thing about pain? It lets you know you're not dead yet.' Clearly, the Roy Batty character, consciously or not, stuck with Scott from *Blade Runner* onwards, a kind of educated monster, maybe the worst kind.

Jordan has a mission to prove her worth. She is not after fame or glory or to become a poster girl. She is an innocent in a world of shady cynicism. When she first enters the soldiers' mess she is confronted by unsurprising and demeaning comments and grief. However, O'Neill shows a lust for life just as so many other Scott heroes do.

We first see Jordan O'Neill at work at the Naval Intelligence Center where she works monitoring military operations. This is a virtually all-male environment. Jordan is in the blue light emanating around the centre, giving it an otherworldly feel. This scene is used to establish Jordan's smart and bold behaviour in a male-dominated world. One male Naval officer says to Jordan, 'Last time I checked you were a topographic analyst not an operations specialist.' Tellingly, she keeps her cool.

During one exercise, O'Neill is given a box to stand on so she can scale the wall. She objects to this and then pushes the box aside. Finally she has to use it but is truly let down when her fellow unit soldier decides not to help her over the wall, for which he is disciplined by Urgayle, who tells him to remember two words: 'team mate'. Urgayle would be most welcome by Maximus on the team that fights in the Colosseum.

O'Neill is like the kid in this story, an innocent, and certainly, like Maximus, she must fight to restore some dignity to the order of an institution and its traditions, in this case the American military, despite being, or maybe because she is, an outsider. Late in the film there is something gladiatorial about her brutal fight with Urgayle on the big training manoeuvre.

O'Neill has to assume a new identity through her journey, notably made physical when she shaves off her hair. When Jordan first arrives at the camp she is initially regarded by the all-male camp as a threat to the established order.

Early in the movie, Chris tells Jordan, 'You need to learn the fine art of detachment, Lieutenant.' There has always been in Scott's work heroes being efficient and effective rather than warm and soft. Their intelligence and commitment to a task is the priority and the drama occurs when the personal and the professional collide.

WOMEN: Jordan O'Neill is a strong woman, determined and bound by honour and duty. Scott also manages to sketch in her femininity. This issue of femininity versus masculinity was well addressed in a *Sight and Sound* article by Linda Ruth Williams entitled 'Body Talk', which explored Demi Moore's screen image and how *G.I. Jane*, particularly, put a new spin on it.

PICTURE PERFECT: One of Scott's neat storytelling devices is not to lay everything out upfront. He allows key elements to emerge, naturally, notably who Jordan's boyfriend is. Scott abides by the golden rule of storytelling, show don't tell.

Scott uses montage to emphasise Jordan's strength as she starts to train privately doing sits-ups and press-ups, intercut with the general training programme. The film slightly critiques the dehumanising, desensitising aspect of military training. Jordan does not want to recognise a kind word at one point – when the female doctor shows some concern, Jordan replies, 'Just fix me up and get me back out there.'

For the Florida training camp segment of the film, Scott creates a sense of it being detached from 'reality' by lending it a steely grey lustre which makes it seem perpetually lodged between night and day. It becomes a real netherworld, contrasting with the far more natural and warm approach to O'Neill's home and even the exterior shots in Washington. For the interiors in Washington, authority figures are placed in shadow and half-light, just as the Commanding Officer is at the training camp where he looms in the darkness like a monster, occasionally rim lighted. O'Neill is moving in a world of vicious and evil men, most notably the Commanding Officer whose face we rarely see in daylight. In the scene where Jordan challenges him in his office about his treatment of her there is just a sliver of light on him, so that he becomes somewhat monstrous in his lair. Even his dialogue here is far from naturalistic when he says to Jordan, 'You're going to get everything you want, let's just see if you want what you get.'

O'Neill's loneliness early on in her training is made clear by the high-level shot looking down at her alone, surrounded by empty space, after the other soldiers have disbanded to their barracks. Two dissolves bring us in to her exhausted face. Jordan goes to see Urgayle who says, 'Lieutenant O'Neill, when I want your opinion I'll give it to you.'

Like Mike Keegan's in *Someone to Watch Over Me,* Jordan's is a very homely environment, with a warm and rustic quality to it, contrasting with the emotional and physical violence and coldness outside the door.

Scott uses emblematic images in all his films and in *G.I. Jane* the most obvious is the one in which we see Jordan striking the camp bell with a baseball bat, trying to break it in a stand of defiance and anger.

The Libyan sequence is shot rather like reportage news footage from war zones (see **Black Hawk Down** where Scott takes this approach to an even higher level). Audiences are so used to this kind of material that any other approach today will undoubtedly seem false. In this battle sequence we see the influence of Oliver Stone and his films, particularly his seminal movies *Platoon* (1986) and *Born on the Fourth of July* (1989), and also an acknowledgement of the audience's familiarity with war-zone footage with its unsteady camera work and crash zooms, slamming in on action caught just in time. Scott's skill at directing action reminds the audience too of James Cameron, with his movies *The Terminator* (1984), *Terminator 2: Judgment Day* (1991) and *Aliens* (1986). Scott laces his battle though with plumes of coloured smoke that make it somehow theatrical and even unreal.

Harking back to his documentary training in New York in the 1960s, Scott immerses us in the regime of the training camp. The

ridley scott

film really feels as though it is documenting the world we are being shown. This part of the film not only establishes the challenge facing Jordan but also suggests the animal-like aspect of the training, sometimes in quite comic ways such as the men in the mess. The camp is a savage place. At the climactic moment between Jordan and Urgayle, the other soldiers take the animal behaviour too far, descending into a caged mob.

TECH TALK: Scott's frequent and more recent production designer Arthur Max designed the look for this film. Notably, Max invented the film's obstacle course, attempting to suggest the aftermath of a WWI battle (see **COLLABORATORS**).

MOVIE TALK:
Jordan: 'I expect a certain amount of pain.'

Urgayle: 'I like to get one quitter on the first day. Until I do that day does not end.'

A concerned politician: 'G.I. Jane . . . Christ, why don't they just get it over with and call her Joan of Arc?'

Jordan: 'The more everybody fucks with me, the more I want to gut it out.'

Senator DeHaven: 'In Washington, you don't even need the Ten Commandments if you're popular.'

Jordan: 'Suck my dick!'

THE BIG IDEA: One of the repeated phrases during the training to the soldiers is, 'Are you ready for the next evolution?' This has a Darwinian air of only the strongest survive, which is what so many Scott films do show. Remember though that Scott is working in Hollywood narratives where all heroes ultimately win and embody the principle of success.

One soldier says of women, 'They can't do what we can do.' In this film men feel threatened by the strong woman and find themselves resorting to jokes and clichés to survive the challenge.

The film ties sexism to racism. Amid the general assault of shouting and screaming in *G.I. Jane* there is a welcome quiet scene after O'Neill is dumped for not being able to climb aboard a boat. As they float in the water, a black soldier talks about his granddad in World War II, when he was told 'Negroes can't see at night' as the reason there were no African-Americans aboard ships. However, O'Neill is also fighting a big institutional prejudice beyond the training camp. In DC, Jordan confronts the corrupt Senator with integrity. Jordan's 'boy scout' quality, á la Jack Ryan (novelist Tom Clancy's hero, from films such as *The Hunt for Red October* [John McTiernan, 1990] and *Patriot Games* [Phillip Noyce, 1992]), spooks the Senator.

For the sequence on Captiva Island, the trainees undergo SERE training: Survival, Evasion, Resistance, Escape. Their mission is to get to a location, retrieve intelligence and get out. When Cortez goes against the unit plan he puts everyone at risk and they all end up in cages and are attacked by 'hostage takers'. This sequence is much more intense than the final real-life skirmish that unfolds at the end of the film on Libyan soil. The SERE training sequence has an eerie otherworldly element to it.

Urgayle finally cannot accept the place of O'Neill in his unit and reverts to a savage sexual assault on her. She gets the mob of soldiers on her side, very much in the way that Maximus does in the Roman arena in *Gladiator*.

As the film's end credits run we hear Urgayle's bird speech again emphasising the film's key concern in true Scott fashion. This is a genre movie, a war movie, with the spin of the strong woman.

The film has a vérité element running through it, especially in the training scenes and really immerses the audience in the drama and intensity of the experience. All Scott's films are environmental in this sense.

'No politician can afford to let women come home in body bags,' the Senator says when Jordan confronts her at a critical moment, and the film's best debate is raised when Jordan replies with the slightly rhetorical questions: 'A woman's life is more valuable than a man's?' and then queries why a woman's death should be considered ' . . . more hurtful than a man's'. It's the best scene in the movie.

CRITICAL CONDITION: '*G.I. Jane* is a more complex and disturbing film than its predecessors . . . *G.I. Jane* remains an exceedingly bleak vision, one that sees civic duty as subordinate to the Nietzschean will to power,' was the assessment of *Sight and Sound*. 'The training sequences . . . are good cinema because Ridley Scott brings a documentary attention to them, and because

Demi Moore, having bitten off a great deal here, proves she can chew it,' confirmed the *Chicago Sun-Times*.

GROSSES: *G.I. Jane* had a budget of around $50 million and grossed around $50 million at the American box office. The film was released on 15 August 1997.

POSTER: Demi Moore's shaven head is focal to the promotional poster for *G.I. Jane*, saying as much about the story as the star's commitment to the role.

HOME ENTERTAINMENT: The film is available on VHS in America and Britain. It is also available on DVD Regions 1 and 2. The American disc includes the trailer and scene access. The British DVD includes a B-roll of behind-the-scenes clips, a short behind-the-scenes documentary and a series of short soundbite comments from the stars and director.

AWARDS: At the MTV Movie Awards the film won Best Fight! At the Motion Picture Sound Editors Awards it won Best Sound Editing.

GREAT SCOTT: Absolutely the worst film Scott has ever made. The character of Jordan O'Neill seems to be an attempt to provide a soul sister for Warrant Officer Ripley in *Alien* or even for Thelma and Louise. Sadly, O'Neill's character lacks the charm of the women in those other movies. She just isn't particularly likeable, despite the rightness of her mission to prove a male elite wrong and out of date. If there had been an equivalent to Ripley singing 'You Are My Lucky Star' as she faces down the alien, then maybe *G.I. Jane* would be getting somewhere in developing our sympathy for the character. Viggo Mortensen as Urgayle is certainly tough and terrifying but there is something questionable about the sequence where he assaults Jordan on the island during training. Scott handled this kind of physical threat much more intelligently in *Thelma & Louise*.

G.I. Jane came along at a time when women's pictures were forming a regular staple of Hollywood production, partly a symptom of Scott's great success with *Thelma & Louise*. Like that film, *G.I. Jane* has a quality of empowerment about it but is not such a strong film. There is an ugly streak to it and it isn't one of

Scott's finest hours. Does the film itself assume the chauvinism of the men in it or does it simply portray it? Demi Moore is perfectly cast in this film and Anne Bancroft as Senator DeHaven is funny and dangerous all at once. In terms of characters and preoccupations it is very much a Ridley Scott film but visually there is nothing there to really alert the audience to his frequently magic touch and the film's outlook on the gender politics is confused. Of the three films made during Scott's 90s trough – the others are *1492: Conquest of Paradise* and *White Squall* – *G.I. Jane* is the weakest.

SCOTT FREE: 'A lot of men have a problem with strong women. I never have.'

'We avoid sex completely. It's completely asexual.'

'I always loved it; Demi always loved it . . . What made it even more interesting was that the film's subject was so provocative too . . .'

Gladiator (2000)

(Colour, 150 minutes)

DreamWorks Pictures and Universal Pictures
Producers: Douglas Wick, David H Franzoni, Branko Lustig
Executive Producers: Laurie McDonald, Walter F Parkes
Associate Producer: Terry Needham
Line Producer: Daniel Wai Chiu
Story: David H Franzoni
Screenplay: David H Franzoni, John Logan and William Nicholson
Music: Hans Zimmer, Lisa Gerrard, Klaus Bedelt
(additional music)
Cinematographer: John Mathieson
Film Editor: Pietro Scalia
Casting: Louis DiGiaimo
Production Design: Arthur Max
Art Direction: Keith Pain
Set Decorators: Jile Azis, Elli Griff, Sonja Klaus, Crispian Sallis
Costume Design: Janty Yates
Make-up: Khalid Alanis, Jo Allen

CAST: Russell Crowe (*General Maximus Decimus Meridius*), Joaquin Phoenix (*Emperor Commodus*), Connie Nielsen (*Lucilla*), Oliver Reed (*Antonius Proximo*), Richard Harris (*Emperor Marcus Aurelius*), Derek Jacobi (*Senator Gracchus*), Djimon Honsou (*Juba*), David Schofield (*Falco*), John Shrapnel (*Gaius*), Tomas Aranu (*Quintinus*), Ralph Moeller (*Hagen*), Spencer Treat Clark (*Lucius Verus*), David Hemmings (*Cassius*), Tommy Flanagan (*Cicero*), Sven Ole Throsen (*Tigris of Gaul*)

BUDGET: $60 million

MPAA: R

BBFC: 15

TAG LINE: What we do in life echoes in eternity.

SUMMARY: It is winter AD 180 and the Romans are attempting to subdue the Germanic tribes. A vicious battle ensues in which the Romans are victorious under the lead of Maximus. Emperor Marcus Aurelius oversees the battle. Aurelius speaks with Maximus who, now the battle is won, only wants to go back home to Spain. Aurelius's son, Commodus, arrives with his sister, Lucilla, but finds he has missed the battle. There is an attraction between Maximus and Lucilla.

Rome began as a Republic ruled by a Senate and it is now ruled by an Emperor. Aurelius says that Rome needs a new leader to remove its corruption. Knowing Commodus is not an appropriate leader, Aurelius wants to put Maximus in charge of Rome. Maximus is reluctant but knows that it is his duty. When Commodus learns of this he is angry as he is preparing to inherit the throne from his father. Commodus kills his father and then, in his position as Emperor, orders Maximus to be ridden from the battleground and killed.

Maximus is taken prisoner and escorted to the forest. Kneeling and ready to die, Maximus outwits the Praetorian guard and escapes. He races back to Spain only to find his wife and young son have been hanged at Commodus's command. Maximus passes out and is taken by strangers from his ravaged farm.

Maximus awakes in a cart crossing the desert. He has been picked up and is part of a convoy of gladiator stock to the north African town of Zucchabar, a Roman province. Among them Maximus befriends a man named Juba. Proximo, a once great gladiator and now trader, buys up the human stock and trains them as gladiators. Soon they are fighting in the small arena at Zucchabar and Maximus displays great strength, making him very popular with the crowd.

Commodus rides into Rome as the Emperor greeted by thousands and by the Senators, some of whom express reservation at the new Emperor. Senator Gracchus is eager to get the new Emperor active in the rebuilding of the city's work and functions but Commodus is not interested. He says that just he and Lucilla should rule without what he sees as the interference of the Senators. This choice would, of course, lead to tyranny. In the palace, Commodus's dubious affection towards Lucilla is made clear.

Commodus announces 150 days of games in the Colosseum which some Senators disapprove of. Maximus is still fighting and joins the best of the gladiators promised glory in Rome by Proximo. The gladiators arrive, enthralled by the scale of Rome. They are soon preparing and masking up for their first battle in the arena where Roman troops and the gladiators are announced as restaging the fall of Carthage to Rome. Influenced by Maximus, the arena battle subverts history as the gladiators acting as the Carthaginians overwhelm their Roman opponents. Commodus goes into the arena to meet the leader of the gladiators. Though Maximus tries not to reveal himself to Commodus he ends up having to. Recognising Maximus, Commodus determines to bring his popularity to an end.

Maximus is put into a cell away from the other gladiators. Lucilla visits and says she'd like Maximus to meet a Senator who wants to revive Rome, in keeping with Aurelius's hopes and aspirations for Maximus. Another fight is staged in the arena and Maximus goes up against Titus, the greatest gladiator. Maximus defeats him and Commodus again confronts Maximus.

In the crowd outside the arena, Maximus sees his old servant from Germania, Cicero. Maximus asks Cicero to rally his old troops with the intention of liberating Maximus so that he can return and take control of Rome. Cicero tracks Lucilla down in the street and tells her that Maximus wants to meet her Senator sympathiser, so Gracchus meets with Maximus.

Proximo grows worried and afraid for his own safety. After Gracchus is taken prisoner by Commodus's soldiers, Maximus is freed by Proximo and heads for his waiting army. He never makes it and is surrounded. In the palace, Commodus lets Lucilla know he is aware of what he sees as her duplicity in helping Maximus.

He then confronts Maximus in the arena but en route injures Maximus to give himself the advantage. A vicious duel ensues and Maximus kills Commodus with his own dagger before collapsing and dying himself.

THE CONCEPT: One of the key inspirations for Scott's epic, and the image that got Scott to commit to the project, was the painting *Pollice Verso*, produced in 1872 by Jean-Léon Gérôme. The image shows a gladiator on the receiving end of a thumbs-down verdict from the crowd. The painting is lush and romantic. Speaking about the painting, Scott commented, 'That image spoke to me of the Roman Empire in all its glory and wickedness. I knew right then and there I was hooked.' The picture resembles something close to a production painting for a feature film. Just look at the slashes of sunlight that are such a part of the painting's atmosphere. This detail was to inform Scott's own creation of atmosphere in the Colosseum sequences where light, shadow and sand combine.

CASTING: For Russell Crowe the film was his breakout role, coming soon after Michael Mann's film *The Insider* (1999) for which he had gained 40lbs (he then promptly shed the weight for the role of Maximus). He had previously appeared in *Romper Stomper* (Geoffrey Wright, 1992), *The Quick and the Dead* (Sam Raimi, 1995) and *L.A. Confidential* (Curtis Hanson, 1997). His more recent movies include *Proof of Life* (Taylor Hackford, 2000) and *A Beautiful Mind* (Ron Howard, 2001). For his role as mathematician John Nash in the latter film Crowe was nominated for a Best Actor Oscar; the film did win both the Best Picture and Best Director Oscars at the 2002 Academy Awards.

Scott had executive produced a film called *Clay Pigeons* which is where he had noted Joaquin Phoenix's skills as an actor. Phoenix had also appeared in *Space Camp* (Harry Winer, 1985), *8mm* (Joel Schumacher, 1999), *U-Turn* (Oliver Stone, 1997), *To Die For* (Gus Van Sant, 1995) and *Parenthood* (Ron Howard, 1989), where he had been billed as Leaf Phoenix, and since *Gladiator* he has appeared in *Quills* (Philip Kaufman, 2000) and *Signs* (M Night Shyamalan 2002).

Danish-born Connie Nielsen had appeared in *The Devil's Advocate* (Taylor Hackford, 1997) and *Rushmore* (Wes Anderson, 1998) before her role in *Gladiator*.

The new, lead performers were supported by stalwart British actors. The most prominent Senators are portrayed by actors such as Derek Jacobi and John Shrapnel as Senators Gracchus and Gaius respectively. As well as being a prolific stage actor, Derek Jacobi has appeared in numerous films and TV series, among them *The Day of the Jackal* (Fred Zinnemann, 1973), *I, Claudius* (Herbert Wise, 1976), *Little Dorrit* (Christine Edzard, 1988), *Henry V* (Kenneth Branagh, 1989), *Gosford Park* (Robert Altman, 2001) and *The Gathering Storm* (Richard Loncraine, 2002). John Shrapnel has appeared in *Fatherland* (Christopher Menaul, 1994), *101 Dalmatians* (Stephen Herek, 1996), *The 10th Kingdom* (David Carson and Herbert Wise, 2000) and *K-19: The Widowmaker* (Kathryn Bigelow, 2002). David Hemmings, star of *Blowup* (Michelangelo Antonioni, 1966) and one of the young stars of 60s British cinema, appears as an 'actor' introducing the first Colosseum gladiator battle. More recently he has also appeared in *Last Orders* (Fred Schepisi, 2001) and *Spy Game* (Tony Scott, 2001).

Richard Harris had starred in *This Sporting Life* (Lindsay Anderson, 1963), *Camelot* (Joshua Logan, 1967), *The Molly Maguires* (Martin Ritt, 1970) and *Patriot Games* (Phillip Noyce, 1992). Since *Gladiator* his career has been revived with such projects as the *Harry Potter* films and *The Count of Monte Cristo* (Kevin Reynolds, 2002). Ironically, Harris, here as Aurelius, had originally been cast by Western director ace Anthony Mann for *The Fall of the Roman Empire* (1964) in the role of Commodus, though the role eventually went to Christopher Plummer.

For all of the tabloid coverage of Oliver Reed's personal life over the years, *Gladiator* was the perfect last film for the talented actor as it reminded everybody jut how strong and captivating a performer he could be. Other Reed films include *The Trap* (Sidney Hayers, 1967), *Hannibal Brooks* (Michael Winner, 1969), *Women in Love* (Ken Russell, 1969), *The Devils* (Ken Russell, 1971), *Tommy* (Ken Russell, 1975), *The Three Musketeers* (Richard Lester, 1974) and *The Adventures of Baron Munchausen* (Terry Gilliam, 1988).

MAKING IT: *Gladiator* is the film that really brought Scott back on to the big-time movie map after a number of less memorable films that failed to connect with the mainstream audience. *1492: Conquest of Paradise*, while possessing moments of greatness, did not come together; at the same time popular interest in Christopher Columbus in 1992 was perhaps misjudged by the media in general. *White Squall* felt a little too much like *Dead Poets Society* while *G.I. Jane* had an ugly streak to it and lacked a level of ambition usually associated with Ridley Scott. *Gladiator* reminded audiences of his skill at fusing spectacle with strong drama. The film was strongly marketed by the studio DreamWorks SKG in the spring of 2000. It was a return to familiar territory for Scott, creating the illusion of something approaching an otherworld so ancient as to border on being fantastic. The emotions and dramas at the heart of the story are very contemporary in the way they are expressed. *Gladiator*'s central drama is simply about a family man who wants to get home and see his family while battling intrigue and corruption.

Scott had spent most of the 1990s fashioning movies that failed to register much anywhere. *Gladiator* restored Scott's standing, and in a way marks a new chapter in his filmmaking career. Like *Blade Runner*, *Alien* and *Thelma & Louise*, *Gladiator* became a movie that transcended its movie roots. Yes, the fight scenes were kinetic and sure and immersed you in the sound and fury of the arena, but this visceral energy was really the icing on a cake that was a tightly written and compelling drama.

THE SHOOT: *Gladiator* commenced filming in early 1999, starting off at Farnham in England with the forest battle that opens the film. For this sequence, when the film's director of photography, John Mathieson, needed the camera to follow the galloping horses the crew constructed a monorail device for the camera to ride along in order to negotiate the undulating landscape.

Over nineteen weeks a crew of a hundred British and two hundred Maltese workers recreated central Rome and a portion of the Colosseum. The CGI work of London-based The Mill expanded the vistas and supplied most of the crowds (see **TECH TALK**).

Rather than hire items, the crew generated all its own costumes, props, weapons and chariots and that ultimately proved cheaper.

One of the key concepts for *Gladiator* was to visualise the Empire in decline, as some of the film's dialogue establishes. Production designer Arthur Max felt this decline was suggested most clearly by the nineteenth-century paintings of ancient Rome. John Mathieson has said that he was able to suggest a cathedral-like atmosphere in the Colosseum sequences because of the combination of light and sand. Consider the wide shot of the arena as the digitally enhanced sunlight filters down from the top left of frame.

Artists such as Sir Lawrence Alma-Tadema (a Dutch-born British artist hugely popular in the nineteenth century with his depictions of ancient world life in work such as *The Pyrrhic Dance*, which depicted a Spartan war dance, and *The Finding of Moses*) and Georges de la Tour (a seventeenth-century French painter who specialised in biblical and classical images) were informing sources for the film's design. Where Scott had previously been accused of allowing setting to overwhelm the human drama (see **Blade Runner, Legend** and **Black Rain**), in *Gladiator* he appeared to strike a balance between grand environments and grand emotion. In keeping with his trademark layering of the image, Scott packs out the background and foregrounds with people and activity giving a strong sense that we really have landed back in time.

COSTUMES: Scott wanted the costumes of the gladiators to reflect their personality traits and it was his suggestion to draw on kabuki theatre and a sense of the magical in the creation of these costumes. For Commodus's marble-like armour Scott's concept was to suggest the character's ambition to evoke the look of his ancestors' statues.

LIGHTING: Scott built each segment of the film around different kinds of lighting. The opening battle was defined by cold, grey tones. A warmer look was designed for the Morocco sequence and finally a bold daylight and shadow scheme was applied for Rome.

LOCATIONS: Production designer Arthur Max scouted England, France, Italy, eastern Europe and north Africa for appropriate locations to film at. The Zucchabar arena set was built at Ait Ben Baddou. Malta doubled for Rome and the Colosseum set (partial only) was built at Fort Risacoli.

Wherever possible, to avoid the feeling of a set those elements that were fabricated by the production team were integrated with existing buildings or environments, for example Proximo's gladiator training school was built into a ruined fortress in Malta.

COLLABORATORS: Screenwriter David Franzoni had written the DreamWorks movie *Amistad* (Steven Spielberg, 1997) and had approached Walter Parkes and Laurie McDonald, Production Executives at DreamWorks, with his plan to write something set during ancient Rome with the arena as the centre of the story. Franzoni had much film history as well as real history to draw on in his fashioning of the screenplay that became *Gladiator*. Films that notably come to mind in the often unfairly maligned ancient-world subgenre are *Spartacus* (Stanley Kubrick, 1960), *Ben-Hur* (William Wyler, 1959) and *The Robe* (Henry Koster, 1953).

Just prior to his involvement with *Gladiator*, Scott had won a Golden Globe as producer of *RKO 281* (Benjamin Ross, 1999), a drama set around the making of *Citizen Kane* (Orson Welles, 1941). *RKO 281*'s screenwriter, John Logan, was brought on board *Gladiator* to further develop the script. A third writer then entered the arena, William Nicholson, who had penned *Shadowlands* (Richard Attenborough, 1993), the play and the screenplay, about part of the life of CS Lewis. Nicholson had also written the screenplays for *Nell* (Michael Apted, 1994) and *First Knight* (Jerry Zucker, 1994). The film's producer Doug Wick and executive producers Walter Parkes and Laurie McDonald all had input into the script alongside Scott. One of *Schindler's List*'s producers, Branko Lustig, served as one of the film's producers. Lustig's other credits include *The Peacemaker* (Mimi Leder, 1997) and 1983's landmark TV minseries *The Winds of War*, a saga of World War II based on the novel by Herman Wouk.

The lead conceptual artist on *Gladiator* was Sylvain Despretz who would base much of his work on Scott's own sketches, known as Ridleygrams.

Neil Courbould provided make-up and prosthetics as he had done on *Saving Private Ryan* (Steven Spielberg, 1998). The film's fight choreographer was Nicholas Powell who had worked in the same capacity on *Braveheart* (Mel Gibson, 1995).

For director of photography John Matheison the key to the film was to put the camera right in the middle of the action as much as possible. Mathieson began his career shooting *Plunkett & Macleane* (Jake Scott, 1999) and Ridley Scott then hired him to shoot an Orange mobile phone company commercial and from there *Gladiator*, *Hannibal* and *Matchstick Men*.

Arthur Max returned as production designer (see **G.I. Jane**).

MUSIC: The film's editor Pietro Scalia (*G.I. Jane*) and composer Hans Zimmer (*Black Rain*, *Thelma & Louise* and *White Squall*) worked, with Lisa Gerrard, in adjoining studios which may partly account for the richly interwoven music and image. Zimmer's music became a hot soundtrack CD. 'I really wanted to avoid a cliché approach,' Zimmer commented, befitting Scott's tradition of not scoring his films in an obvious way.

Scott and Hans Zimmer opt for music that is not heroic. Instead it is more muted and percussive, and without fanfare. In the final duel, Scott and Zimmer choose not to underscore it with any kind of action music, instead depending simply on the sound effects to emphasise the tension. The fight is on a smaller scale than the others but is much bigger emotionally.

This is one of Hans Zimmer's major, and certainly highest profile, scores, significantly enlivened by the melodious vocals of Lisa Gerrard. Gerrard, who has also been involved in the composition of the scores for, among others, *The Insider* (Michael Mann, 1999) and *Ali* (Michael Mann, 2001), provided the haunting vocals for *Gladiator*, which serve as a more emotional and ethereal counterpoint to Hans Zimmer's music. Gerrard's contribution emphasises the film's motifs of the land, of family and of love; Zimmer's material emphasises the bombast of the story while incorporating less clichéd sounds and tones to reflect the cultures that Maximus moves through.

In the rooftop conversation between Maximus and Juba melancholy music underscores the dialogue which expresses one of the film's key themes of family. Sections from Holst's *Mars, The Bringer of War* are integrated into the music track of *Gladiator* during the Germania battle.

One of the not-so-surprising outcomes of *Gladiator* was the success of the music as a soundtrack album. In the film, Scott and Hans Zimmer take a slightly unexpected route. The score does not go for the traditional Roman epic. Instead it is a little more ambient and certainly articulate in its use of ethnic instrumentation. Zimmer leans on conventional devices at key points though, such as the insistent and urgent strains as Maximus rides back home from his execution escape. Zimmer does go for a kind of pomp and ceremony in just one moment, when Proximo's train approaches Rome: it is a buoyant celebratory piece.

THE OPENING: The film opens with burnished logos for Universal and DreamWorks that suggest ancient glory and wrap the audience in the atmosphere for the film immediately. Hans

Zimmer's music rises, with an ethnographic inflection and movie eeriness. A few expository paragraphs establish the extent of ancient Rome's Empire. The first image is of an unidentified man's hand brushing and stroking across wheat lit by the sun – this key shot occurred to Scott late in the shoot. The camera follows the hand's trail in a dreamy and beautiful shot against which we hear the sound of a child.

ON THE SCREEN: Scott contrasts the opening with the main start of the movie – a grey, blue, cold light on Maximus on the battlefield. The shot of a diminutive yet mighty robin on a branch echoes the diminutive ant shot of *1492* and again emphasises the durability of nature against the elements and man's apparent, self-regarding might.

The camera booming up reveals the massed Roman forces and Marcus Aurelius watching. The camera tracks as Maximus walks past his troops preparing them for battle, lending extra energy to the frame which a static shot would not have provided. Films are all about the cumulative effect of details. Maximus is like Sheldon in *White Squall*, a man of action and focus which also harks back to other characters like D'Hubert in *The Duellists*, Keegan in *Someone to Watch Over Me* and Columbus in *1492: Conquest of Paradise*, all men who are tough but emotionally gentle and sympathetic.

HEROES AND VILLAINS: Maximus embodies professionalism and efficiency and great warmth too. He is a primal figure of good, associated all through the film with being in contact with the land. Maximus picks up some earth on the battlefield and rubs it between his hands, just as he does every time he is in the arena. Just prior to battle in Germania, Maximus locks his gaze with a wolf, symbolising Maximus's more primal quality.

Like Columbus, Maximus is an outsider partly because of nationality. He is called The Spaniard a lot during the film. He is an outsider by birth, and also later by choice in two ways: his wish to go home and fight no more and then in his wilful disobedience towards Commodus by not acknowledging him in the arena. The crowd love Maximus as much for his skill as his defiance of the rules and Commodus realises this. If he killed Maximus the crowd would hate it. In Ridley Scott's cinema world, living beyond the rules is where the glory lies. The Roman army code is 'Strength and honour', and Maximus quotes it prior to the battle that opens the film. It resurfaces later in the film and the concept is what binds Maximus to the other gladiators as well as to other heroes in other Ridley Scott films.

Maximus speaks of 'Home. A wife. A son. The harvest'. 'Three weeks from now I shall be harvesting my crops,' Maximus says with satisfaction. His simple dream only heightens the jeopardy of the situation he soon finds himself in after military victory. Marcus Aurelius says to Maximus, 'You have proved your valour yet again, Maximus,' indicating that the aging Emperor wants to know what he can do for the heroic solidier. Maximus replies, 'Let me go home.' Maximus, like Keegan in *Someone to Watch Over Me*, Parker in *Alien*, the soldiers in *Black Hawk Down* and Columbus in *1492* wants to be with his family despite the pressures of his 'mission'.

Maximus, like all Scott's heroes, displays the power of the individual to determine their destiny. Maximus's destroyed homeland, burned and apocalyptic in its wilderness, represents his emotional devastation also. The world is dark and cruel just as he said it was and, like an innocent, he is getting that experience first hand. *Gladiator* has a very melancholy main character and a melancholy ending. Maximus is something of a superman.

Maximus's philosophy is one of unity in the arena, just as Sheldon emphasises unity on *The Albatross* in *White Squall* and Urgayle emphasises teamwork in *G.I. Jane*. Maximus's words during the 'battle of Carthage' have a significance that rings, appropriately, in eternity: 'Whatever comes out of these gates – we've got a better chance of survival if we work together. If we stay together we survive.' He has the oratory of a politician; he is the glue, just like Chuck is the one who holds it all together in *White Squall* and as Eversmann does in *Black Hawk Down*.

Maximus is a man of great faith who symbolises the eternal, just as the land, with which he is associated throughout the film, does. Like Jack O'the Green, Maximus fights a great darkness and tyranny; like Jack, he finds a suit of armour and a sword awaiting him during his adventure. All of Scott's films effectively tell the same story.

Marcus Aurelius watches, and the camera zooms in very slowly on his passive, sad old face. In contrast, Scott immerses us in the frenzy of battle with quick cuts and handheld camera. Scott even finds time for a primally symbolic moment of the wolf leaping through the flames. Like Spielberg, Cameron and Stone, Scott immerses the audience in some sense of the chaos of battle. Some film reviews of *Gladiator* said that the opening battle was confusing to follow. In the subsequent *Black Hawk Down*, virtually the entire running time of the film is concerned with a battle. Scott's efforts to avoid the use of a musical cue are evident in *Gladiator*'s opening sequence so that over slow-motion battle images sync sound is dropped right down, making the moment more and less real all at once.

As in all his films, Scott packs *Gladiator* with skilfully directed performances that often say just as much, if not more, in a look than a line of dialogue. Just look at the relief etched on Aurelius's face as the camera zooms in slowly on him as he watches his troops victorious in the forest battle. To enhance Aurelius's high status Scott frames him so that the sunlight backlights his white hair, giving it a silvery quality. Marcus Aurelius says to Maximus early on, 'Embrace me as my son.' Aurelius is a father figure somewhat like Sheldon to the boys in *White Squall*. After Aurelius's death Proximo becomes the father figure to Maximus. Scott had intended to show Proximo going back to the wilderness at the end of the film but instead has him die after helping Maximus in his attempt to escape Rome and restore order (see **TECH TALK**).

When Commodus fights bare chested in the woods at the beginning of the film in the wake of Maximus's victory, it is his desperate effort as the pretender to the throne to prove his masculinity and strength. Maximus will ace him every time with a combination of physical prowess and emotional resolve. Commodus is clearly uneasy with his father's praise of Maximus and the soldiers cheering their general. And then there is Commodus's desperate effort to convince his father he has virtues. Commodus will emerge as a monster, on a very believable and human scale, and like so much monstrosity he is driven by petty emotions of jealousy and greed. Similarly, Commodus is the lost teenager unable to find a way to please his father – he is like Frank and Dean in *White Squall*, a fragile young man trying to put up a strong front. There is an effeminate quality to Commodus and, in his juvenile angst, he would be very much at home on *The Albatross*.

WOMEN: As in all Scott's films, *Gladiator* features a strong female character, Lucilla. Her face has the same quality as

Sigourney Weaver's and even Mimi Rogers in *Someone to Watch Over Me*. They are all strong women who can withstand the tests placed on them. Maximus confirms this when he says to Lucilla, 'I think you have a talent for survival.'

PICTURE PERFECT: As in his other films, Scott anchors the big pictures with details, ranging from the naturalistic (such as the livestock in the Germania camp or the animals in the backgrounds of the bazaars and streets of Rome) to the expressive (as in the image of Maximus's little figurines of his wife and child and the memory of his farm).

Scott's skill at contrasting colours from scene to scene is evident from the start. Outside in the forest it is grey and in the army tents warm candlelight and the burnished sheen of gold dominates.

Scott's little flourishes enhance the drama in their very visual creation of character. When we first see Commodus we do not see his face clearly, as it is in shadow. He is established and associated with darkness and only half-light, anticipating his amorality and lack of trustworthiness. This device runs all the way through the film for Commodus and Imperial life, represented as a world of duplicity, distrust, paranoia. There is nothing natural and open about it, only menace.

Scott's economic use of intercutting is used powerfully in *Gladiator*, notably to enhance the emotional connection of Maximus to his home as he rides towards it after escaping execution in the forest (see **Top Shots**). It is as if Maximus hears the hooves of the soldiers riding towards his home. Slow motion adds to the intensity and anguish of the moment as the Romans ride on to his property. Scot intercuts again for the scene when Maximus escapes through underground passages as a skirmish unfolds between freed gladiators and soldiers.

Amid the epic scale and sweeping vistas, Scott also includes far simpler, but no less powerful images. A notably simple example is in the Germania segment of the film showing Lucilla and Commodus at their father's bedside. Aurelius lies outstretched along the bottom of the frame which is comprised of vertical and horizontal compositions.

The emotionally epic gesture is found throughout this film, especially when Maximus kisses the charred feet of his wife. In this scene, Scott does not wallow in something obviously grotesque, but instead the camera pulls back to reveal just the feet. Scott repeats compositions and movements through the film but gives them different meanings.

When Maximus awakes on the slave cart he is shot from above and appears to be floating because the audience cannot see the wheels of the cart moving him across the ground. This shot is repeated at the end of the film in his death as he appears to float above the petals strewn on the arena floor. Scott hadn't used this many petals since *Legend*.

When Commodus hugs his son Lucius it echoes the killer hug he gave his father.

The glances and looks of Gracchus and Commodus in the arena communicate their emotions and concerns far better than dialogue would. Scott also captures the fear of the men when they first go to fight just by the looks on their faces. He adds to the sense of threat by using the handheld camera that makes any situation feel unstable. It is also less glossy and because of its imperfect movement is truer to life. It makes the viewer feel as if they themselves are in the mud and blood of the battle.

For a reveal of Rome for the first time in the film, the clouds part in front of the camera and we see the city below. There is something of German filmmaker (and actress) Leni Riefenstahl's work in the framing of the eagle and SPQR with the sky behind it, the camera at low height looking up, emphasising the overbearing majesty of Rome (see **TECH TALK**). Riefenstahl famously recorded the sixth Nazi congress at Nuremberg in 1934 and still continues to make films. There is a silver patina to Rome as Commodus rides in. It is a moment of glory but it is notable for not feeling warm, instead it is simply grandiose.

One shot of the Colosseum has been designed to suggest shots of sporting events that you might see on TV taken from aircraft high above stadia. The shots of sunrise over Rome recall the matte shot of the sun over the cityscape in *Blade Runner*.

Scott enjoys the shadows and layers of fabric in the palace, contrasting with Maximus's elemental and honest rubbing of the arena sand in his hands. To dramatise the moment of Maximus choosing his helmet, he turns his head out of darkness and into a beam of light to mark his transformation.

In the scene just prior to the final showdown between Commodus and Maximus, Maximus is chained up in a crucifix-like way. Both men are lit from above and so their eyes are cast into shadow, giving them a deathly look. The scene has a dead grey pall to it that contrasts with the brightness of the sand and arena above.

TECH TALK: The rising cost of epics made them obsolete by the late 1960s. However, the advent and development of digital effects to make the film medium more painterly than photographic in terms of visual effects, as George Lucas commented in Martin Scoresese's documentary *A Personal Journey Through American Cinema* (1998), made the epic scale feasible again. For Scott the allure was more than sufficient. John Nelson and Nancy St John supervised the visual effects; The Mill generated most of them. Scott had worked with The Mill on *G.I. Jane*. UK-based Audio Motion aided The Mill with motion capture. Practical on-set effects were handled by Neil Courbould's Special Effects UK company.

For the illusion of many soldiers in the opening battle several static VistaVision plates of minimal soldiers were pieced together in a panorama effect.

The production used five tigers, four lions, two zebras, four dogs, two oxen and one elephant. Talking numbers, 16,000 flaming arrows were fired and 10,000 non-flaming arrows followed. More than 2,500 weapons were created for the film. All footwear was made in Rome, and 500 gladiator costumes were made.

The tiger attacks for the arena sequence were always filmed separately and then spliced together with footage of the actors. Special harnesses were fitted allowing actors to attach false limbs for subsequent dismemberment. Collapsing dummies were also designed for the battle scenes. To burn trees for the opening battle sequence, the production team bought a section of Bourne Woods in Surrey so they could set fire to it. Computer-generated enhancements were then made, including adding smoke trails to flaming arrows. Ten shots of Maximus's family were produced by Pacific Title and Art Studio and the flesh tones for his wife and son were given a terracotta look. Skies were replaced and speeding clouds incorporated. Hill towns in France were shot and stood in for southern Rome. Sections of the ancient harbour in Malta were photographed and incorporated into the walls of Rome. Tim Burke went and photographed neoclassical architecture in London that formed part of the illusion.

Scott screened *Triumph of the Will* (Leni Riefenstahl, 1935) to suggest the kind of scale he wanted vis-à-vis soldiers in relation to classical architecture. The scene of Commodus's arrival into Rome was a combination of photos and computer-generated models, with principal actors on steps against blue screen. The illusion of 27,000 extras was generated by computer as were fake vultures for the material shot in Morocco.

Production designer Arthur Max stayed close to the historical accuracy of the Colosseum. Because a full-size replica would have been unfeasible, the first tier was built for real on location and the remainder was a computer image. The computer artists had three main layers to grade on the computer model Colosseum: they had to give the illusion of the flat light given by the sun, a sense of the sun as the lighting source, and they had to judge a way to create a sense of backlighting and other credible light sources. On location there were 2,000 extras for the Colosseum crowd. This number was then digitally expanded by CGI to give the illusion of about 33,000. A Steadicam shot of Maximus and the gladiators entering the arena allowed for the camera to follow and then circle the group 360 degrees so that the illusion of the Colosseum was really sold to the audience.

Computer imaging was also used to build generic statue bodies to which specific arms, legs and toga clothing were added. Rough composites were put together in LA and London and transferred, modified using WAM!NET facility. This way, the time difference was used as an advantage, effectively making it a 24-hour effects production.

Oliver Reed died during shooting with some of his scenes not yet completed so, in post-production, computer animation was used to complete Reed's role. Images of Reed from the background of certain completed shots were taken and composited into the scenes that he had not yet filmed. His features were not reanimated for any dialogue delivery and his speech was cut together from previously recorded dialogue. A body double was used for reverse angles of Reed and at certain points backgrounds from other scenes were pulled in to complete the newly created images of Reed's character. In light of Oliver Reed's death, Scott had prepared a four-minute compilation of Reed clips from the film tracked by 'I Did It My Way' by the Sex Pistols. It had been planned to be included on the DVD but doesn't appear.

MOVIE TALK:

Maximus (to Commodus): 'I think you have been afraid all your life.'

Commodus (to Maximus): 'You simply won't die.'

Maximus: 'What we do in life, echoes in eternity,' and then he adds, 'At my signal unleash hell.'

Proximo: 'Win the crowd and you'll win your freedom.'

Maximus: 'My name is Gladiator.'

Maximus: 'I have seen much of the world. It is brutal, cruel and dark.'

THE BIG IDEA: Innocence to experience is a key Scott journey and in *Gladiator* it is very much part of Maximus's journey.

Duty and military code fuels the drama – Scott had a military father and maybe this had an impact. *Gladiator*, like *The Duellists* all those years before, dramatises themes of honour, worth and heroism, all of them classic Scott preoccupations writ large in ancient Rome. The world of pure aggression is deemed a source of wrong from the very start when Aurelius says to Maximus how much he regrets his history of campaigns: 'I brought the sword, nothing more.' The petals that fall for the final duel between Maximus and Commodus, and which surround Maximus in death, indicate good amid a world of evil, just like the petals swirling in the storm in *Legend*. In his notes for the film during the editing process, Pietro Scalia identified the theme of transcendence as central to the story and worked through various versions and implications of the word.

The film dramatises friendships amongst men, notably in Maximus's friendship with strong but gentle Juba whose first words to Maximus are empowering and cynical: 'Don't die. They'll feed you to the lions. They're worth more than we are.' Juba and Maximus talk on the roof of the gladiator compound in Zucchabar. In the scene both men are lit by golden sunlight that gives them a heroic quality, especially Maximus with the sun rim lighting him. Juba asks Maximus, 'Can they hear you? Your family, in the afterlife?' Like so many other Scott heroes, Maximus wants somewhere to belong.

Scott's comfort with visceral action gets its workout throughout the film. The film mirrors Hollywood filmmaking in that

Maximus is the champion because he wins the mass crowd with spectacular action.

As in *Legend* and *1492: Conquest of Paradise*, the sound of weather in its fury signals doom. When Quintus takes Maximus prisoner and says, 'Your family will meet you in the afterlife,' there is a crack of thunder for transition to a shot of his wife and child, in a very brooding image.

Juba ends the film on an upbeat note that celebrates family as he buries Maximus's figurines in the sand of the Colosseum, uniting Maximus with the earth in a way that echoes Maximus rubbing dirt in between his hands at various moments in the story. The closing shot is an archly Romantic scene of Rome like a Renaissance painting.

In summer 2002, a sequel to *Gladiator* was being talked about in film magazines and on film news websites, though it would obviously be one in which Maximus would not appear.

RELEASE: *Gladiator* was released in May 2000 by DreamWorks SKG and was the first Hollywood-produced epic in 40 years. It was Scott's most successful film since *Thelma & Louise* and re-established his place as one of the most accomplished popular filmmakers.

CRITICAL CONDITION: The *Chicago Sun-Times* was succinct in its summing up of *Gladiator*: 'The storyline is *Rocky* on downers', while *Empire* stressed Crowe's part in the film: 'Ridley Scott has enriched the legacy of sandals, sword and leather wrist thingies to create a magnificent epic . . . Russell Crowe was clearly born in a hard month, in a hard year during a freak outbreak of total hardness,' as did the *LA Times*: 'Crowe has a patent on heroic plausibility . . . *Gladiator* is supremely atmospheric . . . The problem with *Gladiator* is that Scott is so good at creating alternative universes that he hates to leave.' In *Village Voice*, J Hoberman compared *Gladiator* to other Ridley Scott films: '[In its] relentlessly high tech revival of deeply retro material . . . the movie is far closer to *1492* and *Legend* than *Blade Runner*.'

GROSSES: *Gladiator* cost around $100 million to make and grossed $190 million in North America and $434 million worldwide. The film has become an iconic blockbuster movie joining the ranks of *Indiana Jones* (Steven Spielberg, 1981, 1984 and 1989), *Star Wars* (George Lucas, 1977), *Die Hard* (John McTiernan, 1988), *The Terminator* (James Cameron, 1984) and other mainstream classics, which verge on household name status.

POSTER: The film's teaser poster fused the ancient with a modern slogan simply stating in a very contemporary font 'A Hero Will Rise'. In this image, Maximus, with his shoulder pads and surly stance, resembled something closer to Mad Max (from George Miller's 1979 film and its sequels) than some ancient-world fighter. Or is it just that Mad Max was aware of his ancient roots? Another poster was also produced which featured Maximus kneeling with his head bowed, his sword digging into the crowd and a crimson sky behind him.

HOME ENTERTAINMENT: The film is available on VHS but it is the DVD release that offers up a wealth of riches. The DVD contains the following in addition to the feature: interactive menus, scene access, a feature-length commentary by Ridley Scott, the HBO First Look behind-the-scenes documentary (made at the time of the film's original release), The Bloodsport of a Gladiator, twenty-five minutes of deleted scenes, a seven-minute montage of additional deleted scenes, a photo gallery, cast and crew biographies, trailers and storyboards.

DELETED SCENES: There are a number of scenes that were cut from the final edit of *Gladiator*.

After the battle in Germania Maximus walks through the battlefield hospital where his men are wounded and dying. Maximus says nothing, just looks gravely concerned.

Marcus Aurelius, in his tent at night, prays to his ancestors prior to Commodus's deadly arrival.

Proximo, upon arrival at Zucchabar with his new gladiators, is urged to bet against his own men when they fight in the arena.

Prior to going into the Zucchabar arena for a second time, Proximo reminds Maximus to entertain the crowd and not kill all of his opponents too quickly.

In the Colosseum some Christians huddle passively as they kneel on the ground waiting for the lions to come out and kill them. Maximus watches from the gladiators' cell.

In the shadows, Gaius, Gracchus and Lucilla talk about Commodus's wayward plans for Rome and his obsession with the games. It emerges that Commodus is selling Rome's grain supply to fund the games, thereby putting the city in great peril. Gaius suggests they wait for Commodus to make more enemies before striking to end his tyranny.

In secret, Commodus takes a sword to a bust of his father and hacks it to pieces.

Commodus has two Praetorian guards executed at the command of Quintus in a move to test Quintus's allegiance to himself.

Lucilla realises that Falco is Commodus's ally.

The Praetorian guard cause chaos as they go to seize Maximus from Proximo's base.

There are also cut scenes on the DVD that appear in something like a mini movie: it is composed of many other shots not included in the film, dited together to the accompaniment of themes from the film's music. The mini movie charts the narrative of the film and includes further footage of Maximus trekking through the wilderness back to Spain after escaping Germania and more shots of his wife and son as he imagines them waiting for him.

AWARDS: If Ridley and his crew thought they had hit gold with *Thelma & Louise* at awards time, then what could they have made of *Gladiator*'s time in the awards arena? It was a long one.

Oscars went to Russell Crowe for Best Actor, to Janty Yates for Best Costume Design, Best Visual Effects award went to Tim Burke, Neil Corbould, Rob Harvey and John Nelson. The coveted Best Picture Award went to Douglas Wick, Branko Lustig and David Franzoni. Best Sound went to the film also, going to Bob Beemer and Scott Millan. There were also Oscar nominations aplenty, including Best Actor in a Supporting Role (Joaquin Phoenix), Best Screenplay (David Franzoni, John Logan and William Nicholson), Best Art Direction and Set Decoration (Arthur Max, Crispian Sallis), Best Cinematography (John Mathieson), Best Editing (Pietro Scalia) and Best Music (Hans Zimmer).

The awards glut continued when the film was nominated for BAFTAS in Best Performance in a Leading Role, Best Screenplay, Best Sound and Best Supporting Role. The BAFTAS that were won were for Best Cinematography, Editing, Film, Production Design, the Anthony Asquith Award for Film Music, Best Achievement in Visual Effects, Best Costume Design and Best Make-up/Hair.

Pietro Scalia won Best Edited Feature Film at the American Cinema Editors Awards. The film was also nominated at the Empire Awards, UK 2001, in the category of Best British Director for *Gladiator*. At the European Film Awards, 2000, it was nominated for the Five Continents Award, *Gladiator*.

The Chicago Film Critics Association awarded the film nominations for Best Cinematography and Original Score and at the Society of Motion Picture and Television Art Directors awards, the movie won the award for Excellence in Production Design. Golden Globes were also grabbed for Best Motion Picture, Best Original Score, Best Performance by an Actor and Best Performance by an Actor in a Supporting Role.

TRIVIA: Gladiators really did do product endorsements. This was originally to have been referred to in the movie but was dropped because it was felt it would be unbelievable to contemporary audiences.

Connie Nielsen (Lucilla) wears a ring that is actually 2,000 years old.

Crowe's facial wounds after the opening battle are for real: a horse backed into him.

In a very fanciful twist of movie fate, a Yak helmet from *Time Bandits* (Terry Gilliam, 1981) is worn by one of the gladiators.

The real-life Commodus was the only Emperor to have fought as a gladiator.

Originally, the script had Maximus named Narcissus. Not quite the same tough guy associations there!

GREAT SCOTT: Ridley Scott demonstrates his time-honoured skill at pumping new life into time-honoured genres, as he did with *Alien*, *Blade Runner* and *Thelma & Louise*. For some critics, *Gladiator* painted a nice enough picture of ancient Rome but that was all. However, by placing the film in the director's wider body of work, all of the vintage Scott ideas and key images are in place. As with his best efforts it is that sense of an environment vividly brought to life that is so effective – the audience can almost feel the heat and the dust. And, given all the big shots and action sequences, just consider how much of the film is rooted in powerful close-ups and the play of light and shadow on faces.

As an ancient world epic, *Gladiator* is a major addition to a long-dormant genre and, as an action movie, it is as dynamic and sure-footed as *The Matrix* (Andy and Larry Wachowski, 1999) and *Die Hard* (John McTiernan, 1988). Scott finds a way to stay focused on the relationships between the characters without being too distracted by the sound and fury of the ancient world. Another of the film's virtues is that it avoids a cuteness that sometimes works its way into such films – Scott also reminds us of taste for physical intensity where necessary.

With *Gladiator*, Scott proved that he was still able to tell an exciting, action-packed story which did not stint on strong drama. In a way, the film was the ultimate Ridley Scott film with its classical world setting and classical values that have shown up in all his films. The good and evil distinction is also powerfully drawn and his cinematic flourishes remain intact – 'I don't think Ridley could shoot an ugly piece of film if he tried,' John Nelson, visual effects supervisor on *Gladiator,* observed during production on the film. Like other great adventure movies such as *Raiders of the Lost Ark* (Steven Spielberg, 1981), *The Searchers* (John Ford, 1956) and *The Right Stuff* (Philip Kaufman, 1983), *Gladiator* balances kinetics and personal drama. At a time when male movie heroism was not always that sure of itself and when, in the real world, there was a sense of emasculation, Maximus Decimus Meridius was the real deal: tough, sensitive and brave. The perfect combination.

SCOTT FREE: 'Should a hero rise out of the carnage of the arena, his popularity would give him tremendous power . . . he might threaten even the most absolute tyrant.'

Hannibal (2001)

(Colour, 131 minutes)

Producers: Dino De Laurentiis and Martha De Laurentiis
Executive Producer: Branko Lustig
Associate Producer: Terry Needham
Line Producer (Italy): Lucio Trentini
Screenplay: David Mamet and Steven Zaillian, from the
novel by Thomas Harris
Music: Hans Zimmer (additional material by Klaus Bedelt,
Patrick Cassidy, James O'Leary, Mel Wesson), JS Bach *Aria
Da Capo/Goldberg Variations*
Cinematography: John Mathieson

RIDLEY SCOTT Hannibal

Editor: Pietro Scalia
Casting: Louis DiGiaimo and Jim Choate
Production Design: Norris Spencer
Art Directors: David Crank and Marco Trentini
Set Decorators: Crispian Sallis, Cynthia Sleiter
Assistant Director: Julian Brain
Digital FX Artist (Main Titles): Janet Quen
Costume Designer: Janty Yates
Make-up: Greg Cannom, Keith VanderLaan
Unit Production Manager: Pamela Hochschatner
Sound FX Editor: Christopher Assells
Visual Effects Supervisor: Tim Burke

CAST: Anthony Hopkins (*Hannibal Lecter*), Julianne Moore (*Clarice Starling*), Gary Oldman (*Mason Verger – uncredited*), Ray Liotta (*Paul Krendler*), Frankie Faison (*Barney Matthews*), Giancarlo Ginannini (*Rinaldo Pazzi*), Francesca Nerri (*Allegra Pazzi*), David Andrews (*FBI Agent Clint Pearsall*), Francis Guinan (*FBI Director Noonan*), Zeljiko Ivanek (*Dr Cordell Deomling*), Hazelle Goodman (*Evelda Drumgo*), James Opter (*DEA Agent Eldridge*), Enrico Lo verso (*Gnocco*)

BUDGET: $87 million

MPAA: R

BBFC: 18

TAG LINE: Break the silence.

SUMMARY: It is ten years on from Hannibal Lecter's escape at the end of *Silence of the Lambs* (see CONCEPT). Facially deformed rich man Mason Verger is holed up in his Southern mansion talking with Barney, Hannibal Lecter's surviving nurse. Verger is about to buy Hannibal's iconic face-mask from Barney for $250,000. Verger is a man obsessed – he had socialised with Lecter at one time and Lecter had encouraged Verger to mutilate his face beyond all recognition so Verger now wants revenge.

Far from the genteel surrounding of Verger's home, FBI agent Clarice Starling leads an ill-fated operation to bring in a much-wanted criminal. Fatalities ensue and, at the FBI, Clarice is brought before her superiors. A creepy guy from the Justice

Department, Paul Krendler, takes obvious delight in Starling's failing. Clarice is then informed that the subject of her most famous case, Hannibal Lecter, is back on the scene.

Mason Verger has been in touch. Starling goes to meet with Verger and he gives Clarice a package. Starling tracks down Barney who hands over a range of Lecter archive material that Starling pores over.

In Florence an Italian cop, Pazzi, is down on his luck. He approaches an art historian named Dr Fell and asks about the fate of Fell's predecessor. Back at the FBI, Clarice opens a letter artfully addressed to her. It is from Lecter, and updates her on his life and how he has monitored her career since they last met. The letter is marked by a scent, which Starling uses to find out where Lecter is now.

In Florence, Pazzi watches CCTV footage of Dr Fell in a perfume shop, then tracks Fell through cafes and streets. At home Pazzi looks at the video of the CCTV image that was meant to have been sent to the FBI. Pazzi visits the FBI website and deduces the true identity of Fell – Hannibal Lecter – and also that there is a big bounty on Lecter's head.

Back in America, Krendler snoops around Starling's office and then they talk briefly about Lecter. Starling then calls the Florence police and asks them to resend the perfume CCTV footage video. Pazzi goes and sees Lecter at the library. Starling learns that Pazzi has been on the Lecter trail and she calls him to warn him not to pursue Lecter for his own safety. Despite her warning, Pazzi is gruesomely killed by Lecter.

Verger calls on Krendler and agrees to pay him $500,000 to bring Lecter in. Soon after, Lecter arrives in the States. He sneaks into Clarice's home as she sleeps. He then shadows Clarice in public, talking to her by way of mobile communications. Clarice is armed and wants to see Lecter but he remains hidden.

Lecter is then captured by Verger's henchmen who take him to Verger's mansion. Starling finds out what has happened to Lecter and goes to rescue him. Clarice finds Lecter being wheeled into a barn where wild boars are unleashed on him. Starling intervenes and frees Lecter. When she in turn is injured, Lecter picks her up and carries her out of the barn. Lecter prompts Verger's death as he exits by signalling for Dr Cordell to dump Verger into the pit of wild boars.

Hannibal takes gruesome revenge on Krendler while Clarice watches at his side. The police finally intervene; Lecter escapes and is last seen on a plane talking to a child.

RIDLEY SCOTT Hannibal

THE CONCEPT: Thomas Harris had written two Hannibal Lecter novels prior to *Hannibal* – *Red Dragon* and *Silence of the Lambs*. Michael Mann had directed *Manhunter*, an adaptation of *Red Dragon*, in 1986 which starred Brian Cox as Hannibal Lecter, a name that fittingly suggests cannibal and delectation. A second adaptation of *Red Dragon* was released in October 2002. Directed by Brett Ratner, the film starred Anthony Hopkins as Lecter and also featured Philip Seymour Hoffman, Harvey Keitel, Emily Watson, Ed Norton and Ralph Fiennes (see **Ridley Scott: Filmography as Producer**). Jonathan Demme's 1991 adaptation of *Silence of the Lambs* was a massive successs, its story and images easing into the public imagination and Anthony Hopkins's take on the Lecter character becoming as memorable as other horror movie villains, such as Christopher Lee as Dracula. Jodie Foster had won the Best Actress Oscar at the 1992 Academy Awards for her role as Clarice Starling in the earlier film.

In 1999, after a ten-year break, Thomas Harris wrote *Hannibal*. Harris sent a copy of *Hannibal* to Dino De Laurentiis as soon as he had completed it, though at the time of the publication of *Silence of the Lambs* De Laurentiis had opted not to pursue an adaptation. While on location as producer on *U-571* (Jonathan Mostow, 2000), De Laurentiis, who had wanted to work with Scott for years, walked over to Ridley Scott's *Gladiator* set and offered the job to him. When De Laurentiis pitched the *Hannibal* movie to Scott, the director initially thought it was to be a movie about Hannibal and his elephants and declined.

Part of the *Hannibal* film deal was that Harris would have approval of changes to his source material. In the novel, Lecter is living in Florence and is still beguiled by Clarice Starling, though Starling attempts to nail him for good. A bizarre romance develops between the two. Scott read the novel before it was published and responded to its dark romance and black comedy. David Mamet originally adapted the source material for producer Dino De Laurentiis and then Steven Zaillian reworked the adaptation, receiving the screen credit.

For Scott, *Hannibal* would work best as a dark romantic comedy with an ending different to that of the novel – this new ending leaves the movie door open for Hannibal and Clarice. At Scott's request, Zaillian rewrote the ending of the story to have Clarice seduced by Hannibal. Thomas Harris agreed the new ending. When Scott came on board he worked on the script with

Zaillian. 'I love the process with the writers,' Scott acknowledged – this goes way back to his first collaborations with writers such as Gerald Vaughan-Hughes on *The Duellists*, Dan O'Bannon on *Alien* and Hampton Fancher on *Blade Runner*.

Jonathan Demme, who had directed *Silence of the Lambs*, and Jodie Foster had initially been involved in the sequel but Foster and Demme both then departed the project.

Where *Silence of the Lambs* was a slice of high-powered American Gothic, Scott's movie was informed by its Florentine setting, lending the film an ancient-world sense of menace and a kind of florid, operatic violence. Only when back in America does the tone and violence lack invention.

CASTING: Anthony Hopkins returned for this film despite saying he was going to retire from acting, his accent slipping easily from its genteel southern twang to British. During his work on *Silence of the Lambs* he would throw Jodie Foster off balance by never blinking during scenes with her and by improvising lines. Hopkins had appeared in a number of films including *A Bridge Too Far* (Richard Attenborough, 1977), *The Elephant Man* (David Lynch, 1980) and *The Bounty* (Roger Donaldson, 1984), but the 1991 film gave Anthony Hopkins a new high profile and he went on to star in many big Hollywood films, including *The Mask of Zorro* (Martin Campbell, 1998), *Surviving Picasso* (James Ivory, 1996) and *Remains of the Day* (James Ivory, 1992).

Julianne Moore landed the Starling role, after Angelina Jolie, Cate Blanchett, Helen Hunt, Gillian Anderson and Hilary Swank had been considered. Moore had been seen in *The Hand That Rocks the Cradle* (Curtis Hanson, 1992), *The Fugitive* (Andrew Davis, 1993), *An Ideal Husband* (Oliver Parker, 1999) and *The End of the Affair* (Neil Jordan, 1999). Since *Hannibal* she has appeared in *The Shipping News* (Lasse Hallström, 2001).

Ray Liotta broke through with *Something Wild* (Jonathan Demme, 1986) and also co-starred in *Field of Dreams* (Phil Alden Robinson, 1989) and as Henry Hill in *GoodFellas* (Martin Scorsese, 1990).

Gary Oldman, star of *Sid and Nancy* (Alex Cox, 1986), *JFK* (Oliver Stone, 1999), *Bram Stoker's Dracula* (Francis Ford Coppola, 1992) and *The Fifth Element* (Luc Besson, 1997), is uncredited in the film in response to not being given an above the title place alongside Hopkins and Moore.

Frankie Faison has appeared in *Manhunter* as Lt Fisk and in *Silence of the Lambs* and *Hannibal* as the character of Barney. He has also been seen in *Coming to America* (John Landis, 1988) and *The Thomas Crown Affair* (John McTiernan, 1999).

MAKING IT: Michael Mann's 1986 film was austere, featuring a top-flight performance by Brian Cox. However, it was in Jonathan Demme's adaptation of the novel *Silence of the Lambs* in 1991 that the killer character chewed his way into popular culture. The massive success of Demme's graceful and compelling film surely meant that someday there would be another Lecter story.

THE SHOOT: After the dazzling success of *Gladiator* and Scott's resurgence *Hannibal* moved quickly into production with Scott at the helm and filming in Italy and America. In the week prior to shooting, a press conference was held in Italy to bang the drum about the filming soon to commence and the filming received a fair amount of publicity and media coverage.

LOCATIONS: Location shooting began in Florence in May 2000 and the production ultimately shot at around one hundred locations, including the Ponte Vecchio, Florence's oldest bridge, and the Palazzo Vecchio. The Capponi library in Florence is also a rarely filmed location. Back in America, the production shot for six days at Union Station in Washington where one of the novelties to be seen was a carousel not usually found there. Mason Verger's mansion was shot at the Biltmore Estate in Asheville, North Carolina – the location also used in *Forrest Gump* (Robert Zemeckis, 1994) and *Being There* (Hal Ashby, 1979) among others. Scott had also originally considered it for *RKO 281*. Some of the locations were apparently secured by Anthony Hopkins who also found time to cast some of the extras for the Florence scenes.

COLLABORATORS: David Mamet was playwright and screenwriter–director of films such as *The Heist* (2001), *State and Main* (2000) and *Oleanna* (1991) and screenwriter on *The Untouchables* (Brian De Palma, 1987) and *The Edge* (Lee Tamahori, 1998).

Steven Zaillian was screenwriter on *The Falcon and the Snowman* (John Schlesinger, 1985) and *Schindler's List* (Steven

Spielberg, 1993), and director on *Searching for Bobby Fischer* (1993).

Branko Lustig served as executive producer. He had worked with Scott on *Gladiator* and would go on to work on *Black Hawk Down*. Branko Lustig had produced *Schindler's List* (Steven Spielberg, 1993) and had also worked on *Sophie's Choice* (Alan J Pakula, 1982).

Pietro Scalia (**G.I. Jane** and **Gladiator**) continued his collaboration as Scott's editor; Hans Zimmer returned as composer (see **Black Rain, Thelma & Louise, White Squall** and **Gladiator**) and cinematographer John Mathieson reprised his role from *Gladiator*.

MUSIC: *Dante's Sonnet* was put to music by Zimmer and Patrick Cassidy for the opera scene. At the time of the film's release, Hans Zimmer talked about the film's Freudian beauty and the beast aspect and also that at its core *Hannibal* was 'a haunting story'.

Hannibal is a decadent and florid movie at many points. Patrick Cassidy, who composed the music for the Dante opera, conceived for the story – and in fact composed – an entire opera on that theme. *Hannibal* shares a musical reference with *Someone to Watch Over Me* – these are both movies about doomed love after all. The piece of music is 'Aria da Capo' from Bach's *Goldberg Variations*. A score that expressed both the romance and the psychosis in the story, from the melancholy piano theme, to the *Sonnet* music to the disturbing low bass, the *Hannibal* score is memorable for not being an all-out fright movie score. The Lyndhurst Orchestra provide the music.

INFLUENCES: The film's editor Pietro Scalia spoke of the influence of Renaissance poet Dante Alighieri on the adaptation. Florence was Dante's city so Scalia was compelled to think about Dante's concept of Purgatory as a place where souls are tested, just as Clarice is tested by her experience in the film. Scalia also spoke about the motif of Dante and Beatrice in *The Divine Comedy* where Dante is in love with Beatrice but nothing can happen as she is in love with another. *The Divine Comedy* expresses love as an ideal of beauty and purity, corresponding with Lecter's idealisation of Clarice.

An informing image for Scalia as he put the film together was the work of eighteenth-century painter Henry Fuseli, notably the painting *The Nightmare* featuring a sleeping woman on whose stomach squats a goblin, while in the background stands a blind horse. Fear and desire are key motifs at work in the film. Again, Scott's taste for the romantic comes through even in this decadent horror film. For Scalia the mission this time around was to find a way to push the intensity, fear factor and also the romance and beauty of the material.

The film is a very obvious indicator of Scott's career-long interest in classical idioms and motifs. Lecter's relentless precision and contained violence, his quality as a Nietzschean Superman, fits well with Roy Batty in *Blade Runner* and also the strength of Maximus and the obsessiveness of *The Duellists*.

As in all his films, Scott makes his environments into characters, using décor and architecture and place to emphasise the drama and enrich it with clues and devices. Foreground and background elements strengthen the image in their composition and lighting enhances and redefines often familiar environments. In *Hannibal*, Florence is not the city we see in countless tourist images but rather a place of cold stone and shadow.

REFERENCES: In *The Godfather* (Francis Ford Coppola, 1972), characters that are killed are all associated with oranges in the shot. In *Hannibal*, a doomed character eats an orange before encountering Hannibal.

When *Hannibal* was filming in Florence some of the locals objected as they considered the film portrayed Florence as a city of morbid thrills.

THE OPENING: A melancholy piano theme plays as the film begins and the name and title of the movie appear in blood-red handwriting, as though by Hannibal – his signature is seen later in the film. Mason Verger's frail, drawling voice is heard as the black screen fills with a rectangle that widens out to full screen image. The voice-over says, 'I don't consider psychology a science and neither did Dr Lecter.'

A flock of pigeons form to make Hannibal's face in the terrific title sequence. The pigeons disperse and the face goes suggesting Hannibal's mysterious quality, a blink-and-you'll-miss-him persona that is played up through the film.

The shots of Florence in this opening credit sequence have the quality of surveillance camera footage and distorted transmissions and they quicken the pace when they appear.

ON THE SCREEN: Throughout the film, Scott's design is to immerse us in a world of shadows and half-light thereby emphasising the uncertainty of action and murky morality of the story.

HEROES AND VILLAINS: Clarice Starling first appears asleep in the back of an FBI van prior to an operation to apprehend a black woman known for violent crime. Scott stages the action with real kinetic sense. There is a kind of grey pallor to the material. Clarice is established as a strong woman when she challenges Officer Bolton from the local police force. She is clearly in charge and the man can only resort to a snide comment in the hope of silencing her: 'You got a smart mouth, lady.' He doesn't manage. Hasn't the man seen Ridley Scott's other movies?

In the ensuing shootout, Scott mounts the tension and includes a heroic slow-motion shot of Clarice running. The other potent sequence in the image is of Clarice cleansing the dead mother's baby of blood. This washing away of blood is echoed much later in the film when Pazzi washes his head in the boar fountain in Florence.

All through the film, the tension and interplay between Clarice's tough job and fragile character is believably handled. In the wake of the shootout we see Clarice at home crying and appreciate her sadness and guilt. It puts us on her side and soon after we are rooting for her even more when we learn that she is attempting to recover her status in the male-dominated FBI.

As with Maximus in *Gladiator* and Jordan in *G.I. Jane*, Clarice moves through a corrupt world and she is a maverick figure, though not by choice. Also like Jordan, she challenges male supremacy in a very male world. Starling tells her superiors she knows there is a corrupt deal afoot between Krendler and Verger. The embodiment of this corruption is Paul Krendler. He is monstrous in a very mundane and familiar way. He is a chauvinist and homophobic; he lacks politeness. He is perfect Lecter fodder. Scott uses his affinity for the powerful glance between characters, put to great effect in *Someone to Watch Over Me* and *Blade Runner*, to suggest Krendler's creepy feel. He eyes up Clarice's legs and then taunts her by alluding to her recent lack of success at work, adding that by pursuing Lecter again she will 'get to go back on a celebrated case'. One shot of Krendler during a visit to Clarice in her office emphasises his imposing manner – by putting the camera in Clarice's position on her chair. Starling's strength of character is ultimately a threat to Krendler and he gets his just deserts. To what degree Clarice herself is corrupt by the end of the film, though, is open to debate.

Through her adventure Clarice's personal and professional lives collide in classic Scott fashion. Clarice embodies honesty and integrity: 'I resent myself for it,' she says of her failure to capture rather than kill the black woman. Starling is dedicated and focused in her mission. Hannibal's telephone conversation with Clarice, as she tries to find him, raises the classic Scott issues of code when Hannibal says, 'You serve the idea of order.' Lecter also highlights Clarice's maverick status: 'They are weak and murky and believe in nothing.'

Clarice says to Barney about Lecter, 'He's always with me. Like a bad habit.' When Clarice listens to Hannibal on the audiotapes his voice is all-consuming. This connection is amplified throughout the film, for example as we see Lecter writing to Clarice intercut with her reading the letter. And then there is the setpiece of Clarice and Hannibal talking while she tries to find him and he swoops by behind her on the carousel. He is like a dark angel, a necessary evil. He gets Clarice to join him, seducing her rather like Darkness seduces Lili in *Legend*.

The first time Hannibal is seen in the film is when Pazzi approaches him. Lecter turns, wearing his hat, and his face is half-illuminated by sunlight. He is a creature in a world of shadows, a Darkness figure. *Hannibal* is a fairy tale of innocence to experience for Clarice.

When Hannibal tells Clarice that he has 'been in a state of hibernation for some time', it is a comment that emphasises his animalistic character.

As Clarice reads Lecter's letter the images of her have a cold grey pallor and the images of Lecter are as if lit by candle. 'Don't you feel eyes moving all over your body, Clarice?' Lecter asks in the letter, tying the audience back into the surveillance footage that opens the movie and also the film's poster emphasising Lecter's one wide eye.

Pazzi is a cop who has been slightly discredited like Conklin in *Black Rain* going for that one good case.

PICTURE PERFECT: As in his other films, Scott uses intercutting to unite seemingly disparate characters in their shared obsessions. The audience see Clarice watching news coverage of her 'heading up the calamitous strikeforce'; across the country Mason Verger watches the same broadcast. Verger talks about helping Clarice 'cleanse the stigma of your recent dishonour' by which he is referring to the bloody shootout that starts the film.

Scott's sense for creating environments that become more than they are is shown in the design of Clarice's research room at the FBI where she surrounds herself with information about Lecter. The room is like a cave, lit by just a few lamps. In a way it is removed from reality. When we see Lecter writing, he is lit by candlelight in his 'cave' in Florence.

For the shot of CCTV footage showing Lecter attacking a nurse in his cell, there is the sound of an animal in the mix to add to the savagery of the good doctor's behaviour.

Scott visualises Florence with a florid eye. It is shown as a city of shadows and dark romance. Hans Zimmer talked about how he felt the film was deeply romantic and the opera sequence for which Zimmer composed the music demonstrates this and works as a way of symbolising Lecter's feelings towards Clarice.

The scene where it seems as if Lecter will attack Pazzi is creepy and funny simultaneously and demonstrates Scott's skill at building tension exhibited also in his other horror film, *Alien*: Lecter raises the slide remote as he approaches Pazzi from behind and it seems to be a knife to kill with.

LIGHTING: For director of photography John Mathieson the goal was not to overlight anything. Mathieson was especially intrigued about the possibilities of his star's forehead. In an interview with *American Cinematographer* at the time of *Hannibal*'s release he said, 'Anthony Hopkins has lines that run up either side of his forehead from his eyebrows. They look like devil lines so I had fun picking those up . . .'

For the scene where Pazzi is finally killed by Hannibal the action is lit very low key, sourced apparently from the slide projector light. Scott cannot help but play it creepy and funny.

Clarice is always lit beautifully so that at times she appears to look like a marble statue, fitting in terms of the Florence element of the film. There is a *Vanity Fair* photo from the late 1990s that alludes to the actress's classical beauty. When Clarice visits Verger, Scott amplifies the horror in a scene which really does show a beauty and a beast. As Clarice stands talking to Verger we see only the glistening of his eye. He is a monster in the shadows.

TECH TALK: Scott's regular effects house The Mill contributed digital effects to the 35 effects shots required. Keith VanderLaan's Captive Audience Productions, who created the gruesome Krendler model for the film. They have also supplied mechanical effects for films including *Bicentennial Man* (Chris Columbus, 1999), *Ali* (Michael Mann, 2001), *Monkeybone* (Henry Selick, 2001) and *A Beautiful Mind* (Ron Howard, 2001). For the infamous brain-eating scene a life-size puppet of Krendler was integrated with CGI work. Ray Liotta was filmed in position on set with a green skull-cap with tracer markers. All actors were then removed from the set and just the set was filmed (to use as a background plate). A puppet of Liotta was then shot on the set. This material was taken to The Mill whose artists digitally removed the skull cap, leaving Liotta apparently without a top to his head. The background plate of the room was then dropped in behind him and the cowbrain element was integrated into the space on top of Liotta's head. For over the shoulder shots from Lecter's point of view, Liotta was replaced by the model version of him. The final sequence is disturbing, toe curling and pitched somewhere between a laugh and a scream.

For the boars that attack Verger the production used mechanical replicas.

MOVIE TALK:

Verger: 'He comes in the guise of a mentor.'

Verger: 'He thought she was charming.'

Verger: 'Isn't it funny? You can look at my face, but you shied when I said the name of God.'

Barney: 'He preferred to eat the rude. Free range rude.'

THE BIG IDEA: When Clarice opens the envelope from Hannibal it is accompanied by the sound of wind, symbolising Lecter's primal aspect. Later in the film he stands with his face apparently split and distorted by glass and in another instance his coat swirls, accompanied by the sound of a sword slicing.

Hannibal both hunts Clarice and also protects her, knowing when he must let her go. 'You're on your own now, Clarice,' he says after the setpiece sequence around the carousel.

Hannibal is captured by Mason Verger's thugs and is netted like a trapped animal. The wild boars only add to the pervading sense of savagery. The barn to which Hannibal is taken is a shadowy place but very much an arena in which the forces of madness and civilisation confront one another.

CRITICAL CONDITION: Upon its release, many critics dismissed *Hannibal* as lacking suspense; others enjoyed the diabolical humour. Whichever, the film was massively successful.

'Ridley Scott's *Hannibal* is a carnival geek show elevated in the direction of art . . . we must give it credit for the courage of its depravity,' wrote the *Chicago Sun-Times*, and, though *Empire* felt 'it's a thriller devoid of thrills . . . character piece or thriller, love story or psychodrama, *Hannibal* confounds and dumbfounds – an inert spectacle and a frightening waste of modern cinema's juiciest villain', others disagreed: 'Ridley Scott's degenerate but devilishly well-directed work . . .' said the *Evening Standard* and 'Riveting suspense spiced with diabolical laughs and garnished with a sprig of kinky romance add up to the tastiest relish around,' agreed *Rolling Stone*.

GROSSES: The film was a smash success, matched by a media feeding frenzy upon its release. From a budget of $87 million, in North America the film grossed around $165 million.

POSTER: A very simple approach: the poster is filled with just the face of Hannibal, his one eye seemingly watching you as he grins and looms out of the shadow. There is the illusion of the image being printed on a marble surface, tying in with the Florentine location.

HOME ENTERTAINMENT: *Hannibal* is available on both VHS and DVD. As further evidence of Ridley Scott's acknowledged love of the DVD format, the DVD release of the film is packed with informative extra features. These include a feature-length commentary by Scott, five featurettes covering Development, Production, Make-Up, Music and Premiere. Also included are still photographs and trailers.

AWARDS: At the 2002 awards of the Academy of Science Fiction, Fantasy and Horror Films (USA), Hannibal was nominated for a Saturn Award in the categories of Best Actor for Anthony Hopkins, Best Actress for Julianne Moore, Best Horror Film and

Best Make-up for Greg Cannom and Wes Wofford. At the Hollywood Make-up Artists and Hair Stylists Guild Awards, the film was nominated for Best Special Make-up Effects. Meanwhile, over in Italy actor Giancarlo Giannini won the Silver Ribbon for Best Supporting Actor at the Italian Syndicate of Film Journalist Awards. The MTV Movie Awards nominated *Hannibal* in Best Kiss, Best Movie and Best Villain categories.

TRIVIA: The shot of the computer showing the FBI's Ten Most Wanted felons is for real – with the exception of Lecter. Appropriately, the film was released in Britain on 14 February 2001, Valentine's Day.

In Florence a tour guide has been made available for visitors who want to visit the places that Lecter does in the film.

ALTERNATIVE VERSIONS: When *Hannibal* is eventually broadcast for the first time on American television it will apparently be increased from 131 minutes to have a running time of four hours – Scott plans to reinstate about an hour of material cut from the cinema release. A subplot was written and filmed around the Il Motro case that Pazzi is investigating. This material was eventually left out of the final cut as it was felt to be too much story. Three endings were apparently shot. One for De Laurentiis, one for Thomas Harris and one for Ridley Scott.

GREAT SCOTT: For the most part, the film is an involving and effectively creepy piece of work, until the last twenty minutes when the horror is gratuitous and comic all at once. The film is both believable and completely over the top. While the first half is compelling, the second half descends into stupidity and becomes cartoonish. For all its flourishes and moments of interest it is not one of Scott's strongest movies, and yet he does communicate how beautiful Florence is and it is in this section of the film that the drama is at its most powerful.

As always, Scott renders tight and compelling performances from his cast, set against the outlandish events of the story. While Hopkins as Lecter and an uncredited Gary Oldman as Mason Verger play somewhat on the side of hammy, Julianne Moore pitches her performance just right as Clarice – she manages to convey her dented strength and confidence and also her resolve.

Scott's affinity for lighting faces and particularly those of women is evident all through *Hannibal*.

There is something anonymous to much of the film once it returns to America. Anthony Hopkins's Lecter portrayal seems less eerie this time and more comic. At the very least, though, *Hannibal* continued Scott's renewed winning streak and again demonstrated Scott's finesse with opening titles, encapsulating the tone of the film in a short time frame, rather like a commercial.

SCOTT FREE: 'We like Hannibal Lecter because, like a contemporary Nosferatu, he is essentially charming and seductive at the same time he's terrifying us.'

Black Hawk Down (2001)

(Colour, 143 minutes)

Producer: Jerry Bruckheimer
Associate Producers: Harry Humphries, Pat Sandston and Terry Needham
Executive Producer: Branko Lustig, Mike Stenson, Simon West and Chad Oman
Screenplay: Ken Nolan, based on the book *Black Hawk Down: A Story of Modern War* by Mark Bowden
Music: Hans Zimmer (additional music by Jeff Rona and Mel Wesson)
Cinematography: Salvomir Idziak
Editor: Pietro Scalia
Casting: Bonnie Timmerman
Production Artist: Sylvain Despretz
Special Effects Technician: Alistair Anderson
Prosthetics: Cliff Wallace
Lead Digital Artist: Paul Amer
Production Designer: Arthur Max
Art Director: Pier Luigi Basile
Costume Designers: Sonny Howarth-Sheldon, David Murphy
Make-up: Ana Bulajic Crcek
Sound Effects Editor: Christopher Assells
Visual Effects Supervisor: Neil Corbould

CAST: Josh Hartnett (*Staff Sgt Matt Eversmann*), Eric Bana (*Sgt First Class Norm 'Hoot' Hooten*), Ewan McGregor (*Specialist*

RIDLEY SCOTT Black Hawk Down

Danny Grimes), Tom Sizemore (*Lt Colonel Danny McKnight*), Sam Shepard (*Major General William Garrison*), Ewan Bremner (*Specialist Shawn Nelson*), William Fichtner (*Delta Sgt First Class Jeff Sanderson*), Charlie Hofheimer (*Ranger Corporal Jamie Smith*), Tom Hardy (*Ranger Specialist Lance Twombly*), Tom Guiry (*Ranger Staff Sgt Ed Yurek*), Jason Isaacs (*Ranger Captain Steele*), Ron Eldard (*Chief Warrant Officer Mike Durant*), Orlando Bloom (*Ranger Pvt First Class Todd Blackburn*), Hugh Dancy (*Ranger Sgt First Class Kurt Schmidt*), Johnny Strong (*Delta Sgt First Class Randy Shughart*), Gregory Sporleder (*Ranger Sgt Scott Galentine*), Brian van Holt (*Ranger Staff Sgt Cliff Strencher*), Jeremy Piven (*Chief Warrant Officer Cliff Walcott*), George Harris (*Atto*), Abdibashir Mohamed Hersi (*Somalian Spy*)

BUDGET: $95 million

MPAA: R

BBFC: 18

TAG LINE: Leave no man behind

SUMMARY: Somalia, 1993, 300,000 Somalians are dead at the hands of warlord Mohammed Adid; the United Nations are engaged in peacekeeping operations and the American military have a presence there too.

Intelligence has been gathered about the hideaway location of the lieutenants of two wanted warlords and the American military have hatched a plan of attack to go in and extract the wanted men. As the operation prepares, Eversmann is upgraded to Sergeant by Captain Steele who emphasises the gravity of the job.

In Mogadishu, a contact locates and identifies the hideout for Adid and his men and the call to action is given in operation Irene. The date is 3 October 1993.

The mission is planned to last about thirty minutes. The American Rangers are fired up and confident in the ease of the mission. But flying into Mogadishu things begin to go wrong. One soldier falls from a Black Hawk helicopter as others rope in on to the streets. The Somalian militia are ready and well armed and an all-out skirmish commences which takes a lot of American casualties. Everything gets worse when a Black Hawk is knocked out of the sky. The Rangers on board hole up in the wreckage as Somalian crowds rush in.

On the ground, troops engage in gunfire and a convoy of American vehicles closes in. The unit gets split up and back at base Major General William Garrison realises that the situation is getting out of control and orders the men to be pulled out of the battle before they are fighting the whole city. A second Black Hawk is downed soon after and its pilot, Durrant, holes up in a bombed-out building. He is eventually attacked by Somalians and taken to Adid's camp where he is held for eleven days. Desk jockey Grimes and supercool Sanderson find themselves working together to get to safety while Nelson and Twombly, who had been charged with holding a position on the street, suddenly realise that the convoy of Humvee jeeps is not going to arrive to pick them up any time soon. They make a run across town to get to one of the fallen helicopters.

With his breakaway unit, Eversmann holds a position in a building and his crisis moment comes when he has to help clamp a ruptured femoral artery in one of the other soldiers. The battle continues and eventually night falls. Garrison sends in more troops to extract the American soldiers. Amidst the ruins of the city a massive rescue mission is undertaken led by Colonel Danny McKnight. The soldiers are all rescued. As they exit the city, they are waved at and cheered by those Somalians opposed to Adid's reign.

The soldiers return to the American base at the former Pakistani Stadium. Some are tended in the makeshift hospital while others go into the city to retrieve the last remaining troops. The nineteen American coffins are taken on board a plane to be flown home; many more Somalians died.

THE CONCEPT: Jerry Bruckheimer bought the rights to Mark Bowden's source book, *Black Hawk Down: A Story of Modern War*, and Bowden made a first pass at a draft of the screenplay. Then a new writer Ken Nolan was brought in, having had contact with Bruckheimer's offices previously. Nolan had written and sold several unproduced screenplays and had been developing material. *Black Hawk Down* marked his first credit. His first task was to write a treatment of his version of the Bowden's book. Nolan made three drafts of this at sixty pages each time out. He then wrote a draft screenplay.

Once Scott was involved, he brought in screenwriter Steven Zaillian to do an uncredited polish of Nolan's material, specifically on the dialogue. Stephen Gaghan, who had written the screenplay for *Traffic* (Steven Soderbergh, 2000), also had some involvement and Sam Shepard contributed many of his own lines. Screenwriter Eric Roth came in to focus some of the dialogue between Hoot and Eversmann at the end of the film.

INFLUENCES: The film's source is the book by *Philadelphia Enquirer* writer Mark Bowden, *Black Hawk Down: A Story of Modern War*, itself based on the testimonies of those soldiers who were involved in the mission. Bowden also went to Somalia to obtain eyewitness accounts of the battle.

Ridley Scott's film is centred around the unforeseen chaos that was the American intervention in Somalia in late 1993. One hundred and twenty-three soldiers were sent in to capture two top lieutenants of a renegade Somalian warlord. American military intelligence planned it as a manoeuvre that would last about thirty minutes. Instead, the operation became an eighteen-hour all-out battle between American soldiers and guerrillas on the streets of Mogadishu. Scott's film plunges the audience into the battle, with little emphasis on administration or context.

At the time of the film's release, Scott commented that the rules and processes of combat were of real interest to him. Many of his other films (*The Duellists*, *Black Rain* and *White Squall* particularly) examine the dramatic implications of this same issue. This was the first all-out war film Scott had made and therefore the most obvious expression of the military themes and motifs he had built into films like *White Squall*, *G.I. Jane* and *Gladiator*. For producer Jerry Bruckheimer the film was his second big war story after the sudsy and expansive *Pearl Harbor* (Michael Bay, 2001). *Black Hawk Down* is a very different kind of war film, essentially a two-and-a-half-hour, almost real-time dramatisation of a moment in an oft-forgotten US military operation in 1993.

In talking about the film, Scott would sometimes refer to the photographs taken by James Nacthwey of Somalia as an influence, in particular his collection of images titled *Inferno*.

Black Hawk Down has a washed-out look to it for its battle sequences. Polish cinematographer Slawomir Idziak gives the images clarity and chaos in equal measure.

CASTING: Billy Bob Thornton and Gary Sinise had both been considered for the role of General William Garrison. Sam Shepard, who eventually got the role, brings an association of the toughness and can-do masculinity associated with the American West. This is based on several movies he has appeared in through his long and distinguished career, none more so than *The Right Stuff* (Philip Kaufman, 1983).

Of the bigger name performers, Tom Sizemore was one of the first actors to sign on board the project and his appearance in the film is similar to his role in *Saving Private Ryan* (Steven Spielberg, 1998). He can also be seen in *Born on the Fourth of July* (Oliver Stone, 1989), *Point Break* (Kathryn Bigelow, 1991) and *Natural Born Killers* (Oliver Stone, 1994).

William Fichtner has also been seen in *Strange Days* (Kathryn Bigelow, 1995), *Armageddon* (Michael Bay, 1998), *The Perfect Storm* (Wolfgang Petersen, 2000) and *Pearl Harbor* (Michael Bay, 2001).

In a film starring men, the notably female presence is that of Giannina Facio, as the wife of a ranger – the audience sees her listening to an answerphone message from him. Facio had portrayed Maximus's wife in the flashback sequences in *Gladiator*.

Like *White Squall*, *Black Hawk Down* is an ensemble piece featuring some of the biggest younger names in the movie star game confirming once again Scott's sure eye for casting rising stars, namely Ewan McGregor, who had appeared in *Trainspotting* (Danny Boyle, 1996), *Star Wars: Episode I – The Phantom Menace* (George Lucas, 1999) and *Moulin Rouge* (Baz Luhrmann, 2001), and who was apparently keen to be in a film where he ran around with a gun. Josh Hartnett had been seen in the Bruckheimer-produced *Pearl Harbor* (Michael Bay, 2001), and Eric Bana has gone on to star as *The Hulk* in the film directed by Ang Lee (2003).

MAKING IT: It's a little-known piece of Ridley Scott's career but he and Hollywood producer Jerry Bruckheimer had worked together once before, thirty years before *Black Hawk Down*: they made a tyre commercial together. Over the years, Bruckheimer had tried to get Scott on board one of his productions but Scott had always been busy on some other film.

For Ken Nolan the biggest challenge was in condensing the range of storylines that would then be given added clarity and organisation by Scott. For Nolan, the fact that the soldiers were just ordinary guys was compelling and in order to give audiences some sense of who they would be following through the ensuing chaos, where it can be difficult to distinguish soldiers, he conceived all of the barrack and pre-mission scenes at the American base. In the seven days prior to filming, Nolan and Scott went through the material one last time and then Nolan stayed on location for the four-month shoot to adjust and revise the screenplay and work in suggestions from the actors.

THE SHOOT: The film was shot in early 2001, beginning on 3 March and wrapped in early July.

On the shoot, Scott used multiple cameras to cover the action which meant the film had cameras running simultaneously, allowing him to go for a documentary look. Given Scott's taste for this kind of approach, *Black Hawk Down* is a real celebration of this style.

For the actors there was an intensity to the shoot – as much of the filming centred on the re-creation of the battle. The set was literally something of a war zone that apparently had actors quite spooked by the rounds of gunfire going off. Of the resulting footage, Scott has said that 'there should be a confusion'.

COLLABORATORS: As on *G.I. Jane*, *Gladiator* and *Hannibal*, Scott's editor was Pietro Scalia and the production designer was Arthur Max; as on many previous films Scott's composer was Hans Zimmer (see **Black Rain**). Sound design editor, Jon Title, returned, having previously also worked on *Gladiator* and *Hannibal*.

On location in Morocco, editor Pietro Scalia had a mini edit suite in Rabat, comprised of three Avid edit suites and in another room a G4 to render bare bones FX. Jon Title to whom Scalia would hand over scenes as they were being cut, set about cleaning up the audio on location. This meant that Scott and Scalia would know what lines would be needed as there was an impending actors' strike which might have thrown recording and looping dialogue later in the year.

The film marked Scott's first collaboration with Polish director of photography Slawomir Idziak who had previously worked with the late, great Krzystof Kieslowski on the landmark Polish TV series *Dekalog* (1988) and then on *The Double Life of Veronique*

(Kryzstof Kieslowski, 1991) and *Three Colours Blue* (Kryzstof Kieslowski, 1993). In Hollywood he has worked on *Proof of Life* (Taylor Hackford, 2000).

MUSIC: The score for *Black Hawk Down* confidently combines east African rhythms and sounds with a more conventional synthesiser approach to suggest the collision of cultures shown in the film.

For editor Pietro Scalia, the vocals of Senegalese singer Baaba Maal serve as 'an unseen observer, who represents more of the humanity of the silent Somalis'.

Yes, that is a Stevie Ray Vaughan cover of Jimi Hendrix's 'Voodoo Chile (Slight Return)' as the Rangers head out for Mogadishu.

For the music, Hans Zimmer supplies an almost constant low-end hum which is utterly sinister. At key points Lisa Gerrard's mournful vocals (see **Gladiator**) come in and, at other moments, a mournful piano plays. For the film's penultimate scene of Eversmann talking to the dead body of Ruiz, the music recalls that from the end of *Gladiator*, indeed the whole tone of this scene recalls Juba burying the little figures in the dirt. It is both mournful and celebratory.

THE OPENING: *Black Hawk Down* opens with an eerie sound and the Plato quote 'Only the dead know the end of war.' In keeping with Scott's previous images of apocalypse the film's 'prologue' sequences establish the Somalian dead against a desert backdrop that looks like the end of the world. The camera tracks slowly alongside the corpses and a grey pallor washes over the images. There is a sense of mourning and also of savagery. A series of on-screen text passages establish the fundamentals of the Somalian situation as of early 1993.

ON THE SCREEN: With *Black Hawk Down*, Scott reaffirmed his skills as a director at ease in all genres. *Black Hawk Down* takes the military codes explicitly played out in *G.I. Jane* and alluded to in many other of his films and uses that as the basis for this dramatic version of a real event. Or rather of a moment during a real event. *Black Hawk Down* was well received for immersing its audience in, and giving them some sense of, the chaos and carnage. It is perhaps Scott's most constant and consistently visceral film to date.

Numerous interweaving narratives tell the story, the first time Scott has run this approach. One soldier falls from their helicopter; another leads a team; another is an administrator thrown into fighting. To help the audience and the characters of the military intelligence follow the chaos an aerial camera lays out the geography of the skirmish. In effect, the American soldiers are cornered by their enemy just like the crew of the *Nostromo* were cornered by their enemy in *Alien*.

Tom Sizemore is the experienced and wise older soldier; William Fichtner's character is the model soldier. In this film, the soldiers are not so much deeply complicated characters but instead identifiable types. The film uses dramatic shorthand to make us familiar with each key character so that we can empathise with them during the battle. That said, Scott wants us to feel like we are in the battle zone where only action matters. There is not time to pause and take stock.

Scott captures the might of the out-of-control helicopters as they swoop and spin to the ground. The film follows innocents in a dangerous world through which they must struggle. Rather like other highly visual directors, Scott likes to anthropomorphise inanimate objects. To help us identify the number of soldiers, who all look the same in their uniforms, Scott breaks with fact and has the soldiers' names written on their helmets.

In terms of Ridley Scott's cinema the most important pieces of text here are not so much descriptive but emotional so that we read of 'famine on a biblical scale' and a description of Adid's tyranny: 'Hunger is his weapon'. This sequence then cuts to images of an American helicopter flying over the Mogadishu area where chaos reigns at a food distribution centre. Scott immediately establishes the youthfulness of the soldiers through close-ups; there is also the sense early on that the situation is not really that serious.

As the first half hour of the film progresses, Scott plays up this naïvety and also through many close-ups makes us appreciate just how young so many soldiers are. The viewers are soon introduced to Sam Shepard's granite-faced General Garrison. Scott's casting here does half the job of communicating the man's strength and resolve. Framed with golden sunlight on his face, Garrison certainly looks heroic, thereby amplifying the tragedy of his command later in the film. His classic hero quality comes out early on when he says of Adid and the mission, 'We're not leaving here until we find him.'

The film creates its characters through the action rather than through dialogue. For Josh Hartnett, one of the most important parts of the film is that the audience find out about each character during the battle; that is where their qualities are displayed, rather than at any earlier point in the film. As such this is a highly cinematic film, breaking away a little from conventional dramatics and the establishment of characters through dialogue.

Scott immerses us in the battle so intensely that the audience feels exhausted by the end.

HEROES AND VILLAINS: Garrison is a tough character who has a fatherly side too, evidenced in his farewell to the troops as they head off for Mogadishu. In this he shares something of the same qualities as Sheldon in *White Squall* and like him is a man who has to deal with events getting out of his control.

The character of Eversmann is the film's moral focus in terms of the Americans and he is the true Scott hero of this film. Early on he is described as 'a bit of an idealist'. He is particularly like Chuck Gieg in *White Squall*, recognised as having to hold everyone together. In being promoted to lead a unit his situtation mirrors Jordan O'Neill's at the end of *G.I. Jane*. Eversmann is keen on control and there is a stillness to Josh Hartnett's performance. Towards the end of the battle, holed up in a bombed-out building with some of his men, Eversmann is evidently anxious about the losses. His fellow soldier Hoot gives him a pep talk to keep him strong.

Amid all the gunfire, Scott even finds a place to frame some tension between Jason Isaacs (Steele) and William Fichtner's laidback soldier (Sanderson) about professionalism. Their one heated exchange between bullets recalls Ripley and Ash way back on the *Nostromo*. Steele says, 'You let me do my job, I'll let you do yours.'

To some degree the audience's representative on screen is desk jockey Grimes (Ewan McGregor) who has not been involved in action before. As the American soldiers head out for Mogadishu it is through the eyes of Grimes that we get acquainted with the feel of a mission and the grunt humour that fills the film. We share his unease and anticipation.

PICTURE PERFECT: Scott cannot help but add his flourish to this truly gritty, down and dirty story. His use of colour filters has a symbolic aspect that fits with the story's use of symbolic characters. To enhance the drama, Scott focused the film on a crossroads where the Rangers get caught in crossfire over a couple of hours.

For the scenes at the American base there is bright sunlight, contrasting with the heat, dust and shadow of the Mogadishu streets where the viewer sees the militia gathering their arms. Scott gives us a sense of the network of spies and intelligence gathering at work and the fear involved. He also threads information along so that the audience is beginning to wonder early on why a man marks an X on the roof of his car.

Scott maintains our sense of the geography of the battle. He often keeps a building called the Olympic in shot and in intercutting with Garrison overseeing the mission we are able to see aerial footage of the operation and maps marking out the plan which rapidly fails.

Scott uses slow motion to amplify tension, such as a trooper rushing across a bombed-out street. He also uses freeze frame for a few moments such as when a hand is blown off or when Grimes is blown to the ground. The camera then crashes into his one open eye beneath the dirt and he is awake and alive.

As with *Saving Private Ryan* (Steven Spielberg, 1998), *Born on the Fourth of July* (Oliver Stone, 1989) and *Full Metal Jacket* (Stanley Kubrick, 1987), there is a throwaway feeling to the violence and horror that is recreated, suggesting the way in which there must be no time to think too much during battle. Unlike *Saving Private Ryan* there is no sense of a guiding hand ensuring the soldiers' surival. It is purely their own efforts and teamwork that saves the day.

Scott captures the eeriness of the empty streets and the sense of threat lurking everywhere. Amid the sound and fury he finds chances to play it quieter such as when the one trooper, hiding from a Somali fighter, hides out in a room where a mother and her children huddle. The Ranger gestures for them to remain quiet, which they do. He waves to the kids as he heads back out and they wave back.

Grimes and Sanderson take a quiet moment to drink some coffee as the battle experiences a lull. Finally, Grimes is able to prove his real worth in the field – making a good drink. The respite is short lived.

For the final night-time battle Scott lends the action a great theatricality which contrasts with the far more reportage-like frenzy of the majority of the film. At night, the darkness comes alive with gunfire, explosions and smoke that is lit with green and blue light. The theatre of war is alive and well in *Black Hawk Down*.

SOUND: In contrast to the raging noise of the battle, Scott plays up the silence and respite at the end of the film in a surreal way. As Eversmann returns to the relative safety of the Pakistani Stadium, he and his men are greeted by men delicately carrying silver trays with glasses of water like waiters.

As the film develops, there are opportunities for humour, notably around Nelson and his loss of hearing.

Prior to the unit heading into Mogadishu one of the troops is shown making a call home to his wife in America and the viewer is shown the family home as his answerphone message is heard. The home is empty and ghostlike as the curtains flutter which foreshadows the deaths that will follow. This scene humanises the Rangers further, reminding the audience of the lives they have left behind and might well sacrifice.

TECH TALK: The live action footage certainly recalls that of *Saving Private Ryan*, but in a way feels more vivid because of the amount of real war-zone footage the audience have seen. Given Scott's liking for certain documentary-feel elements in parts of all his films, *Black Hawk Down* allows him to go into full flight with this approach.

Small digital adjustments, primarily through the use of digital matte paintings, were made to the Sale location in order to expand the number of buildings and also to distress the buildings that were filmed in and around. Production designer Arthur Max created Mogadishu in Morocco where Scott had filmed *Gladiator*. The streets were realised in Sale and lots of smoke was used to enhance the believability of sets.

A computer animation system was used to create fake smoke clouds to thicken and expand what had been achieved practically. There were many practical smoke effects on the location shoot. The effects for the film were provided by Asylum FX in LA and The Mill. One restriction the American military made on the shoot was that the production was not allowed to attach smoke canisters or anything else to the helicopters (supplied by the military) as a safety precaution and so any shot in which a helicopter trails smoke had that element added in post-production. Certain shots featured computer-generated helicopters and crew.

At The Mill, animatics of helicopters crashing were created and then sent to the editor who incorporated them into his picture cut for references. The Mill then begain detailed animation work. Scott had seen research footage of a helicopter crashing and particularly liked the way it appeared reluctant to die, rather like a huge beast.

For the film's opening scene Scott shot 1,000 extras but on screen wanted it to look like 8,000 so the crowd was digitally expanded. To enhance the believability of this illusion still photos of extras' faces were mapped on to fake figures for variety. Walk and run cycles (computer animation programmes simulating movement that run over perhaps twenty seconds in a loop) were blended to avoid uniformity and give some sense of the randomness that defines real.

Prior to filming the actors attended some training sessions in how to fire weapons and some time was spent at Fort Benning in Georgia. Stunt co-ordinator Phil Neilson was himself a Force Recon Marine and many of the film's military stunts were executed by Rangers. For the scene where Danny Grimes is knocked across the street by a missile, Ewan McGregor did the stunt himself.

MOVIE TALK:

Hoot: 'You can't control who gets hit – it's just war.'

A Somalian (to Garrison): 'This isn't the KO Corral.'

Danny Grimes: 'I made *coffee* through Desert Storm.'

THE BIG IDEA: Fidelity to the unit in the widest, least military sense runs all the way through the film, as it does through so many of the director's films, especially *The Duellists*, *Alien*, *White Squall*, *G.I. Jane* and *Gladiator*. Garrison repeatedly talks about leaving nobody behind and there is a fatherly quality to him. Like so many war stories, *Black Hawk Down* is really about peace as the Plato quote upfront (see **THE OPENING**) suggests. The film also acknowledges a certain amount of hubris and nemesis on the part of the American operation – the thought that it would take thirty minutes to extract the warlords. A humorous scene shows the Rangers quipping about not needing to take certain pieces of kit such as bottled water.

Details suffuse the film, for example the soldiers taping the name of their blood type to their boot. Jerry Bruckheimer described the film as being '. . . about the bravery, courage, honour and commitment . . . after 9/11 it becomes more important because you need these young men to go out there and protect our shores'.

Ridley Scott's familiar Nietzschean element of the Superman and survival of the fittest plays a part in this film. More than any other Scott film, *Black Hawk Down* celebrates professionalism. The film has such a strong sense of putting the audience in an almost real-time apocalypse. Building on *G.I. Jane*, *Gladiator* and *White Squall*, *Black Hawk Down* affirms group action and the tightness of the interdependent unit. The film shows how the group is formed and they function as one.

The youth of the soldiers emphasises the film's dark fairy-tale quality as the soldiers go from innocence to experience through the course of the film, finally emerging with a sense of what is important. When Hoot heads back to bring out the last men remaining in Mogadishu Eversmann cannot believe it so Hoot sums it up for him, and for us, saying, 'It's about the man next to you. And that's it.' The film comes full circle, all the way back to the tag line, Leave No Man Behind.

RELEASE: Initially the plan had been to release *Black Hawk Down* in early 2002. However, a degree of understandable patriotic fervour in America in autumn 2001 – there was a huge surge of American national pride welling up in the aftermath of the terrorist attack on New York on 11 September 2001 – prompted the film to be released a little earlier. Also, by being released prior to the end of 2001 (just) the film qualified for Oscar consideration.

CRITICAL CONDITION: Some critics felt the film was simply a two-and-a-half-hour battle sequence with no obvious character work or any real effort to give a sense of the political. Scott is working in a film system that always makes the political personal. But in a battle where everybody is masked, how easy is it to differentiate between one soldier and another? This film immerses you in some sense of the chaos of a skirmish. It is a pure film, sound and vision, putting the audience right in the middle of the action in a vérité way and challenging them to just try and keep up. Terminology and 'slang' is simply presented but not explained.

The key complaint about the film was its failure to humanise the Somalians portrayed in the film. Certainly we see them marauding or killing, but there are quiet occasions where the film emphasises their loss, notably towards the end of the film when on their way home the Rangers watch an old man carrying a dead child in his arms. With the capture of Durant the film sketches out some sense of the issues the Somalians had with the Americans.

For others it was nothing less than a piece of American propaganda, the second such produced by Jerry Bruckheimer in 2001. In 2000, a similarly plotted film – *Rules of Engagement*, directed by William Friedkin and starring Tommy Lee Jones and Samuel L Jackson – was released and, much closer to the release of *Black Hawk Down*, was the based-on-fact film *Behind Enemy Lines* (John Moore, 2001), about an American soldier who had to escape from the Bosnian war zone.

Perhaps the biggest criticism the film faced was that it did not define or acknowledge the wider political and cultural aspect. For some, the key criticism was that the film had too much John Wayne American swagger to it.

For some the film was an all-out immersion in the chaos and carnage of a military skirmish. Reservations expressed were that the battle was incoherent and that overall *Black Hawk Down* was overly patriotic and seemingly pointless. The point of the film is that it surrounds you in an experience. The film is very much about the American soldiers' experience and courage in a situation that, over time, has been portrayed as a failure of military intelligence.

The film recalls *The Duellists* in its use of an historical wartime setting to explore a single theme. There was also some reservation about excluding any kind of reference to dead American soldiers being hauled through the streets of Mogadishu but Scott argued that it did not need to be shown as it occurred outside the timeframe of the events portrayed in the movie. Such an image would have acknowledged American fatalities and at the time of the film's release the American audience were understandably seeking images that would empower their national pride.

Despite all this, reviews for *Black Hawk Down* were generally fairly complimentary: '[Scott's film] is a triumph of pure filmmaking, a pitiless, unrelenting, no excuses war movie so thoroughly convincing it's frequently difficult to believe it is a staged re-creation' (*LA Times*); 'Scott keeps things disorientating yet understandable . . .' (*Total Film*); 'Ridley Scott provides us with a pure war movie, remarkable in some ways for the severity – even asceticism – of its utter concentration on deafening and relentless action. There is no backstory for anyone and an eerie absence of political context' (*Guardian*); 'one of the most convincing, realistic combat movies I've ever seen' (*Observer*); 'Ridley Scott's achievement is to render [chaos] comprehensible to the audience' (*Chicago Sun-Times*); 'Scott abandons a black and white stance for an exposé of the unilateral tragedy of war . . . a barrage of uneasily believable horrors. Ambitious, sumptuously framed and frenetic . . .' (*Empire*); 'No war movie I have ever seen so vividly shows battle from differing perspectives' (*USA Today*) and 'Like Mr Scott's *G.I. Jane* but this time with an all-boy cast' (*New York Times*). However some were less positive: 'an endless battle scene in search of a movie' (*Salon.com*); and an action movie dressed up like an art film' (*PopMatters.com*).

GROSSES: The film was very successful, especially in America. In the US it brought in $29 million in its opening weekend, and grossed around $108 million in total in America.

POSTER: The film's teaser poster was like a snapshot caught in blurred freeze frame of American troops running. It recalled a Robert Capa photo from the Normandy landings of World War II, albeit with a more contemporary feel. Capa's blurry and intense photographs of the Normandy beach landings inform, to some degree, the visualisation of the whole battle in *Black Hawk Down*; they were also a similar source of inspiration for *Saving Private Ryan* (Steven Spielberg, 1998).

The release poster featured Josh Hartnett, his rifle across him, sitting in the doorway of a Black Hawk helicopter looking muted. The poster, like the film, has a sandy patina.

HOME ENTERTAINMENT: The film is available on VHS, and on DVD Regions 1 and 2. The DVD extras are production notes, trailer, an on the set short documentary and scene access.

AWARDS: The film was widely recognised as an awards contender. At the American Film Institute Awards in 2002 it was nominated for Director of the Year and also gained a nomination in the category of Movie of the Year.

At the Directors Guild of America awards Ridley Scott was nominated for the DGA Award for Outstanding Directorial Achievement in Motion Pictures. At the Oscars the film was nominated for Best Director.

The film garnered many other nominations, notably from the American Film Insititute who nominated it for AFI Cinematographer of the Year, Director of the Year, Editor of the Year, Movie of the Year and Production Design of the Year. At the Academy of Science Fiction, Fantasy and Horror Awards, the film was nominated for a Saturn Award in the category of Best Action/Adventure/Thriller category. The American Cinema Editors Awards awarded Pietro Scalia Best Edited Feature. The film was nominated for BAFTA awards in Best Cinematogrpahy, Best Editing and Best Sound.

TRIVIA: Eversmann was 26, whereas Josh Hartnett was 23 when he made the film; the average age of the soldiers under Eversmann's lead was 19. In the film, Hoot is to Eversmann what Conklin is to Vincent in *Black Rain*, an older, wiser character.

In something of a first, the American Department of Defense sent military support to the production, the first time this had been done for an American movie shot outside America.

In *Black Hawk Down* all Black Hawk and Little Bird vehicles were from the 160th Special Operations Aviation Regiment and most of the pilots involved in piloting them for the movie had done the job for real in Somalia in 1993. Many of the Rangers on screen are indeed real Rangers. In *Black Hawk Down*, real-life army pilot Keith Jones re-enacts the real-life rescue of trooper Daniel Busch. For the photograph held by an imperilled soldier, Durant, the prop department had failed to provide one and so Eric Bana's wife and child stepped in front of a stills camera at the location.

Disney would not agree to distribute the film because of its R rating and so Joe Roth – one-time Disney studio chairman – agreed to distribute it under his Revolution banner.

At one point part of the text at the end of the film informed the audience that some of the soldiers engaged in Mogadishu were by late 2001 engaged on the post-11 September campaign in Afghanistan. Test-screening audiences had mixed feelings about this and so the text was cut.

GREAT SCOTT: Alongside *The Duellists*, *Alien*, *Blade Runner*, *Legend*, *Someone to Watch Over Me*, *Thelma & Louise* and *Gladiator*, *Black Hawk Down* is the most recent Scott film that could be added to a Desert Island Flicks list for this director. The film combines a reportage aesthetic stunningly with fleeting moments of conventional movie heroism. Beneath the pyrotechnics there is a warm sympathy for the young men under fire – it is as if Scott has taken the spirit of the boys from the *Albatross* of *White Squall* and transplanted it to Somalia. There is something very appropriate about the film's concentration on a particular moment in the battle and it builds on the work done by Oliver Stone and Steven Spielberg in their war movie efforts. Despite what some critics may have said, the viewer does feel for the soldiers as they negotiate the crossfire. In the film's opening sequence at the military base Scott works hard to introduce us to the main characters and, most importantly, his emphasis is on the youthfulness of the soldiers.

Black Hawk Down received mixed reviews. Many cautioned that it lacked a political context – in film magazine *Sight and Sound*, Philip Strick commented that 'the film is inclined either to simplify or to omit altogether . . .' – and others acclaimed its more inherently cinematic qualities (see **CRITICAL CONDITION**). *Black Hawk Down*, however, is one of Ridley Scott's best films and perhaps the best film of the three (*Gladiator* and *Hannibal* are the other two) that have marked his resurgence. Scott's war movie is deeply cinematic with its emphasis on motion, sound and atmosphere. Complaints about not being able to identify characters are unjust. This is pure cinema that is totally immersive. It is not classical drama and yet Scott skilfully establishes the characters of all these soldiers, notably when they are in the mess at their base. Kinetics and a sense of environment are the key stylistic elements.

SCOTT FREE: 'It's all about the men. First of all, this is closure for those who were at it because they were withdrawn so fast. I showed this film in four military bases . . . It was closure for them.'

'It's as near to the edge of a documentary as I could make it.'

'. . . the idea of a pocket war which was meant to take 39 minutes, but developed into a 22-hour battle, fascinated me.'

'If you're left with questions at the end of it, that's good.'

Top Shots

All of the sequences discussed below are emblematic of Ridley Scott's best work as a director. Any director whose cinematic vision endures will have, in their body of work, scenes – or better still sequences – where their genius at fusing performance, composition, sound and editing will shine through and convey the essence of a given movie. Kubrick does it, Lynch does, Burton does it, Spielberg does it, Hitchcock does it. So too does Ridley Scott.

This section takes a closer, appreciative look, at examples of key sequences across his films that represent his finest moments. Think of these sequences as the heart of the film. Or maybe think of them simply as a greatest hits list – they are the sequences that sum up the film in a 'sound and image' bite.

What all of these sequences have in common is a fitting emphasis on visual atmosphere rather than dialogue. In keeping with Scott's affinity for fairy-tale forms, disguised as cities, future worlds and battlefields to name a few variations, most of these sequences play up that sense of characters lost and trying to find their way out of a given, threatening forest.

This section is a chance to take a closer look at how Ridley Scott applies his film craft in the very best examples of his work. These sequences demonstrate the cumulative effect of a sequence of shots; the psychological impact of the way a shot is framed is rarely an accident and Ridley Scott has always been quick to remind audiences that a film is not just the human interest on screen but also where they are placed and how they are framed and lit.

THE DUELLISTS: the sequence where D'Hubert duels with Feraud on horseback

This sequence marks something of a climax for the story and certainly a defining moment for both main characters. It is the one and only duel that they fight on horseback. A wideshot starts the sequence – it is the same shot that features on the VHS video cover image – and D'Hubert rides in down the slope of a vineyard. There is then a cut to soldiers in a wood eating breakfast around

223

tables. It is a very elegant set-up. It also looks incredibly cold – like *The Lion in the Winter* (Anthony Harvey, 1968), *The Duellists* really does feel cold as you watch it. The camera pans right to left as D'Hubert trots by and then moves faster into the woods. Grey skies brood.

The scene then cuts to a shot of D'Hubert on his horse and there is a slight zoom in to intensify D'Hubert's sense of menace as Howard Blake's score pounds and Feraud is shown riding in. A close-up reveals D'Hubert's hand furiously shaking with nerves as he holds on to the reins and then he pulls his sword. The music slides and skitters atonally, suggesting the generally unpleasant nature of the event at hand.

Two cuts show Feraud and then D'Hubert kissing the hilt of their swords. The camera again zooms in slowly on D'Hubert in profile as his upper lip quivers. The two men then ride towards one another in alternating wide shots. Their charge is intercut and intensified by several flash images from D'Hubert's memory of Feraud at his most ferocious in the three previous duels. The intensity builds with three more flash images, this time of Laura, smiling, laughing and finally saying, 'Kill.' The sequence is an explosion of simply built energy and anxiety.

There is a shot of Feraud's hat falling to the ground. The horseback duel is over, in a flash. A cut to D'Hubert shows him pulling up and then there is a quick cut showing the treetops against the sky, communicating a sense of disorientation. The charged music drops out and there is blood being wiped from D'Hubert's sword, just as he wiped lipstick from it earlier in the film. A close up of Feraud shows his head bloody and his expression registering anger and shock. This is intercut with an image of D'Hubert continuing to ride away from the scene of the duel and a close-up of him sheathing his sword. D'Hubert then rides towards camera and a cut reveals a cart stacked with hay. D'Hubert vaults his horse over the bales and the music rises victoriously.

D'Hubert has finally defeated his nemesis and in the process probably slayed a few demons too.

ALIEN: this sequence occurs late in the film, prior to Ripley's final confrontation with the alien

With the demise of the rest of the *Nostromo* crew, Ripley finds herself all alone and anxious to escape in the shuttle ship. To enhance the terror and believability, Scott eschews too much use of Jerry Goldsmith's threatening music. Instead, there is a reliance on a sparse range of sounds, particularly Ripley's almost feral breathing; backing her anxious escape effort is the sound of the emergency siren.

As Ripley commences the detonation protocol, Scott delights in detailing the process in almost real time. A series of extreme close-ups of Ripley's hands opening panels and pulling levers enhances the intensity of the moment – these are vital gestures and the detail that so much marks all of Scott's filmmaking is evident in the beads of sweat on Ripley's knuckles. There is something highly believable about the readout of the computer protocol. (Interestingly, Dan O'Bannon, who designed the protocol, also designed the readouts on the screens of the X-Wing Fighters in *Star Wars: A New Hope* [George Lucas, 1977].) Enhancing the sympathy we feel for Ripley is her evident fragility as she does all she can to restrain her tears. Her face grimaces with pain and terror and steam rises apocalyptically in the background behind her.

The sequence then shifts from elegant and intense close-ups to handheld camera work as Ripley enters frame from the left into a menacing corridor; steam bellows in the foreground and the camera hurls forward. This initial phase of Ripley running is then intercut with a slow and menacing zoom in on the detonation device as the countdown continues. Ripley looks ever more primal, her hair loose and sweaty as half her face is lit by orange light and the other side by blue light. This fire and ice look is a scheme used by more recent directors such as Michael Bay (*Armageddon*, 1998).

With Ripley in the corridor, the angle shifts and the camera tracks ahead of her as she runs; still there is no music, only the breathing of the now almost childlike Ripley. A strobe lighting effect kicks in as Ripley rounds a corner and leans against a wall, her face becoming to some degree frightening in itself. Suddenly Goldsmith's score rises and there is a cut to a shot of the alien just a step or two away from Ripley as its mouth looms into view around the corner. Goldsmith's insistent music drives the action along while the camera tracks smoothly behind Ripley as she flees the alien. With just one minute before the ship detonates a claxon wails and the sound and visuals combine to create a war-zone effect, which Scott would take to an operatic extreme at the close of *Black Hawk Down* (2002).

From the claustrophobia of the tunnel chase, Scott cuts to a super-wide shot of the *Nostromo* exterior and there, in the centre of the frame, is a window and Ripley's tiny figure moving by, further emphasising her loneliness. Back inside, Ripley closes off the detonation system and screams when she realises she has not been able to override it. She wails at Mother (the computer controlling the ship) like a helpless child let down by a parent.

Ripley leaves the room and there is a cut to her re-entering the darkest recesses of the ship. She is introduced through a close-up on her hands and face as she rises up from a portal. The closeness of the camera primes us for a possible immediate scare (James Cameron in *Aliens* does use this kind of close-up for that reason when one of the grunts checks out an alien detected above them in a ceiling vent) but the film then cuts to a wide shot to reveal Ripley armed with the incinerator gun. There is no music again, and an overriding vérité sense dominates the terror. There is an occasional point of view shot that momentarily makes the audience Ripley – these intensify the sense of danger. As in *Black Hawk Down*, Scott immerses the audience totally in the believability of the environment.

At this point, the ship is now almost alive itself – claxon wailing, vents blasting steam, lights flickering and piping and cables like musculature and organs. Ripley makes it to the escape shuttle in the belief that she is free. There is a fantastic optical effects shot of the undercarriage of the *Nostromo* as the shuttle rockets out from below that completes the sequence – but Ripley's troubles are far from over.

BLADE RUNNER: this sequence takes place soon after Rick has met Rachel – the first replicant he encounters in the movie

As with *Someone to Watch Over Me*, *Blade Runner* puts a lot of weight on the looks and gazes that fly and drift between characters.

Deckard's car pulls up to camera in the pouring rain and the sequence cuts to Rick returning to his apartment, the first time he has been seen at home. A low-key, downbeat mid-shot shows Rick in the vestibule of his apartment block; the space is apparently lit by just the bright white light on the wall.

The shot cuts to Rick in the lift, filmed from a low height as the camera circles him, and just the beep and hum of the lift taking him upwards are heard. There is the slightly threatening sound of the lift door opening and the sound of Rick's gun clicking as he turns around and points the gun towards the open door so that it fills the foreground of the frame. Rick looks anxious, then retracts the gun as there is clearly no threat. Does he pull a gun every time he heads out of the lift?

The next shot reveals Rachel in close-up, her face part lit by a strand of light, the rest of her lost in the all-encompassing darkness of the hallway.

Rick is shot in the foreground and it's obvious to the audience how confused and thrown he is by Rachel's appearance. Rick's face is only half lit by strips of light coming through a window – there is a very noirish ambience to the scene. With a sense of sadness and need, Rachel tells Rick that 'I wanted to see you.' Rick blinks and reaches for his key card but drops it. Rachel's appearance has thrown him. There is a quick cutaway of the key card being inserted in the lock and then a cut to a mid-shot that shows Rick opening his apartment door, going in and shutting the door on Rachel. There is a pause and the door re-opens and Rick lets Rachel come in. A brief shot shows Rachel looking at Rick before she goes in.

The scene then moves into the apartment. A wide shot with a block of white light centre frame through the only window pitches the apartment into silhouette as Rick fixes himself a drink. There is another cut to Rachel in close-up, partly in shadow: 'You think I'm a replicant, don't you?' A cut shows Rick looking sceptically at her.

Rachel hands Rick a photograph, saying it is of her and her mother though Rick then narrates a series of memories that belong to Rachel as evidence that she is a replicant. Rachel's reaction is very human as Rick upsets her and a beautiful close-up reveals tears glazing her eyes as a gentle piano theme whispers on the soundtrack. Rachel truly seems childlike at this point, quite in contrast with her initial femme fatale appearance in her first scene. Rick offers her a drink and Rachel sniffs back a tear. A wide shot shows Rick going into his kitchen as he looks back into the living room where Rachel stands in lonely silhouette and then leaves.

A close-up of Rick shows him looking at the pictures Rachel left behind, and then sitting down and picking them up. He studies the picture of Rachel and her mother as Vangelis's melancholy music plays on the soundtrack. The camera moves in slightly on Rick as

227

he looks at the pictures and then the image cuts and Rick, wearing a dressing gown, moves out of the shadows, cradling a drink. A saxophone plays and a wide shot reveals Rick looking down into the nightmare of the city.

The sequence cuts to a wide shot of one of those mean city streets and a young woman approaches coming right into the foreground, doll-like in her appearance. It is the replicant, Pris. She hides in the rubbish and garbage as the film's legendary rain falls. A vehicle pulls up and out of it steps the man-child JF Sebastian. There is a close-up of Pris watching and anxious.

Sebastian discovers Pris; she tells him she has no home and JF takes her inside the building, an eerie and impressive piece of architecture where the Off World ship's lights sweep the darkness. They enter JF's apartment where a close-up reveals Pris's delight in the teddy bear and Kaiser automata that greet them. A wide shot reveals several menacing, silhouetted mannequins, as the film continues its fine creation of a world that is terrifying and beautiful.

The sequence then cuts back to Rick's apartment where the camera tracks slowly right to left to reveal a piano, on top of which sit many photographs. Deckard is slumped over the keyboard, repeatedly striking one note.

There is a dissolve to a slow motion, daylight shot of a unicorn running through a forest. The shot then dissolves back to Rick stirring from his reverie.

Fantasy, characterisation, doom and sadness all come together brilliantly in this extended sequence which is the heart of the movie.

LEGEND: this sequence occurs late in the 96-minute version

Darkness has decided he will seduce Lili – this is revealed by a menacing voice-over, accompanied by an image of the fire in his lair. It then cuts to the first shot in an impressive and almost abstract (certainly too abstract for a mainstream fantasy adventure) sequence where the narrative stops and the film divests itself of dialogue and traditional drama, trading that in for a dance. The first image is a wide shot in slow motion of Lili – in rags that suggest something of Cinderella – running into a massive dark chamber of huge pillars. She runs down an aisle between the pillars (another kind of forest) and a shaft of white light slices into the darkness. Jerry Goldsmith's score emphasises the eerie dreaminess of the moment and the sequence then cuts to a close-up of the fairy Oona (now full-sized) as, in slow motion, she peers out and watches Lili disappear into the darkness. There is a grey pallor to the image that plays up a sense of death. Another shot shows Lili running out of sight and then there is a cut back to Oona, in close-up, looking greatly concerned; she exits the frame.

A wide shot shows Oona running between the pillars to follow Lili. The sequence then cuts to a beautiful tracking shot past the pillars as Lili runs by, again in slow motion. Oona stays on Lili's trail, as protective of her as she is of Jack. Lili runs towards camera as it tracks back in front of her and she raises her arms in a gesture of freedom and submission that makes her vulnerable.

She looks up; for the first time the sequence is with synchronous sound – she stops running and two huge doors slam shut behind her. The chamber Lili finds herself in is lit by firelight and a wide shot shows Lili starting to run again. The possibility that Lili is in danger is emphasised by her tininess in comparison to the enormity of the environment.

A cut back to Oona shows her creeping up to the closed doors as a sliver of brilliant golden light can be seen where the door meets the floor. Back inside the chamber the camera tracks behind Lili, following her through, as she hides behind a pillar. An extreme close-up of Oona's face follows, most of her face in darkness and only a strip of light from the gap between the two doors lights one of her eyes. On the soundtrack there is the creepy spirit voice that speaks to Darkness (wherever he may be): 'You should see your Princess now.'

There is a wide shot of Lili in front of a huge fireplace and then a cut to a close-up of her – she looks terrified and ragged as she turns her face, just half of it visible as her glorious dark hair cascades down her cheek. She is sweating and her breathing is nervous at this moment of uncertainty and terror. It is the beginning of Darkness's attempt to seduce her: beauty and the beast colliding.

Lili looks anxious. What is it she is seeing that the audience are not? Lili looks and sees a table of jewellery boxes set for her. Jerry Goldsmith's previously eerie score for this scene starts to emphasise the sense of discovery and we hear voices interlaced with the music, though it's not clear what they are saying. Lili approaches the table and the camera is at low height as she walks towards it, revealing the majesty and imposing architecture of the chamber all around her. It is not an inviting place. A brief point of view shot suggests Lili's view of the table, placing the audience directly into Lili's visual and emotional place. Spookily, a sprite on a long table in the shadowy background watches and shifts position, like a statue awakening.

The camera drops down as Lili reaches the table and approaches the riches. There is no music to be heard on the soundtrack, only a fanciful jingling sound. Lili lifts a necklace from a box and a bright white light emanates magically from it. It illuminates her face from below, throwing spooky shadows off her chin and eyebrows so that, for all her beauty, there is now something uneasy in Lili's face – the hint of danger. It's a soft-edged horror moment. Lili's breathing is emphasised again.

A cut reveals the table sprite watching and suddenly a dark fairy dancer appears in front of the huge fire. Lili turns and watches. Interestingly, in Jim Henson's far lighter fantasy *Labyrinth* (1986), the heroine experiences a dream in which she is seduced through dance by the villain of the story. The music starts again, with a waltz-like tempo and a rumbling sound underscores this, as does another voice-over saying, 'Make her one of us.' The features of the dark dancer are undefined and the character is more a shadow, an abstraction, representing seduction and danger. Lili presses herself against one of the pillars, terrified; the dancer closes in on her and comes right up to the camera, her dark robes filling the frame. The dancer touches Lili. There is a close-up of Lili's anxious eyes and the shadow of the dancing spirit's hand falling across Lili's smooth face. Darkness and firelight fuse.

Lili appears to have been lulled into a deep sleep, hypnotised by Darkness, and she starts to dance. The camera booms up somewhat joyfully as the waltz develops and Lili dances with the spirit. A cut reveals that Lili has been transformed (symbolically) and she now wears a dark dress with a menacing-looking fan coming off the shoulders behind the neck and her chest revealed slightly.

Lili is dancing, but then the music stops. There is the sound of ripping and crumbling; something is breaking through the mirror next to Lili. On the left of frame, with her at the centre, a blood-red hand pushes through and appears by magic. Lili collapses and a close-up reveals a horrifying hoof pushing through and coming to rest down on the ground. Darkness has arrived.

SOMEONE TO WATCH OVER ME: this sequence of the film combines the detective thrills and spills with the warmth of the relationship between Claire and Mike at the moment when Venza sends a hitman to kill Claire

The first shot of the sequence is a handheld shot of the hooded hitman entering Claire's apartment; he moves through the icy blue light and shadow. There is a cut to Claire's bedroom where Mike is awake at her side, his hand on her shoulder as she sleeps. Contrasting with the blue of the hallway, the room has a candlelit warmth to it, suggesting the safety of the room yet also emphasising its vulnerability.

One of Mike's colleagues is on watch at Claire's apartment. The sequence cuts to show him going into the kitchen. The hitman sees him and kills him; the death's silence is played up by the close-up of a glass of water on the side and the overwhelming quiet of the sequence is what enhances its threat.

The sequence then cuts back to the hitman, showing only his feet in a brief shot that tracks behind at ankle height. The hitman puts his hand to another door and opens it. In Claire's bedroom, Mike has sensed something and is out of the bed and pulling his trousers on. He goes out into the threatening blue light of the hall. He sees that a door has been opened and, for the first time in the sequence, there is a slight rise of music. The sequence cuts back to the bedroom where Claire lies in bed. Mike enters frame from the right, in an abrupt way, and puts his hand over Claire's mouth as he gets his gun.

The sequence then cuts to Claire's closet, stacked with perfume bottles and a real maze of mirrors. Scott is able to keep the audience aware of which character is where but also plays up the confusion and disorientation that Mike feels when he enters the closet. The music track is at its most intense, with its string emphasis and nod to Bernard Herrmann. There is a close-up on Mike's eyes as he tries to see the intruder. Another shot reveals the distorted reflection of the hitman but it is not clear who has seen whom first, so the threat that Mike is under increases.

Mike shoots the hitman and the music is very atonal at this point. Everything is off balance. Mike then checks out the rest of the apartment and goes to the kitchen where he finds his partner dead on the floor. The sequence ends with a flourish: with the camera at the side of the dead cop looking up at Mike as he leans in over the body, the frame is enlivened and made more intense by the cascade of water spilling over the sink.

BLACK RAIN: this standout sequence occurs midway through the film and is the real turning point in the drama

As in several other Scott movies, the action hinges on a character who is effectively lost and very vulnerable and therefore threatened because of their disorientation. As with *Blade Runner*, Scott visualises an urban environment in such a way that its exotic quality becomes almost alien.

The first shot of the sequence shows Nick and Charlie after a late night out, stumbling home through a mall. It is a cathedral-like place with its archways, columns and highly polished floors. With Nick and Charlie on the right of frame, their backs to camera, they do not initially register an apparently innocuous biker as they pass by the camera and then exit frame.

A reverse wide shot on the two cops reveals the biker weaving in between the pillars on his bike, to which Nick says, 'What the hell is that?' By degrees, Scott builds a sense of unease and tension. In a mid shot, Charlie turns and holds up his coat to the approaching biker like a bullfighter in a moment of macho bravura that will be his undoing. A close-up reveals a helmeted biker, his eyes covered by dark glasses. He looks menacing.

A wide shot then follows as the bike pushes closer to Nick and Charlie, this time taking Charlie's coat as he passes. Nick laughs but the laugh soon fades when Charlie announces that his passport is in the coat. The sense that this was a game has suddenly shifted. Typically, Scott holds off on any menacing music, allowing the virtual silence of the mall to convey the creepiness. All the audience hears are the footsteps as Charlie runs after the biker.

There is a wide shot showing Charlie and Nick's point of view as the biker, up ahead of them, stops and swings the bike around and then spits on Charlie's coat. A long lens shot, an alternative to the deeper focus of the preceding (and more melodramatic shots), shows Charlie running to the bike to try and retrieve his coat. The following shot emphasises Nick as he suddenly realises that everything is not fine. He runs after Charlie, who is pursuing the biker beyond the well-lit mall.

The sequence now cuts to an escalator area. In contrast to the warm look of the mall, this space is dominated by a steely blue feel and neon lights. Layer by layer, the journey of these two lost cops through the 'dark forest' is becoming creepier. The biker rides down the escalator and the following brief shot has the camera track left to meet the bike as it hits the ground at the bottom of the escalator with Charlie in pursuit. These camera moves energise the frame and have the effect of making the audience more immediately part of the action. The next shot is a quick close-up of the biker smiling nastily as he leads Charlie towards a dangerous unknown.

The sequence then cuts to Nick at the top of the escalator as he begins to race down. Only at this point does Scott introduce any score and composer Hans Zimmer provides an eerie and atonal track. There is a sense of frightening emptiness about the location, only adding to the helplessness of the American characters. Nick looks around, his face cast in a soft but icy-blue light.

The sequence cuts to an underground car park, its darkness enlivened by flashing lights on the ground. The biker roars left to right across frame and there is a cut to Charlie furiously pursuing on foot. His cockiness is going to be his downfall. Again, the use of a long lens of Charlie adds a documentary-style believability to the sequence, which is heavy with a sense of 'fantasy' in its creation of a culture that is quite alien to the heroes.

A wide shot of the biker follows and then there is a cut back to Nick who hears the bike and is alerted to the direction he needs to run. An overhead shot plays up Nick's loneliness in this underworld. Like Ripley in *Alien* and Lili and Jack in *Legend*, Nick and Charlie have descended from the 'real' world to be confronted by a source of evil and terror. Hans Zimmer's music kicks in with more force before a cut to an eerie, rain-strewn street. Down the centre of the street are brightly lit discs, perhaps advertising a product.

A wide shot shows Charlie confronting the biker, who finally turns and faces him. There is another long lens shot of Charlie, this time retrieving his coat from a puddle. A medium wide shot tilts up from the wheel of the bike to the rider as he revs the bike, partly in aggression, partly as a signal to his fellow bikers. For all its contemporary, urban edge, the scene has a more primitive feeling to it, of a tribe coming to evict an intruder.

Nick rushes into the underground car park and the music skitters in a classic thriller-style score. Another shot reveals several new bikers entering the scene and there is a close-up of Charlie looking very apprehensive. Scott then releases the audience from the tension of Charlie's face to the impressive arrival of the bikers, with their banners rising from their seats. Charlie thrashes out at one biker with his coat. His situation is clearly becoming helpless. A close-up of Charlie turning as he is surrounded is not amplified by any music, just the violent roar of the bikes.

The sequence cuts back to Nick searching for Charlie. He hears the bikes again and the edgy music kicks in once more. Nick runs towards the confrontation but is blocked by a grille between him and the street. Nick, for all his usual bluster, looks frightened and helpless. A close-up of Nick shows him shouting to Charlie, 'Get out of there.' A wide shot then shows how far Charlie is from Nick (who is seen far in the background), as the biker stands between them. The scene then cuts to a wide shot from Nick's side of the street as the bikers close in on Charlie and with two blows bring him to the ground. A close-up shows a biker pulling his sword and the music pounds. With the camera at wheel height the next shot gives the scene real spark, literally, as the sword tip is dragged along the tarmac, sparks flying from its tip, while Charlie is helpless and out of focus in the background as the bike approaches.

A mid shot shows the very unfussy beheading of Charlie. This is a gladiatorial scene that Scott returned to with the barbarism of *Gladiator* (2000). A slow-motion close-up shows Nick looking on and another close-up shows him shutting his eyes and his head leaning against the grille. The bikers depart victoriously. The final shot of the sequence plays up the loneliness and helplessness of Nick, in silhouette, clinging to the grille, he is almost on his knees. Above him a bright neon logo dominates the scene. Nick is tiny and helpless; the scene is utterly silent in contrast to the sound and fury that preceded it.

THELMA & LOUISE: this sequence occurs late in the film as the plight of Thelma and Louise deteriorates with every dirty desert mile

Driving into the night, the camera follows Louise's car. There are then a series of close-ups that dissolve between Thelma and Louise as they look straight ahead, sure of what they want to do but uncertain of how it might turn out. On the soundtrack Marianne Faithfull sings 'The Ballad of Lucy Jordan'. This sequence allows Scott to send the film into its dreamiest phase, the characters somehow at their most disconnected from the real world. The fact the sequence occurs at night only adds to this sense and the audience is shown the imposing and wonderful mesas of the desert and the tiny speck of light that is the car passing by at the bottom of the frame. It recalls the speck of light that was the three crew approaching the relic in *Alien* (1979).

The wide shot cuts back to the bonnet of the car effectively making the audience look in through the windscreen as Louise drives. The camera pans left to Thelma asleep but the shot binds the two women together in one move. There is no sync sound at this point.

A wider shot has the car pulling up to the camera and the first sync sound of the sequence is heard in the form of the nightlife of the desert. Louise looks around in close-up and there is then a wide shot of the glorious dawn sky. Louise looks more concerned than content and still the silence of the scene is what lingers. A wide shot follows – Thelma and Louise stand away from the car, the two of them backlit in the darkness. Thelma asks, 'What's goin' on?' to which Louise replies, 'Nothin'.'

Another cut reveals the massive mesas in silhouette and the next cut brings it back to daylight as, in the car, Thelma and Louise continue on their way. As they drive along, Thelma remains concerned by Louise's silence and soon begins to realise why Louise shot Harlan, beyond her reaction to the moment.

This sequence is notable for its silence in what is, overall, a noisy movie of cars rumbling along, trucks thundering by and the car radio playing. The sequence reminds the viewer of Scott's passion for framing landscapes and suggesting their secret might. With the desert he is able to suggest a world removed from the real lives that Thelma and Louise lead. The sequence is very simple and far from busy and yet it remains one of the film's best.

WHITE SQUALL: the sequence occurs reasonably early in the film once the *Albatross* is out to sea and the crew is beginning to gel together

The ship strikes a stormy sea. A long lens shot of the ship emphasises the overpowering nature of the waves as they seem to press the ship down between them. Chuck Gieg is at the wheel.

A series of quick cuts intensify the sense of interruption that nature has started to wreak on the apparently easy ride. A sail rips and chaos immediately engulfs the ship. One boy is thrown overboard, desperately hanging on for his life as he grips hold of a rope. A wide shot of the ship shows it rising higher still on the turbulent sea. The boy overboard is rescued and the action is completed with a close-up of the captain, Sheldon, laughing with his wife. Chuck is seen in close-up as a gentle piece of music underscores his relief at the storm passing and also emphasises the bond between him and Sheldon.

The action then cuts below deck, the calm after the storm, and the area is bathed in warm, orangey light, suggested by the lamps. Chuck fills out his journal entry, while the viewers hear Chuck's voice as he writes. The sequence cuts to a shot of the ship on the silvery night sea, both beautiful and dangerous. A cut back inside takes us to a close-up of a Coke bottle rolling back and forth and there is the sound of wind and creaking wood. Chuck lies awake writing and the calm is then broken, not by a storm, but by one of the other boys having a nightmare. Chuck wakes him and in this moment demonstrates his ability to hold everyone else together. It is Chuck's defining moment and goes unseen by the others on board. The boys talk in tight close-ups as soft music underscores the moment. For anybody who thinks Ridley Scott only does flash and big pictures this sequence proves the opposite.

GLADIATOR: this sequence occurs early in the film and marks the first stage in Maximus's transformation into a gladiator

As part of Commodus's effort to ensure that Maximus is no longer around to interfere in his own running of the Empire, he has Maximus taken to the woods close to the Germania battlefield to be executed by the Praetorian guard. Maximus proves his valour and courage in the sequence, the second half of which foregrounds the centrality of his family and home.

The sequence begins in the wintry surrounds of the forest. A mid shot shows Maximus kneeling as a soldier raises his sword to kill him. The shot is a neatly composed image of the strong lines of the trees and the shapes of Maximus and the guard. The camera zooms in on the Praetorian guard as he walks to the back of Maximus ready to plunge the sword into his neck. A close-up shows Maximus bowing – surely he has a plan? It's already been shown how resourceful and tough he is on the battlefield. A series of quick cuts do indeed show Maximus evading death and meting out vengeance on those who have betrayed him.

RIDLEY SCOTT Top Shots

Contrasting with the locked-off and very steady shots of the first images of the sequence, Scott at this point chooses to go for a handheld camera to invest the action with real urgency as Maximus must ensure his handiwork is not cut short. A slow motion shot shows a Praetorian guard on a horse charging towards Maximus and a close-up of Maximus registers his determination to survive. Hans Zimmer's score builds as Maximus, his sword raised, in what Scott has acknowledged as a nod to samurai tradition, clashes with the guard.

Maximus is victorious and he mounts the horse and races away. Hans Zimmer's score rides with him, increasing the sense of speed. The action shifts to the desert as Maximus makes his vast journey back to his wife and child in Spain and there is a feeling to the sequence that recalls biblical movies. One wide shot of a thunderous, lightning-slashed sky sells the film's epic status once and for all. Maximus, his hair thicker with the passing of weeks, is shown at a campfire and then slumped on his horse as it crosses the desert.

There is a cut to a dreamy tracking shot left to right across the lush fields of Maximus's villa and the audience is shown his wife and child, with several servants looking on. It is an ideal scene, the perfection of it made all the stronger by the elegance of the sweeping camera move. This blissful scene is interrupted by a wide shot that reveals Praetorian soldiers thundering on horseback along the track leading to the villa.

The sequence intercuts between the villa and Maximus continuing his trek home and the sense the viewer gets is that he begins to feel what is unfolding at home. The edit does not just tell stories happening simultaneously in different locations, it also fuses the emotions of the characters. The music score thrashes violently as Maximus heads home. There is a slow-motion shot of his wife running up to her son as the soldiers ride in.

When Maximus arrives it is too late. As he enters the frame of a wide shot of the villa, smoke is billowing from the property in the top left of the frame and Maximus falls from his horse. There is a dissolve as he crosses the burned remains of his farmland and the camera tracks back as he approaches home. He kneels and the camera lifts up slightly to reveal the charred feet of his wife and son. A close-up on Maximus shows him crying; there is a wailing accompaniment on the soundtrack. A slow zoom in on Maximus intensifes the moment as he puts his hands to the feet of his loved

237

ones. There is then a shot of two burial mounds, topped with flowers and a dissolve reveals Maximus lying next to them, his hand touching the soil – an echo of a gesture in which Maximus touches the earth that we have seen once in the film and which will be seen again.

A time lapse of the sun setting brings the sequence to a close. Maximus the Roman soldier is dead and his resurrection will begin in the most unlikely of circumstances.

Soundtrack Listing

Ridley Scott has always emphasised the place of music in his films and has worked with Hollywood great Jerry Goldsmith twice. Scott's most fruitful collaboration has been with Hans Zimmer, beginning with their work together on *Black Rain* at a time when Zimmer was beginning to make his mark in Hollywood. The Scott–Zimmer collaboration continues today. The music to Ridley Scott's films is a vital component, never treated as an afterthought. Below is a listing of the soundtracks currently available including their track listings.

The Duellists
There is no soundtrack available for *The Duellists*.

Alien
Composed by Jerry Goldsmith
Main Title
Face-Hugger
Breakaway
Acid Test
The Landing
The Droid
The Recovery
The Alien Planet
The Shaft
End Title

Blade Runner
Composed by Vangelis
Main Titles
Blush Response
Wait for Me
Rachel's Song
Love Theme
One More Kiss, Dear
Blade Runner Blues
Memories of Green
Tales of the Future
Damask Rose
Blade Runner (End Titles)
Tears in Rain

Legend
Composed by Jerry Goldsmith
Silva Screen
Main Title/The Goblins
My True Love's Eyes/The Cottage
The Unicorns
Living River/Bump and Hollow/The Freeze
The Faeries/The Riddle
Sing the Wee
Forgive Me
Faerie Dance
The Armour
Oona/The Jewels
The Dress Waltz
Darkness Falls
The Ring
Reunited

Someone to Watch Over Me
Composed by Michael Kamen
Soundtrack comprised of various artists
Someone to Watch Over Me – George and Ira Gershwin
Johnny Come Home – Fine Young Cannibals
Suspicious Minds – Fine Young Cannibals
Eight Little Notes – Audrey Hall
Cry – Johnny Ray
Freedom Overspill – Steve Winwood
What More Can I Ask? – Ray Noble and his Orchestra
Marie, Marie – The Blasters
Smoke Gets in your Eyes – Irene Dunne
Memories of Green – Vangelis
Walk Right By – Ted Seneka
Someone to Watch Over Me – Sting
Someone to Watch Over Me – Roberta Flack
Aria by Alfredo Catalani
Duo *Viens Mallika* from Lakmé by Delius

Black Rain
Composed by Hans Zimmer and various artists
Livin' on the Edge of the Night – Iggy Pop
The Way You Do The Thing You Do – U2
Back to Life – Soul II Soul
Laserman – Ryuichi Sakamoto
Singing the Shower – Les Rita Mitsouko/Sparks
I'll Be Holding On – Gregg Allman
Black Rain Suite: Sato – Hans Zimmer
Black Rain Suite: Charlie Loses His Head – Hans Zimmer
Black Rain Suite: Sugai – Hans Zimmer
Black Rain Suite: Nick and Masa Hans Zimmer

Thelma & Louise
Composed by Hans Zimmer and various artists
Part of You, Part of Me – Glenn Frey
Badlands – Charlie Sexton
House of Hope – Toni Childs
I Can't Untie You From Me – Grayson Hugh
Better Not Look Down – BB King
Little Honey – Kelly Willis
Kick the Stars – Chris Witley
Wild Nights – Martha Reeves
Tennesee Plates – Charlie Sexton
The Ballad of Lucy Jordan – Marianne Faithfull
Thunderbird – Hans Zimmer

1492: The Conquest of Paradise
Composed by Vangelis
Opening
Conquest of Paradise
Monastery of la Rabida
City of Isabel
Light and Shadow
Deliverance
West Across the Ocean Sea
Eternity
Hispaniola
Moxica and The Horse
Twenty-Eighth Parallel
Pinta, Niña, Santa Maria (Into Eternity)

White Squall
Composed by Jeff Rona
Still Waters
Departures
The Journey Begins
Power of the Wind
On the Water/Dolphins
A Wonderful Sail
Ringing Out
The Cubans/New World
Galapagos
The Test
White Squall
The Return Home
Teenage Ska – Baba Brooks
I Want to Walk You Home – Fats Domino
The Skye Boat Song
Yellow Basket – Tommy McCook
Be My Guest – Fats Domino
The Twist – Chubby Checker

Somethin Else – Eddie Cochrane

G.I. Jane
Composed by Trevor Jones and various artists
Hollywood Records
Goodbye – The Pretenders
Homecoming – The Pretenders
Mama Told Me – Three Dog Night
Feel Like Makin' Love – Bad Company
Dimples – John Lee Hooker
Two Wrongs Won't Make Things Right – Tarnation
The Future Is A War – Auntie Christ
Conspiracy
Time to Reflect
Endurance

Gladiator
Composed by Hans Zimmer, with Lisa Gerrard
Progeny
The Wheat
The Battle
Earth
Sorrow
To Zucchabar
Patricide
The Emperor is Dead
The Might of Rome
Strength and Honour
Reunion
Slaves to Rome
Barbarian Horde
Am I Not Merciful
Elysium
Honour Him
Now We Are Free

More Music from the Motion Picture Gladiator
Duduk of the North
Now We Are Free (Juba's Mix)
The Protector of Rome
Homecoming
The General Who Became a Slave
The Slave Who Became a Gladiator
Secrets
Rome Is The Light
All That Remains
Maximus
Marrakesh Marketplace
The Gladiator Waltz

Figurines Ya Ching
The Mob
Busy Little Bee
Death Smiles At Us All
Not Yet
Now We Are Free

Hannibal
Composed by Hans Zimmer
Dear Clarice
Aria da Capo
The Capponi Library
Gourmet Vaise Tartare
Avarice
For a Small Stipend
Firenze di Notte
Virtue
Let My Home Be My Gallows
The Burning Heart
To Every Captive Soul
Vide Cor Meum

Black Hawk Down
Composed by Hans Zimmer
Hunger
Barra Barra
Vale of Plenty
Chant
Still
Mogadishu Blues
Synchrotone
Bakara
Of the Earth
Ashes to Ashes
Gortoz A Ran J'Attends
Tribal War
Leave No Man Behind
Minstrel Boy
Still Reprise

Ridley Scott: Filmography as Producer

Since *The Duellists*, Scott has had an active role in the development of his films, with the notable exception of *Black Rain*, so in a sense he has always, unofficially to start with, operated as producer and from *Blade Runner* onwards he has received a producer credit on those films he has directed. However, starting in the mid-1990s, he began producing other directors' work and now functions as producer or executive producer on feature films and television material.

1994
The Browning Version – producer. Scott collaborated with Mike Figgis.
The story is a period piece focusing on a public school teacher, Andrew Crocker Harris. He is at the end of his career and is also having to confront his wife's infidelity. The film starred Albert Finney as Andrew Crocker Harris, Greta Scacchi as Laura Crocker Harris, Matthew Modine as Frank Hunter, Julian Sands as Tom Gilbert, Michael Gambon as Dr Frobisher and Ben Silverstone as Taplow. Other cast included Derek Jacobi, Tom Wilkinson, Ronnie Barker and Jim Broadbent.

Monkey Trouble – executive producer.
A family film starring Thora Birch and Harvey Keitel, the film is about a girl's pet monkey who has been trained as a pickpocket and is on the run from a gypsy. It starred Thora Birch as Eva Boylan, Harvey Keitel as Shorty Kohn, Mimi Rogers as Amy Gregory and Christopher McDonald as Lt Tom Gregory.

1997
The Hunger TV series – executive producer. Scott collaborated with his brother Tony Scott.
The series' episodes were hosted by Terence Stamp and for a period David Bowie, who had appeared in Tony Scott's debut feature *The Hunger* in 1983, of which this TV series is a spin-off. Tony Scott directed the pilot episode 'The Swords'. Horror writer

Poppy Z. Brite contributed several scripts. Ridley Scott's cinematographer on *Gladiator* and *Hannibal*, John Mathieson, worked in the same capacity on the series.

1998
Clay Pigeons – producer. Directed by David Dobkin.
Clay is a young man living in a Montana town. He witnesses his friend kill himself and soon after a serial killer arrives and befriends Clay. As numerous murder victims pile up, Clay keeps finding the victims. A double-crossing black comedy. The film starred Joaquin Phoenix as Clay Bidwell, Gregory Sporleder as Earl, Vince Vaughn as Lester Long, Scott Wilson as Sheriff Moon, Georgina Cates as Amanda, Vince Vieluf as Deputy Barney, Wayne Brennan as Minister, Nikki Arlyn as Gloria and Janeane Garofalo as Agent Shelby.

1999
RKO 281 – executive producer. Directed by Benjamin Ross.
This TV movie centres on the drama about Orson Welles facing opposition from the real-life subject of his film, the newspaper tycoon William Randolph Hearst. The film starred Liev Schreiber as Welles, James Cromwell as William Randolph Hearst, Melanie Griffith as Marion Davies, John Malkovich as Herman Mankiewicz, Brenda Blethyn as Louella Parsons and Roy Scheider as George Schaefer.

2000
The Last Debate – producer.
Directed by John Badham (*War Games*, *The Hard Way*), *The Last Debate* is a TV movie starring James Garner. It is set behind the scenes of a Presidential debate where all the protocols of the process are abandoned.

Where the Money Is – producer. Directed by Marek Kaniewska.
A crime drama starring Paul Newman and Linda Fiorentino in which Newman is an old-time thief and Fiorentino is a bored rest home nurse.

2002
Six Bullets From Now – executive producer.
The plot is based around a real event on New Year's Day in 1972 when bank robbers got away with $10 million in cash and

jewellery from New York's Pierre Hotel. Stephen T Kay is to direct and Robert Downey Jr is to star.

Red Dragon – executive producer: a prequel to *Silence of the Lambs* based on Thomas Harris's source novel. The screenplay is being written by Ted Tally.
In this story, FBI Agent Will Graham seeks the help of Hannibal Lecter in solving the case of the Tooth Fairy who murders families when there is a full moon. Brett Ratner directs the film, which features Edward Norton, Ralph Fiennes as the bad guy, Dolarhyde, Harvey Keitel, Emily Watson, Mary Louise Parker and Philip Seymour Hoffman. Dino De Laurentiis produces.

The Gathering Storm – executive producer.
Directed by Richard Loncraine, this TV movie centres on the love story between Winston and Clementine Churchill just prior to the beginning of World War II. The drama is set against the rise of Nazi power but the focus of the story is the struggle Winston must face between his personal life and his professional duties. *The Gathering Storm* won the Emmy award for Best Made for Television Movie at the 2002 awards ceremony in September 2002.

AFP: American Fighter Pilot TV series – executive producer.
This is a high-profile American reality TV show that follows three men as they undergo the intense training programme to become F15 pilots. In effect, this is real-life Top Gun stuff. It is produced by Tony Scott, who directed *Top Gun* (1986), Ridley Scott, Jesse Negron and Brian Gadinsky, and has been broadcast on CBS.

Ridley Scott On TV

Over more recent years, Ridley Scott has been seen in several documentaries about film.

He has appeared as an interviewee on *Murder By Numbers* (2001), *AFI's, 100 Years, 100 Thrills: America's Most Heart-Pounding Movies* (2001), *Hollywood Halloween* (1997), *Reflections on Citizen Kane* (1999) and *The Horror Hall of Fame* (1990).

Of most interest, though, are the documentaries he has contributed to about *Alien* and *Blade Runner*. Scott appears in the British documentary written and hosted by Mark Kermode, *Alien Evolution*, which charts the life and success of the *Alien* series from the first film through to the fourth instalment. There are also interviews with James Cameron, David Fincher and Jean-Pierre Jeunet as well as with Sigourney Weaver. Mark Kermode wrote and presented a similarly themed documentary again on Channel 4 called *On the Edge of Blade Runner* in 2000. *The Alien Legacy* was another documentary, specifically about the making of *Alien*.

Ridley's Unrealised Visions

As of the time of writing, Scott is in a position where he has more freedom than ever before to select his material. There has been the recent suggestion that he will direct the fifth instalment in the *Alien* series or maybe a movie about Alexander the Great or maybe a pirate movie or maybe an expansive movie, *á la* Lawrence of Arabia, called *Tripoli*. Scott has fashioned stories expressly for the screen and has also vividly adapted, in the truest sense of the word, novels. He uses film to transform the source material rather than dumbly transpose it, which seems to be what too many people expect of an adaptation. Here are some films that have yet to see the light of day.

I Am Legend

At the time *Gladiator* was being worked up at DreamWorks, Ridley Scott was over at Warner Brothers developing *I Am Legend*, a futureworld tale for Arnold Schwarzenneger to star in. When the budget went to $100 million the studio pulled the plug. It would have been perfectly suited to Ridley Scott. The source material was Richard Matheson's novel of the same name which had been previously adapted as *The Last Man on Earth* starring Vincent Price (1964) and as *The Omega Man* (1971) starring Charlton Heston. The adventure is based around the last surviving human in a world ravaged by the effects of a biological war; all other humans have been transformed into undead vampires. Scott felt the script needed work. He came on board the project in summer 1997, with a planned autumn start on the shoot under the Scott Free banner. Tom Cruise and Mel Gibson had both apparently been interested. In Mark Protosevich's script the vampires were called Hemocytes and they lived in a tribe around San Francisco. The screenplay remained faithful to the novel until the last thirty pages or so where it became much more of an all-out action film. In autumn 1997, the plug was pulled. At present Michael Bay may direct Will Smith in the project.

Knight

The Tristan and Isolde project based on the medieval romance
which occupied a lot of Scott's attention in the first few years of
his career. If nothing else, its very obvious romantic scope fits
neatly with all that he has made. After work on *The Duellists* was
completed, Scott turned his attention to developing his *Tristan
and Isolde* project. He intended to shoot it in the Dordogne.
Gerald Vaughan-Hughes wrote a screenplay and Paramount put
the film into development in spring 1977. Scott was being
influenced by *Heavy Metal* magazine in his look for the film: he
wanted a beat-up, ragged, almost cowboy-like quality to the look
of the characters so that there was a kind of used historical look
that was far from pristine. When David Puttnam and Ridley Scott
went to see *Star Wars* in Los Angeles, Scott realised that Lucas
had somehow been thinking similarly about a look for space. The
Tristan and Isolde project was abandoned at this stage.

In the late 1990s the project resurfaced for a short time,
apparently targeted at a 2001 release. Kevin Reynolds (*Robin
Hood: Prince of Thieves*, 1991) was involved as director in the
development process and Ridley Scott, because of other
commitments, was due to produce. Again, the project never made
it past the fires of development hell. The project under Kevin
Reynolds is now due to shoot in Ireland, possibly in 2002, most
likely at Aardmore Studios as a co-production of Octagon Films
and Scott Free.

Crisis in the Hot Zone

A thriller based around the Ebola virus, which everybody was
talking about in the late 1990s. In 1995, Scott had just signed a
deal with 20th Century Fox and had begun developing an
adaptation of the book *Crisis in the Hot Zone* by Richard Preston
about the discovery of the Ebola virus. Jodie Foster and producer
Lynda Obst came on board. Scott was a big fan of Jim V Hart's
script and a little later Robert Redford became a possibility to
star. At the same time, producer Arnold Kopelson got the film
Outbreak, also based on Ebola virus, off the ground. It was
directed by Wolfgang Petersen and starred Dustin Hoffman and
Rene Russo.

Mulholland Falls

Scott read the script for *Mulholland Falls* at the same time as discovering the *White Squall* material, and it was *White Squall*'s focus on young men growing up that was the more appealing story. This period drama was eventually made starring Nick Nolte and directed by Lee Tamahori (*Once Were Warriors*, 1994 and *Die Another Day*, 2002).

The Metropolis project

From the way Scott has briefly described it, the proposed film sounds very much like a science fiction piece but the specifics remain unclear, although several drafts of the screenplay have been completed. Perhaps it was inspired by Fritz Lang's 1926 masterpiece.

The Shape of Films to Come

As of summer 2002, Ridley Scott is looking to realise a range of films for which he has secured deals. With Scott shooting two new movies back to back in 2002/2003 (*Matchstick Men* and *Tripoli*), the possible follow-ups might include *Perfume*. But there's also talk about *Captain Kidd* which was announced as a Disney feature in autumn 2000 with Jerry Bruckheimer producing. Jude Law was mooted as taking the lead, but it remained just a rumour. A pirate adventure, Captain Kidd was described as being conceived as an anti-establishment hero. Sadly, the once popular pirate genre has sunk at sea more recently with Roman Polanski's *Pirates* (1986) and Renny Harlin's *Cutthroat Island* (1995). Only *Waterworld* (Kevin Reynolds, 1995) managed some semblance of success and to this writer it is always surprising that Scott never directed that movie. Captain Kidd has previously been portrayed by Charles Laughton. For the proposed new version, the plan has been to make it something resembling Errol Flynn and Michael Curtiz's movie *The Sea Hawk* (1940) with the studio emphasising some kind of cast to equal the star-studded line-up in Steven Soderbergh's *Ocean's Eleven* (2001).

Alongside *Captain Kidd*, Scott was then mentioned as being attached to the currently in-production *Terminator 3*. An adaptation of Ben Elton's novel *Popcorn* was also mooted. This would have been intriguing – its premise is of a producer of violent movies being kidnapped by a couple of maniacs inspired by his films. In the wake of *Hannibal*'s success, Scott was then named as the director of first *Hannibal* outing *Red Dragon* though that is now being helmed by the director of *Rush Hour*, Brett Ratner, with Scott as executive producer. For many though the most appetising prospect was *Alien 5* which Scott said would give him a chance to return to a favoured subplot that never made it into the original film, namely the source of the aliens. Scott even went so far as to meet and discuss the project with Sigourney Weaver in late 2001. As of this writing, though, there is no confirmed *Alien 5* due with Scott on board. Other than *Perfume*, the other movie that seems likely is *Tripoli*, a Lawrence of Arabia scaled piece based on real events that happened in the early nineteenth century when William Eaton, an American (Russell Crowe), helped the rightful heir to the throne of Tripoli lead a rebellion and overthrow a corrupt ruler.

There may even be an epic based around the Crusades that Scott has apparently signed on to direct. Given the amount of time it took for Paul Verhoeven to try and develop a Crusades project in the 1990s, however, it remains to be seen whether this project will get off the ground.

Films That Have Influenced Ridley Scott

As with many of the most well-known film directors – Martin Scorsese, Steven Spielberg, Jane Campion and Baz Luhrmann are examples – Ridley Scott is always happy to refer to those films that influenced his concept of what cinema can be. Certain other movies also have a more specific impact on a particular film in terms of how a scene might be staged, lit or edited together. Evidently, some of the films listed below have also been referenced elsewhere in this book.

Ridley Scott's favourite films include:

Metropolis (1926)
Directed by Fritz Lang, *Metropolis* is a future world drama of a mega city with flying transports and mile-high buildings. As with *Metropolis*, *Blade Runner* not only gives a sense of the grim aspects of urban life but also finds a way to suggest the element of fun there would be in driving a flying car and living alongside robots. *Blade Runner* raises the issue of slavery; in *Metropolis* there is an underclass working below ground and it is they who keep the machine of the city running. Rotwang, the creator of Metropolis, has his equivalent in Tyrell in *Blade Runner*.

Fantasia (1940)
An animated feature produced by Walt Disney and directed by Samuel Armstrong, James Algar, Bill Roberts, Paul Satterfield, Hamilton Luske, Jim Handley, Ford Beebe, Walt Disney, Norman Ferguson and Wilfred Jackson, the film fuses classical music with 1940s classical animation. Mickey Mouse famously puts in an appearance but, for Ridley Scott, the memorable segment, as it also appears to have been for Steven Spielberg, is the 'Night on Bald Mountain' sequence (set to Mussorgsky's music of *Night on Bare Mountain*). Scott acknowledged that the design of the 'devil' in *Fantasia* informed his design of Darkness for *Legend*. Interestingly, given the tie between Scott's emphasis and delight on creating a strong visual atmosphere, the *Fantasia* sequence is

itself clearly inspired by images from FW Murnau's movie version of *Faust* in which Mephistopholes lords it over a village.

Beauty and the Beast (1946)
Directed by Jean Cocteau, the film is a classic adaptation of the 1757 fairy tale by Marie Leprince de Beaumont, in which a beautiful young woman saves her father's life by agreeing to visit the Beast – whom she then comes to love. *Hannibal* and *Legend* most clearly give expression to the influence of this film on Ridley Scott's cinema.

Gilda (1946)
Scott referenced *Gilda* in his concert for Rachel in *Blade Runner*. Given *Blade Runner*'s film noir qualities, the *Gilda* connection is important. Directed by Charles Vidor, the film is as much a cornerstone of film noir as *Blade Runner* is of the science fiction genre.

The Seventh Seal/Det Sjunde Inseglet (1956)
Directed by Ingmar Bergman *The Seventh Seal* focuses on a knight, Antonius, who, home from the Crusades, grapples with his thoughts about faith. Antonius is confronted by the figure of Death and they play chess as the debate about the existence of God unfolds. The impact of the film's historical setting and austere style reverberates throughout Scott's career.

The Searchers (1956)
When Scott was preparing *The Duellists*, he mused on setting it in the American West. John Ford's films had been some of the first where Scott, as a child, had begun to develop a sense of what a director did on a film. Beyond that, Ford's affinity for military codes (in films such as *Fort Apache* and *She Wore A Yellow Ribbon*), rebel heroes (such as Ethan Edwards in *The Searchers*) and the rich seam that history can provide for stories (going as far back as his silent classic *The Iron Horse*) all find their echoes in Ridley Scott's movies.

Paths of Glory (1957)
Directed by Stanley Kubrick, this film is set on the Western Front of World War I as an Allied unit makes an assault on a German position. The film is noted for its tracking shots along the trenches. The military setting clearly echoes with Scott and, in the

opening of *Gladiator*, there is a shot of Maximus walking along his line of soldiers, the camera tracking in front of him, just as it does in *Paths of Glory*.

Spartacus (1960)
Directed by Stanley Kubrick and starring Kirk Douglas, who had also starred in *Paths of Glory*. *Spartacus* is set in ancient Rome amidst the world of gladiators among whom there is a slave rebellion. The comparisons to *Gladiator* are obvious.

Lawrence of Arabia (1962)
Directed by David Lean, this film is a vital touchstone for many directors who came to prominence in Hollywood in the 1970s. Scott, like Lean (in his later films at least), has an affinity for stories set against so-called epic backgrounds but where the main characters are given time to develop as individuals.

A Man for all Seasons (1966)
An adaptation of Robert Bolt's stage play by Bolt himself, this film was directed by Fred Zinnemann. Like several of Scott's films, notably *The Duellists*, the movie achieves a terrific balance between historical realism, spectacle and compelling personal drama. For Ridley Scott the film is a model of great screenwriting and, like some of Scott's films, concerns a main character who must reconcile duty with desire.

2001: A Space Odyssey (1969)
Directed by Stanley Kubrick, this film was an adaptation of Arthur C Clarke's source novel of the same name. It is hard to find a modern director who has not been influenced and inspired by this film. Scott's *Blade Runner* similarly provided a shot in the arm for the science fiction genre some years later.

The Wild Child (1969)
Directed by François Truffaut, the film dramatises what happens when a boy found in a forest is socialised. The influence of this can, of course, be seen in *Legend*.

Badlands (1974)
Directed by Terrence Malick, the film is based on the actual killing spree of Clarence Starkweather and Carol Fugate across

Nebraska, and was an influence on Scott's *Thelma & Louise*. The film is notable for its voice-over and also the lyricism the director brings to his vision of the American landscape.

Barry Lyndon (1974)
Directed by Stanley Kubrick, the film was an adaptation of William Makepeace Thackeray's novel *The Luck of Barry Lyndon* (1884). The film's intense and deliberate pace is legendary, as was its use of newly developed high-speed film to allow filming to occur using just candlelight with no extra lighting. The film follows Barry Lyndon's adventures through the army and high society and Kubrick's still-life-inspired images are clearly acknowledged throughout *The Duellists*.

The '1984' Apple Commercial

It is not usual to dwell on a sixty-second movie. However, when Ridley Scott directs it at the high point of the first phase of his career and when it is to launch a massive computer company that remains the byword for cool, it is worth talking about.

Scott had established himself as a major commercials director by the mid-1970s and one of his commercials had really made an impact in America: the 'Chanel Share the Fantasy' ad. However, by 1982 Scott was a major feature film director with three smart, inventive and memorable movies to his name.

With Ridley Scott Associates still very much a concern, in 1983 Scott was approached personally by Steve Jobs, CEO at Apple computers.

At the time, Apple were in need of a dose of success and Scott was commissioned to make something truly memorable. Scott had one minute to communicate this. He shot the commercial at Shepperton Studios. With a budget of $400,000 and with a further $500,000 doled out to buy airtime for the ad on American television the 1984 Apple piece was going to be special. Not only was a major moviemaker on board but the commercial would screen just the once, a unique and unprecedented approach which worked. Its one-off status immediately meant it received extensive coverage on news programmes and in print media. The commercial's other significance was in fuelling the event commercial and it raised the bar for the industry.

Casting for the Apple commercial took place in Hyde Park because the producers needed to cast women partly on their ability to throw a hammer – apparently, one woman's hammer nearly collided with an elderly passer-by. Eventually, though, the star of the commercial was cast. Her name was Anya Major and she was both a model and an experienced discus thrower.

When the Apple commercial was screened on CBS during the Superbowl it sparked a frenzy and switchboards were jammed at the American network, at Apple and at the Chiat/Day advertising agency with people who had seen the mini movie and phoned in wanting to know more. What Apple had not predicted, given the fact that when the ad was screened to Apple's board of directors it was widely disliked, was that they would generate so much free advertising: after the one-off screening, news items and magazines and newspapers went on to cover the commercial. Estimates put the worth of the free publicity at around $5 million.

The commercial went on to win the Grand Prix at the Cannes advertising competition and for many it remains the best TV commercial yet made.

Just as the great Beach Boy Brian Wilson talks about his songs being 'pocket symphonies', so too Ridley Scott has described commercials as 'pocket versions of feature films'. The 1984 commercial feels more like a micro movie and is in the mode of *Blade Runner*. Whilst only sixty seconds long, the commercial is very much a Ridley Scott movie. In succeeding years some of Hollywood's most successful directors would come out of commercials, notably Michael Bay and David Fincher.

This is what happens in the commercial:

A vast unidentified future-looking chamber inside of which can be seen enormous transparent walkways which criss-cross the depths; as the camera zooms in, an ominous sound rises on the soundtrack and far below figures move through the tunnels. The ad cuts to inside one of the tunnels and bald-headed, grey-outfitted men march along and stare straight ahead, somehow deadened. On the soundtrack the voice of a 'Big Brother' figure says, 'Today we celebrate the first glorious anniversary of the information purification directives.' Thereafter there is a brief, slow-motion shot of a blonde-haired athletic woman, wearing a white T-shirt with the Apple logo on it, red shorts and in red trainers, running towards the camera. She is bronzed and she holds a hammer.

The ad then cuts back to a close-up of the workers, some of whom wear face masks. There is then a cut to a slow-motion shot of menacing police officers in visors, obscuring their faces. They wield bars and are all dressed in black, light glistening on their visors. The ad then returns to one of the tunnels as the men continue marching by, the camera at foot height. There is the voice of Big Brother again, saying that 'a garden of pure ideology where each worker may bloom secure from the pests . . .' The ad then cuts back to the woman running and then to a wideshot of the workers gathering in a massive chamber and all of them looking up at a screen on which they see the 'Big Brother' figure. Some text on the screen suggests the face is named Prophet

Mentor and he looks a little like Tyrell from *Blade Runner* with his big glasses. Text runs across the screen that the men watch. Scott then cuts to a wide shot of the woman running towards the camera down a corridor, the police chasing her. The ad cuts to the camera tracking along a line of seated workers. The next shot is a point of view shot of the screen from amongst the men. The camera tracks past the workers again and then the ad cuts to a wide shot of the woman running into the chamber. This slow-motion shot is hugely symmetrical and designed, with two walls on either side of the frame, a block of light above, text on the walls. The woman runs down the central aisle between the men and the Prophet is heard speaking again. Another long lens shot shows the police in pursuit of the woman. On the Prophet screen we then see the text 'one resolve' in dead centre of frame. The Prophet says: 'We are one people. One will. One resolve. One cause.' The woman swings her hammer and there is another shot of the cops who are now approaching behind her. The woman yells out and hurls the hammer.

One shot isolates the hammer arcing through the darkness. A cut to a wide shot of the monitor shows the hammer smashing against it, destroying the image and voice in an explosion. The men sit watching aghast as dust covers them. It is not clear what happens to the woman. Text appears on screen, read out in a mysterious-sounding voice-over: 'On January 24th Apple Computer will introduce Macintosh. And you'll see why 1984 won't be like "1984".' The image dissolves to the Apple logo.

The commercial is vintage Scott. There is the futuristic feel of the environment, based in part on popular culture's understanding of what George Orwell's novel *1984* suggested as a future. The workers were recruited from a group of two hundred skinheads. The Big Brother face was shot on video and composited into the footage in post-production.

The science fiction of *Blade Runner* certainly fits the approach of the commercial and the policemen look as though they have wandered in off the streets of LA 2019. Even in the space of sixty seconds, Scott packs in a real sense of the ominous and the heroic. With Scott at the helm it is no surprise the hero of the commercial is a woman of physical strength and presumably courage as she flees from the authorities. She is an athlete and the hammer suggests the classical, the gladiatorial. She is the only point of colour in the commercial. All else is steely blue and grey and throughout the ad there is a low rumbling on the soundtrack. The marching sound contrasts with the quieter moments when the woman runs gracefully along the corridor. The ending of the commercial is apocalyptic. Like most Scott films, the commercial fuses the ancient and the modern.

Famous for starting his career in television commercials, Ridley Scott has contributed several other all-time classics to the medium. Prior to his feature debut, *The Duellists*, Scott directed, among others, the famous Hovis commercial. This commercial showed a young boy pushing a bike up the hill of a Yorkshire village delivering bread. It depicted an archly romantic realisation of rural England, the cobbled street bathed in golden sunlight. Ironically, the image of rustic Yorkshire was realised on location in the village of Sherborne in Dorset.

Ridley Scott's Business Ventures

In 1995, Ridley Scott and his brother Tony became owners of Shepperton Studios in Middlesex. Then, in February 2002, an announcement was made that the Scott brothers were in the process of making a deal that would allow them to build a studio in the run-down dockland area of Toronto in Canada. In May 2002, in a list compiled by *Screen International* (and excluding actors), the Scott brothers were together named the richest and most powerful people in the UK film industry, thanks largely to their part in making, but also financing, films in the UK.

This industrial element of Ridley Scott's career puts him on a similar footing with film directors, and sometime 'movie moguls', George Lucas, Steven Spielberg and Francis Ford Coppola, who have committed themselves to building worlds beyond the screen in order to help them continue making movies.

Index of Quotations

53   'the more sophisticated . . .' and 'Every moment . . .' Ridley Scott quoted in
     The Book of Alien by Paul Scanlon and Michael Gross, Star Books

Blade Runner

57   'Blade Runner was . . .' Richard Yuricich quoted in *Blade Runner: The
     Inside Story* by Don Shay, Titan Books, 2000, p. 71; reprint of original
     Cinefex issue from 1982

58   'a very romantic writer . . .' Ivor Powell quoted in 'The Blade Runner
     Chronicles Part 1', *Starburst*, October 1982, interviewed by Phil Edwards

59   'Knight, a medieval film . . .' Ivor Powell quoted in 'The Blade Runner
     Chronicles Part 1', *Starburst*, October 1982, interviewed by Phil Edwards

60   'My argument with Ridley . . .' Harrison Ford quoted in *Empire*,
     November 2000

61   'There should be total integration . . .' Ridley Scott quoted in 'Blade
     Runner: Production, Design and Photography' by Herb A Lightman and
     Richard Patterson, in *American Cinematographer,* July 1982

62   'every Blade Runner set was . . .' Lawrence G Paull quoted in *Future Noir*
     by Paul Sammon, p. 137

71   'social theory was that . . .' Syd Mead quoted in *Blade Runner: The Inside
     Story* by Don Shay, Titan Books, 2000; reprint of *Cinefex* article from July
     1982

76   'It is not the unicorn . . .' Ridley Scott quoted in *Future Noir* by Paul
     Sammon, p. 377

78   'a bleak but hypnotic . . .' review of *Blade Runner* by John Brosnan in
     Starburst, volume 5, number 2, October 1982, pp. 12–13

78   'Much to its own detriment . . .' review of *Blade Runner* by Tom Milne in
     Monthly Film Bulletin, September 1982, volume 49, number 584, pp.
     194–195

78   'Rubbished on its intitial release . . .' review of *Blade Runner* (Director's
     Cut) by Ian Freer in *Empire* – see www.empireonline.co.uk archive

78   'Ford is always good . . .' review of *Blade Runner* by Roger Ebert in
     Chicago Sun-Times

78   'the special effects . . .' review of *Blade Runner (original release)* in Screen
     International

78   'The script has some . . .' review of *Blade Runner (original release)* by
     David Pirie in *Time Out*

78   '*Blade Runner* has nothing . . .' review of *Blade Runner* by Pauline Kael in
     the *New Yorker*, 12 July 1982; reprinted as 'Baby, The Rain Must Fall' in
     Taking It All In: Film Writing, 1980–83, An Arena Book, 1987

80   'this is a real Ridley-ism . . .' Ivor Powell quoted in 'The Blade Runner
     Chronicles Part 1', *Starburst*, October 1982, interviewed by Phil Edwards

83   'my most complete . . .' Ridley Scott quoted in 'Scott's Corner', an
     interview with Lynn Barber, *The Observer*, 6 January 2002

83   'The elevator door . . .' Ridley Scott quoted in *Starburst*, November 1982,
     interview by Phil Edwards and Alan McKenzie

Legend

91   'the way that Tom's arms . . .' Alex Thomson quoted in *Labyrinth and Legend: Big Screen Fairytales* by Ron Magid in *American Cinematographer*

94   'like *Blade Runner* . . .' review of *Legend* by Kim Newman in *Monthly Film Bulletin*, number 623, December 1985, p. 380

94   'Let it be said that . . .' and 'It is so effective . . .' review of *Legend* by Roger Ebert in the *Chicago Sun-Times*, 18 April 1986

94   'And lo, it came to pass . . .' review of *Legend* by Anne Bilson in *Time Out*

95   'many of the lingering moments . . .' Terry Rawlings quoted in 'Terry Rawlings: Cutting Fantasy Film' by Anthony Timpone, *Starlog*, issue 103

97   'It is not a film of the future . . .' Ridley Scott quoted in *Starburst*, number 87, November 1985, p. 10

Someone to Watch Over Me

106   'The final image . . .' review of *Someone to Watch Over Me* by Julian Petley in *Monthly Film Bulletin*, January 1990, volume 55, no. 651, p. 119

106   'A cliché maybe . . .' review of *Someone to Watch Over Me* in *Empire* – see www.empireonline.co.uk

106   'With its stunning . . .' review of *Someone to Watch Over Me* by Rita Kempsley in the *Washington Post*

106   '*Someone to Watch Over Me* does contain . . .' review of *Someone to Watch Over Me* by Roger Ebert, *Chicago Sun-Times*

106   'Scott's gleaming . . .' review of *Someone to Watch Over Me* by Brian Case in *Time Out*

106   'Ridley Scott's thriller . . .' review of *Someone to Watch Over Me* by Pauline Kael in the *New Yorker*, 2 November 1987; reprinted in *Hooked*, Marion Boyars Publishers Ltd, 1990, p. 386

106   '*Someone to Watch Over Me* is far richer . . .' From *A Biographical Dictionary of Film*, Andre Deutsch, 1995, p. 681

108   'I figured . . .' Ridley Scott quoted in *Ridley Scott: Close Up* by Paul Sammon, Orion Books, p. 87

Black Rain

111   'Any way you look . . .' Steve Pond, 'Black Rain: Shot by Shot', *Premiere*, October 1989, pp. 105–107

116   'We didn't want . . .' Jan De Bont quoted in 'High Crime Culture Clash in Black Rain' by David Wiener from *American Cinematographer*, September 1989, number 9, p. 42

118   'Is Ridley Scott the new . . .' review of *Black Rain* by Richard Combs in *Monthly Film Bulletin*, volume 57, number 672, January 1990, pp. 8–10

118   'Scott distracts us . . .' review of *Black Rain* by Roger Ebert in *Chicago Sun-Times*, 22 September 1989

118   'obvious stuff . . .' review of *Black Rain* by Colette Maude in *Time Out*

118   'Don't expect . . .' review of *Black Rain* by Mike Clark in *USA Today*

118   '(Scott) approaches this prickly action thriller . . .' review of *Black Rain* by Rita Kempsley in the *Washington Post*

Web Resources

www.alien-moves.com – official 20th Century Fox website for all
of the *Alien* films
www.hrgiger.com – official site for *Alien* concept artist
www.rsafilms.com – official site for Ridley Scott's company
Blade Runner sites
www.bladezone.com – voluminous fansite dedicated to the film
Blade Runner, features interviews with cast and crew
www.geocities.com/Hollywood/Pavilion/3504/scottridley.html
www.kzu.stanford.edu/uwi/br
www.devo.com/bladerunner/blade-runner.html
Legend
www.bluewyrm.com/legend/legpage.html
www.figmentfly.com/legend/index.shtml
The *Alien* soundtrack
www.planetawp.com/alienshive/amr/music/a1music.html

Bibliography

Andrew, Geoff, *The Film Handbook*, Longman, 1989

Bakutman, Scott, *BFI Modern Classics: Blade Runner,* BFI Publishing, 1997

Bouzereau, Laurent, *The Cutting Room Floor: Movies Scenes Which Never Made It to The Screen*, Citadel Press, 1994

Bullock, Alan et al., *The Fontana Dictionary of Modern Thought* (Second Edition), Fontana Press, 1988

Foster, Alan Dean, *The Alien Omnibus*, Time Warner Paperbacks, 1993

Giger, HR, *HR Giger's Film Design* intro by Ridley Scott, Titan Books, 1996

Jenkins, Gary, *Harrison Ford: Imperfect Hero*, Simon & Schuster, 1997

Jeter, KW, *Blade Runner II: The Edge of Human*, Gollancz, 1996

Kerman, Judith B (ed.), *Retrofitting Blade Runner: Issues in Ridley Scott's Blade Runner and Philip K. Dick's Do Androids Dream of Electric Sheep*, Bowling Green University Press, 1991

Khouri, Callie, *Thelma & Louise* and *Something To Talk About*, Grove Press, year

Kuhn, Annette, *Alien Zone: Cultural Theory and Contemporary Science Fiction Cinema*, Verso Books, 1990

Lacey, Nick, *York Film Notes: Blade Runner*, York Press, 2000

Lyon, Christopher, *The International Dictionary of Films and Filmmakers: Directors*, Papermac, 1987

Nolan, Ken, *Black Hawk Down: The Shooting Script*, Newmarket Books

O'Bannon, Dan, *Alien: The Complete Illustrated Screenplay,* Orion, 2001

Robb, Brian J, *The Pocket Essentials: Ridley Scott*, Oldcastle Books, 2001

Sammon, Paul M, *Future Noir: The Making of Blade Runner*, Orion Books, 1995

Sammon, Paul, *Ridley Scott: Close Up*, Orion Books, 1999

Ridley Scott: Eye of the Storm, BBC documentary 1992

Schwartz, Richard A, *The Films of Ridley Scott*, Praeger Publishers, 2001

Shay, Don, *Blade Runner: The Inside Story*, Titan Books, 2000

Shay, Don and Norton, Bill, *Aliens: The Special Effects*, Titan Books, June 1997

Sturken, Marita, *BFI Modern Classics: Thelma & Louise*, BFI Books, London, 2000

Thomson, David, *Biographical Dictionary of Film*, André Deutsch, 1996

Thomson, David, *The Alien Quartet*, Bloomsbury Publishing, 2000

Picture Credits

The following pictures are from the Ronald Grant Archive:
Page 1 (top) courtesy of Scott Free Productions; Page 1 (bottom) courtesy of 20th Century Fox; Page 2 (bottom) courtesy of the Ladd Company; Page 3 (bottom) courtesy of Columbia Pictures; Page 4 (bottom) courtesy of MGM; Page 6 (bottom) courtesy of DreamWorks SKG; Page 6 (top) and Page 8 courtesy of Hollywood Pictures.

The following pictures are from the Kobal Collection:
Page 2 (top) courtesy of Kobal Collection/the Ladd Company/Warner Bros; Page 3 (top) courtesy of Kobal Collection/20th Century Fox; Page 4 (top) courtesy of Kobal Collection/Paramount; Page 5 (top) courtesy of Kobal Collection/Due West Legend Cyrk; Page 7 (top) courtesy of Kobal Collection; Page 7 (bottom) courtesy of Kobal Collection/Columbia Revolution Studios.

Suggested Further Reading

The following have not necessarily been referenced directly for this book but offer up yet more coverage and responses to Ridley Scott's films.

Assayas, O and Le Peron, S, 'Ridley Scott cinéaste du décor', an interview with Ridley Scott in *Cahiers du Cinema*, September 1982

Bassan, Ralph and Lefevre, Raymond, interview with Ridley Scott in *Revue du Cinéma* (Paris), February 1986

Biodorowski, Steve, 'Legend Makers', *Cinéfantastique*, vol 15, number 5, January 1986, pp. 25–27

Brown, Clive, 'Ridley Scott Changes Direction', *Screen International*, number 504, 6–13 July 1985

Buckley, M, 'Interview with Ridley Scott' in *Films in Review* (NY), January 1987

Caron, A, 'Les archetypes chez Ridley Scott' in *Jeune Cinema*, March 1983

Coleman, John, 'Horses for Courses', *New Statesman*, volume 110, 1985, pp. 30–31

Davis, Brian, 'Ridley Scott: He Revolutionised TV Ads', *Ad Week*, 2 October 1989

Desowitz, Bill, 'Brazil, Legend Stay on the Shelf', *Hollywood Reporter*, 3 Sept 1985

Doll, Susan and Faller, Greg, 'Blade Runner and Genre: Film Noir and Science Fiction', *Literature/Film Quarterly*, number 2, 1986

Durgnat, Raymond, 'Arts for Film's Sake', *American Film*, May 1983

Johnston, Sheila, 'Interview with Ridley Scott', *Films and Filming*, November 1985

Jones, Alan, review of *Legend* in *Cinéfantastique* volume 15, number 4, October 1985, pp. 9 and 53 and *Cinéfantastique*, volume 15, number 5, 1986, pp. 22–24

Kellner, Douglas and Leibowitz, Flo and Ryan, Michael, 'Blade Runner: A Diagnostic Critique' in *Jump Cut*, number 29, 1983

Kennedy, Harlan, 'Designer Genes', *Films*, London, September 1982

Larson, Randall D, 'The Score/Tangerine Dream in the Shadow of a Legend', *Cinéfantastique* Volume 16 number 3, 1986, pp. 42 and 61

Lofficier, Randy and Jean-Marc, 'Tom Cruise: Fairy Tale Hero' *Starlog*, number 107, June 1986, pp. 30–33

Milmo, Sean, 'Ridley Scott Makes the Details Count' *Adverstising Age*, 21 June 1984

Nashawaty, Chris, 'Best Director – Ridley Scott', *Entertainment Weekly*, 22 February 2002, Issue 640/641, p. 92, Best Director

Natale, Richard, *Madison (USA)*, May 1999, volume 1, issue 6, pp. 74–77

Niogret, Hubert, 'Interview with Ridley Scott' in *Positif* (Paris), September 1985

Olsen, James, *Legend review, Starburst*: Volume 8, number 1, Sept 1985, p. 16

O'Neill, Patrick Daniel, 'Mia Sara: Innocence with an Edge', *Starlog*, no. 105, April 1986, pp. 16–18, 72

Ostria U, review of *Legend* in *Cahiers du Cinéma*, Volume 376, October 1985

Palmer, Martyn, 'Action Hero', *The Times Magazine*, 21 November 2000, volume 6, issue 23 p. 36–37, 39–4

Pirani, Adam, 'Ridley Scott: The Nightmare of Fantasy Filmmaking', Starlog, number 107, June 1986, pp. 28, 29

Pulleine, Tim, *Legend* review, *Films and Filming*, number 37, December 1985, p. 43

Rabkin, William, 'Tim Curry: Eight Foot Tall, Bright Red Demon', *Starlog*, no. 106, May 1986, pp. 23–25

Rafferty, Diane, 'Ridley Scott and the Forces of Darkness', *Millimeter*, Volume 14, July 1986, pp. 150–154, 156

Scapperotti, Dan, 'Hjortsberg on Legend', *Cinéfantastique* Volume 17, number 34, 1987, p. 122

Sikker-Rasmussen, *Peter, Tjeck Magazine (Denmark)*, June 2000, Issue 103, p. 47

Szikora, Eszter, *Vox (Hungary)* June 2001, issue 50, pp. 46–51

Szikora, Eszter, *Vox (Hungary)* July 1999, issue 27, pp. 58–59

Index